COSMON NEWSLETTER FOR THE YEARS 1961-1964

Gloria Lee

SAUCERIAN PUBLISHER

ISBN:978-1-7366564-9-5

© 2021, Saucerian Publisher

Al rights reserved. No part of this publication maybe reproduced, translate, store in a retrieval system, or transmitted in any form or by any means, electronic, mechanical, photocopying, recording or otherwise, without prior written permision from the publisher.

PLEASANTON SPACE CRAFT CONVENTION PERSONALITIES

Among the many speakers featured at the Northern California Space Craft Convention were, from left, Orfeo Angelucci, Otis T. Carr, Gloria Lee, and Reinhold O. Schmidt.

Gloria Lee Byrd and other speakers at the Northern California Space Craft Convention in 1959

PROLOGUE

It is generally a good idea to return to the classics in any genre. This also goes for UFO literature. Rereading a book after ten or twenty years is a rewarding experience. You will discover new data and ideas you didn´t notice before. The reason, of course, is that you are, in many ways, not the same person reading the book the second or third time. Hopefully you have advanced in knowledge, experience, intellectual and spiritual discernment. A good starting point is to reread the classics of the early 1950s, in order to understand the deeper mystery involved in what happened during that era.

Gloria Lee Byrd (March 22, 1926 – December 3, 1962) was an American airline flight attendant and a follower of Oahspe who became part of the 1950s contactee movement in 1953.

Lee, a native of Los Angeles, claimed to be in telepathic communication with an entity known as JW, who lived on the planet Venus, and began to assemble a book of his spiritual teachings as dictated to her. At his direction she founded the Cosmon Research Foundation for the purpose of publication and study of JW's superhuman wisdom, much of which bore some resemblance to the 1882 teachings of Oahspe.

Membership in Lee's organization rose sharply after advertisements were regularly carried in Ray Palmer's monthly occult magazine Fate. She hit the contactee lecture circuit and attracted considerable public attention. During her lectures, Lee sold copies of her book of revelations, Why We Are Here! (1959). The year of her death, a second "JW" book was published, The Changing Conditions of Your World! (1962).

She developed a plan for world peace and a space station design and took them to Washington D.C. in late 1962 in an attempt to bring them to the attention of officials. However, after being rebuffed, she launched a hunger strike or protest fast, telling others in the UFO contactee community that she expected to enter a coma resembling death, then "return" with renewed spiritual energy to carry on her "great work". However, the press were not notified of Lee's hunger strike until some time after it had begun, and she attracted no publicity. After approximately 66 days without eating, she was taken to George Washington University Hospital. She died there on December 3, 1962 at the age of 36.

After her death, Charles Boyd Gentzel, the founder of Mark-Age, Inc., and his partner Pauline Sharpe (also known as Nada-Yolanda), claimed to be channelling spirit messages from Lee on behalf of their own UFO-contact cult. Lee is not the only contactee or would-be contactee to starve herself to death. In November 1982, LaVerne Landis, a member of the UFO cult Search and Prove, died of starvation while waiting in her car in the northern Minnesota woods for over 40 days for a flying saucer to land, after reportedly being told to wait there during psychic contact with a Space Brother.

Saucerian Publisher was founded with the mission of promoting books in Science Fiction, Paranormal, and the Occult. Our vision is to preserve the legacy of literary history by reprint editions of books which have already been exhausted or are difficult to obtain. Our goal is to help readers, educators, and researchers by bringing back original publications that are difficult to find at a reasonable price while preserving the legacy of universal knowledge. This title is an authentic reproduction of the original articles printed text in shades of gray. **IMPORTANT**, although we have attempted to maintain the integrity of the issues accurately, the present reproduction has missing and blurred pages, poor pictures from the original scanned copy. Because this material is culturally important, we have made it available as part of our commitment to protect, preserve and promote knowledge in the world

This edition is a collection of the issues of COSMON NEWSLETTER for the years 1961 to 1964 published by Gloria Lee as Editor. Some issues are missing. The issues published here are: December (1961), January-March (1962), June (1963), July (1963), August (1963), October (1963), April (1964)

Great, but unpretentious, these issues are hard to find these days and are a rare symbol by themselves of what was going in the dawn of the modern UFO phenomena.

Kenneth Arnold
Saucerian Publisher, 2021

COSMON

SPECIAL EDITION
DECEMBER, 1961

RESEARCH FOUNDATION
P.O. BOX 55
PALOS VERDES ESTATES, CALIF.

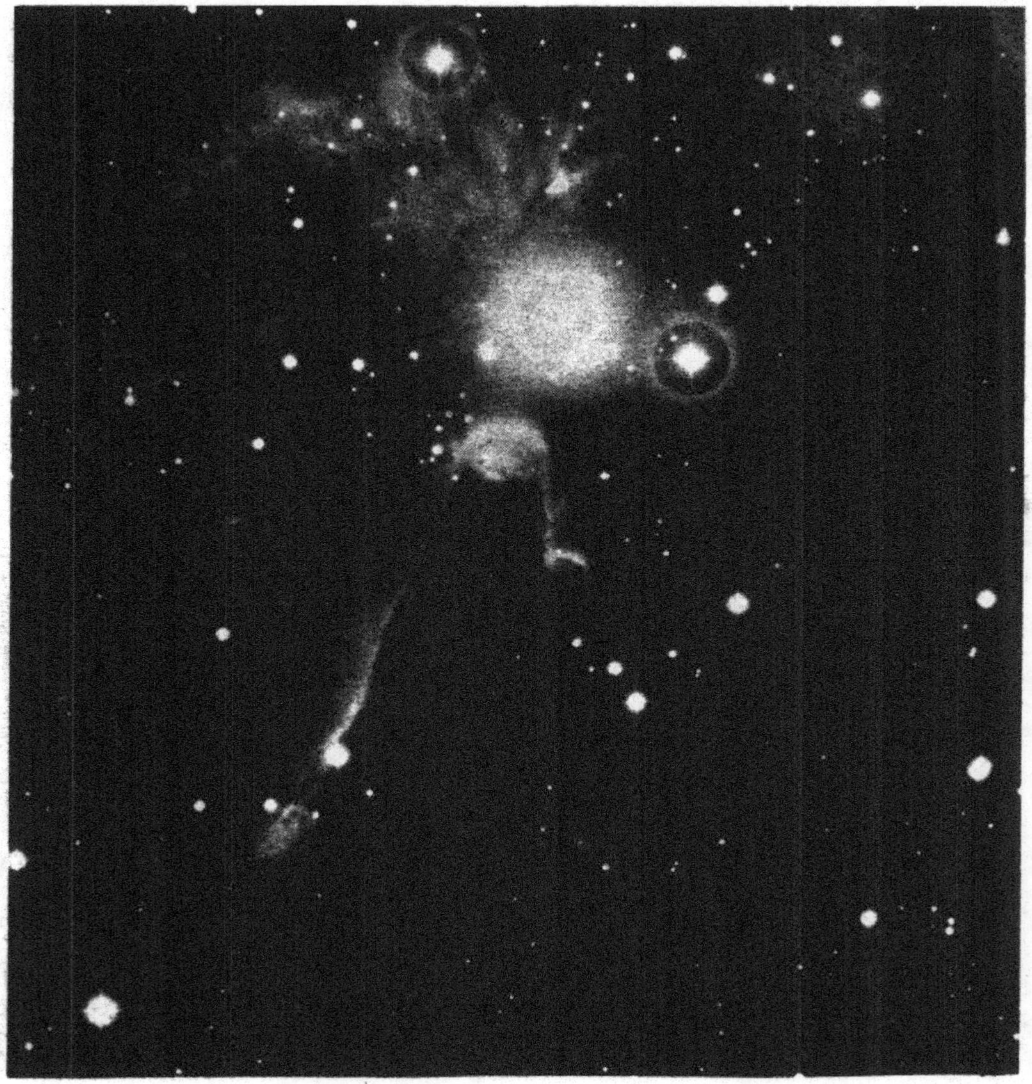

𝔅𝔢 𝔬𝔣 𝔤𝔬𝔬𝔡 𝔠𝔥𝔢𝔢𝔯: 𝔈𝔥𝔯𝔦𝔰𝔱 𝔖𝔭𝔦𝔯𝔦𝔱 𝔦𝔰 𝔥𝔢𝔯𝔢.

TABLE OF CONTENTS

Space Communication..................3

Message from a Master (Jesus).......6

Cosmic Art by Albert Roger..........8

Message from an Archangel...........9

Message from Mother Mary...........11

Prayer of St. Francis of Assisi......12

Our Thanks to You...................13

☥

About Our Cover........

    The beautiful picture shown on our cover is the Nebulosity in Monoceros. Situated in south outer region of NGC 2264. Photographed in red light, 200-inch photograph.
    We like to call it the "Madonna and Child" picture because if you look closely, you will see the cosmic dust actually forms a Madonna holding a child on her right shoulder. We hope the reproduction will clearly show this. It is a favorite of ours and is enjoyed by all in our Cosmon offices.

☥

    Cosmon Research Foundation is a non-profit organization dedicated to developing mankind spiritually and physically and is incorporated under California law. This is a Special Edition for all who are members or on our mailing list and is by donation only.

Copyright © 1961 by Cosmon Research Foundation. All rights reserved.

Printed in U.S.A.

SPACE COMMUNICATION

Beloved Children of Earth,

This season of Christ Spirit will be long forgotten when you have established the true Christ Spirit within your consciousness. You will forget the suffering and anxiety of earth consciousness in a world torn with strife and turmoil. The inception of the Christ Spirit does not take place over-night, nor does it take place over a period of time designated by earth concepts, but is an inherent part of you already established by divine law.

The awareness of this Christ Spirit will be the ultimate in the sudden rise of race consciousness over your whole planet this season and in the months following this prelude to Spring or the out-bursting of this divine consciousness in all manifestations of eternal power as exemplified in the simple awareness of the first bud of Spring.

It will be like the individual has found within himself, the simple awareness of the Christ bud of spiritual wakefulness stirring within him and his first recognition of this phenomenon will occur in those who have reached the specific stages of evolution that will grant unto them this "spring" awakening, beginning in the time of now and more forcibly in the projected power of the Christ "sun" during the February planetary pattern which will stimulate the dormant bud into ever greater awareness of that inherent divine Sonship with God.

We have given ourselves to the projected power of Christ in order to be of assistance in any situation in which, you of the earth plane, may require help in the pangs of this Spring "birth." We will project love, understanding, and divine guidance to those of you in utter turmoil of consciousness when you reach that point of this divine awakening. It is not an easy matter to throw off the shackles of earth consciousness, for indeed, you may have accustomed yourselves to accept that which is false in so many ways, you do not view the true sun (light, truth) with your physical eyes but only the false glitter of REFLECTED glory from earth objects. Because of this mishap, the light within will shine brighter and you will be forced to re-evaluate your motives, concepts, ideals, morals, and preconceived notions of understanding the spiritual side of life which will leave you, but only temporarily, as one lost in a maze of misconceptions and with no place to rest the weary mind. Because of this, we have instigated many plans which will grow in proportion to the need, of educating the people upon your planet.

Many of you now reading this article, have already conceived of the Bud of Christ consciousness within yourselves and so you will not suffer the pangs of the new experience, however, you will suffer the pangs of "growing pains" as your individual buds burst forth into greater array of the light and understanding under the projected power of the Christ Spirit.

This energy of the Christ Spirit is withheld by many who are incapable of resisting truth, yet they fight to maintain their preconceived ideas and reach a level of consciousness beyond their capacity. This is true of many disciples who do not want to follow the path of truth, but who want the light and cannot distinguish between light (truth) and darkness (falsehood), nor do they wish to suffer the pain of expanding their consciousness which would take them beyond the door of their present understanding. Instead, they wish to maintain their equilibrium and still insist that truth come to them, not realizing, truth is, but THEY are the ones who must open the door of their consciousness to allow it to enter in. The prefer to sit and wait, hoping someone else will open the door and go thru all manner of suffering, not necessary to the ultimate development of their own Christ expression. These are the ones with whom we have the most trying times!

We have others who do not know the meaning of any of our teachings, and yet are most receptive to anything brought forth in like manner, because they are not clinging to any preconceived ideas. Then there are those who must feel that what they have, IS the truth and will not recognize anything new, no matter how it is placed before them! These are the ones who will be hit the hardest, for a concrete consciousness or mind will be the first to break under the weight of absolute truth. We pray for them, we extend our light, but know in divine wisdom, there is much that will be learned in the long run, that would not be accomplished by any degree of understanding at this point of their evolution.

We know too, many of you will be able to gracefully turn to the light of full Christ consciousness, even though it may blind you, you will persevere to maintain a vigilance which will open your inner eye to the real conception of the Christ Spirit.

Conceive of the Christ Spirit as being one part of our Father who pushes His awareness thru all forms so He may understand the motion of the universe in even the smallest of form. He may distinguish the part of Him being made manifest thru His children by projecting, as a finger of light, into the consciousness of any individual who will accept His truth and light the way for others to recognize this same light inherent, but perhaps dormant, within each one. This is the meaning of Christ Spirit, in a word picture... the rays of one aspect of God, gleaming forth THRU the individuals ready to accept that point of light as it is given unto our dimension of life.

There are, of course, many dimensions of light, but each one has a greater "finger" of light awareness that will give impetus to the creative structure of divine Mind. This is why we are called Sons of God, because we are His instruments to promote the Great Plan according to His divine illumination, but in being Sons, we are free to promote free-will. However, it is found by all Sons of God, who went on into greater Christ awareness, it is to their advantage, to follow the Plan of the Father and be in tune with these inherent powers to at last emerge the master of self and life upon the physical plane of manifestation.

Which way do you choose? Do you choose to go with the Sons of God who have traveled the path before you, or do you choose to delay your progression by admitting defeat before you have even begun? You have so much to gain and little to lose, but within the confines of earth consciousness, it is difficult to distinguish between the true sacrifice of self and the sacrifice of selfishness! It may seem difficult to partake of the riches of Christ awareness, as the peasant who does not wish to give up his rags for finery because he has become accustomed to rags, or the nobleman, finding his riches are of no true value, will not give up his supposed status, while not earning what should rightfully be his. He has come to one conclusion, and the peasant to another, but both could live in perfect understanding, were they to behold the true riches of spiritual elegance and not bind themselves with opposite conceptions of the same thing! We do not find life in rags, nor do we find it in false elegance, but we find it in truth. We must begin to recognize what is the false glitter and which is the false pride, and let both fall by the wayside and continue in our search for truth.

This is again the true meaning of Christ Spirit, when we are all one under the eyes of God and particularly, in the eyes of each other! God does see us as equal, but in His ability to use us as instruments there is a vast difference, until we, as His children, can recognize that spark of life inherent within each object, whether in form or not, and to be able to decipher the meanings behind the various patterns with which we come in contact. We are all on the brink of a new awakening. Some into greater horizons than others, but nevertheless, we are on our final pathway, as a complete Solar System, to withstand those energies of God which will place us amongst the "stars of heaven" in greater light and inspiration than ever before.

We are here to place ourselves at His disposal, to release that which may be our blessing as well as a blessing for an entire Solar System. So often we consider ourselves, such an infinitesimal part of any plan, but if we could view the whole picture, within our finite consciousness, we would be able to see where upon the whole machine is regulated by each "wheel" no matter how seemingly insignificant we may feel. That is why it is our privilege, as individuals, to fulfill that part of the plan which will help our whole Solar System to progress.

Does it not seem like a grave responsiblity to set in motion some part of this unique Solar System? And yet it is done with the greatest of love and understanding that we may fulfill our very own desires of destiny whether it be in a manner of greatest ease or by climbing the ladder of spiritual illumination in the fastest way possible. We all have equal opportunity, but we do not have equal desires, and so we listen to that part best played by us and if we succeed where others have failed, then we are able, by our very momentum to help carry them along into greater illumination, where they too, will be able to visualize the greatest of all opportunities...that of consciously developing Christ awareness and promoting this great and glorious divine Plan of an entire Solar System!

You have begun to stretch your own awareness to include other planets, but there are still many among you who do not give even a thought as to whether there is life in any form upon the other planets. However, the recent plans that are attempting to be fulfilled by reaching the moon, have at least accomplished that awareness of being able to bridge the mental consciousness of worlds beyond the Earth. Unfortunately, so much of what is being attempted is with the thought of promoting the greater power for whoever is able to reach the moon first. This is not the proper way to expand our conscious awareness, but God is even able to use our weaknesses to advantage!

Learn to use your strengths, overcome your fears of greater development. Many do not wish to develop because they fear what it will bring them. They do not realize the thing it brings is well worth the agony of mental turmoil and assimilating truth and being able to distinguish the false and at last be free of all that binds with the earth ties of misconceptions and false beliefs. We have not accomplished anything that you will not be able to do. But we have accomplished it in greater strides in some ways because we did not hinder our teachers as greatly as some of you have done.

Yet, we have planets upon which there is even greater hindrance to the truth and so you of Earth need not feel alone! We are never truly alone except within our own consciousness, and if we allow ourselves the improper condition of separateness, we cannot see what beauty we are surrounded with. We pity ourselves and others and we do not pity God for the tremendous job of educating His millions of children in preparing them for their divine Sonship! He has placed us in those circumstances which will best prepare us for those chores we would like to help Him with, and yet we recognize it not. We are looking for an easy way to become omniscient, omnipotent, and all-knowing, and it cannot be without first going over the lessons of life and applying ourselves to the situations that will best place us as co-creators, working at the right hand of God and helping Him to fulfill the grand plan of the ultimate purpose of our Beingness.

Take each day for what it may bring you and instead of complaining of its difficulties, bless them, that you may grow in greater stature to complete your understanding of divine perception and allow that indwelling Christ Spirit within you to be stimulated by its outer manifestation of power which will awaken the very Bud of reunion with the Father and greater awareness of our universe.

Be in Christ light, be in Christ spirit and be that Christ spirit within. My love and blessings to spur you on in greater understanding.

J.W. of Jupiter

MESSAGE FROM A MASTER

Beloved Brethren,

This is the time of great rejoicing! Do not allow yourselves to think otherwise for one minute. We are in the time of great projection of the Christ Spirit and are casting out the devils of miscreation in the minds of men. Do not let yourselves resist the oncoming illumination of Christ awareness for it will be the greatest blessing you will ever have while yet in physical form. Be ever content to learn your earthly lessons as they come to you and learn to let go of your earthly concepts that bind you to the illusion of earth consciousness.

Many have strived to accomplish what you are now privileged to accomplish. We have met many upon the path who forsook the very necessities of life in hopes of accomplishing the awakening of the Christ Spirit within them. My Brethren, it is not necessary to prove to God the desire within your hearts by sacrificing many of the necessities of life. He already KNOWS what the desires of your hearts are. There have been many disciples in the past who have tried to prove to man they were so desirous of achieving that ultimate illumination, they gave up all earthly belongings and desecrated the body to prove a point to the world of men. But they proved nothing to God. They gave of themselves in sacrifice to impress the world but they achieved nothing but what the effort made in their hearts...that of impressing men.

God knows better than they what is within their hearts! He knows when one is struggling within himself to achieve a note of truth, they do not know wherein truth lies and falsehood begins, and many times, they do not really know that the note of truth even, is false upon which they base is but earthly concept. But does God forsake you? Never! He did not forsake me upon the cross although popular opinion has it that I believed so! This is not true. We forsake only our selves, by not recommending God help us when we need Him the most. This, unfortunately, is the way of men. To forsake the flesh in hopes that the world of spirit will come to them. But are you not living within that temple of flesh? Are you not a part of it and does it not have a use?

I did not forsake the temple of flesh. I proved it could be "taken up" in greater manifestation of LIFE, not death. Remember, you are now at that threshhold, wherein you are challenged by the keeper of keys, to lay aside your earthly fears and illusions and enter into the realm of eternal LIFE. There is no death, and so what do you fear? There is no fear except what is conjured up in the minds of men. Learn to be with God and not the earth-born fears and illusions. Learn to be in harmony WITH Creation. That is the real secret of overcoming death...to be in tune with Creation. Inharmony with this great Creative Force that permeates our Universe, is what promotes the idea of death. It is non-existent. It exists only within the minds of men.

What must be understood in the days ahead, is that "death" may bring a change of form, but even in living in a world beyond physical form, there are "changes." And as one learns to recognize the change called death, he will begin to recognize the great universal law of constant change at cyclic intervals. This is a great Law and will be understood in the days ahead, but now you are passing thru a period of transitional change within your consciousness and as the race consciousness changes, so shall the outer forms. You will see these changes coming about in your present life pattern.

There are many things to tell you about God and His Creative force, but it is beyond your comprehension at this time. As your consciousness changes, you will also note a change in your ability to comprehend change itself. You will also note the changes coming in the earth consciousness, as it adjusts itself to the onslaught of Christ Spirit and the greatest change will seemingly be within the individual. This of course will be true, but YOU are the ones that must first instigate the change within your own mental makeup and ALLOW the influx of Christ power to become manifest within you.

When I was in my fleshly abode, such as you presently manifest, I did not see many of the things MY teachers told me about, but as I learned to change within my THINKING I was given insight into the many truths that came my way in preparing me for my earthly ministry. They are not truths that come easily unto the earth consciousness. And does it seem strange to you I was one who also complained about not being able to "see" the light plainly either? Yes, I was prepared many lifetimes, but could not give of my knowledge completely until I had relived the earthly experience of life in much the same way that you have done. My life pattern was entirely different perhaps, but nevertheless, I achieved within my lifetime the necessary experiences to acquaint me with the weaknesses of man and the illusions that try to bind us into the abyss of darkness within our own consciousness.

These were the reasons I could truthfully say upon the cross (And this I did say!) "Father, forgive them, they know not what they do." For verily I did pursue the foibles of flesh until I was led into the path of light and able at an early age to distinguish between the false and the true. I was blessed with an early understanding of God principles, because that was my life pattern to be able to comprehend the basic truths of God-given energy, but it was not within my power to heal all those who came to me in demand of their freedom. I gave unto those within my karmic pattern of revelation and unto those whose faith was so great as to release the karmic pattern that bound them and unto those who released their emotional hindrances of evil which allowed the beginning of light to flood their consciousness.

Many were turned away as being unfit to accept universal light, not because I did not have compassion for them, but because they were not able to release THEMSELVES for the glory of God. They wanted to be free and proven to that God did exist and yet with all the seeming "miracles" around them, they would not believe. So it was my duty to bring light and show the way to that light, but it was not my obligation to free those who had bound their own souls.

You see, we have many obligations unto the Father, and one is that the right of the individual's free-will must not be interfered with. It is not easy to distinguish between free-will of the PERSONALITY and the free-will of the soul. There is a vast difference. The free-will God has endowed man with is actually the free-will of the soul, and many disciples speak of free-will when the path becomes difficult, but it is within their power to break the will of the soul by exercising the ultimate will of the personality. This leads to much chaos. Do you remember my struggle within the garden of Gethsemane when I asked that the "cup" be taken from me? That was the will of the personality, but I knew within that my soul had already made the decision to forego the comforts of the personality and that it was my duty unto God and humanity to fulfil my prearranged pattern. It was not an easy task, and it is not an easy task for those of you upon the path to go on in the face of all manner of obstruction, but let me say unto you, the personality will never know peace until the soul has allowed itself the fulfillment of its own individual pattern.

If we do not allow ourselves the privilege of seeking attunement with our soul activity, we do not allow ourselves the greatest chance of self-progression. We dawdle until the time of awakening and then the greatest of tumult ensues. Then we blame God and everyone else for the problems that beset us! Are we not human in nature? Then let us first understand the human nature and let our God-selves overcome that lower nature of ourselves and lead us into the appointed glory of self-conscious realization. This is

(Please continue on page 9)

MESSAGE FROM AN ARCHANGEL

Beloved Children of Cosmon,

Today is the time of great rejoicing. We have gathered as the "Host of Heaven" to watch over you disciples who are joined in thought at this time of awakening the Christ Spirit within. We see many who are not aware of the import of this year's occasion and are struggling on alone, without knowledge, to ascertain the feeling that grows within them.

We hope, as angels of God, to be able to carry our messages of love and joy to the earthly ones who could cease their struggles against the darkness by admitting the light of golden illumination. We are here in our sphere of activity to bring you the courage and upliftment necessary for your spiritual strength to reach millions not yet cognizant of the Path and to help them, even if unknown, to partake of the glories of Heaven.

We are not in the Heaven of man's thinking, but within the Heaven of divine authorization. We are within that sphere of activity wherein all tumult of the earthly heart is heard and we hasten to reject the doubts that enter the minds of men. We hear the protest of unaccustomed life, and the cries of mothers who worry about their children and the impatience of men, who long for a better life. We are here to project that living light which will bring illumination unto the soul sick with fears and worry and to eliminate, as man will let us, this dis-ease or tumult of their souls.

For many eons we have fought the tyrants of darkness with my flaming sword of truth, and today I offer it to you as individuals, to call upon me in your hour of stress, to allay your fears and shut out the darkness by cutting the earthly ties that bind you to the illusion of your world. Let me be your master of light who would look down upon my stars of Earth to enlighten your own lights with a burning and purging of the false within to bring greater illumination within your own star-like souls so that we of this heavenly sphere can look down and see your lights, as indeed the bright stars of Earth they should be.

You must be the warriors of light for Earth now. You must be the ones to fight the karmic darkness as it closes around you, and you must be the ones to overcome the evil that lurks within the hearts of so many. Learn to be the soldier upon this great battlefield who wields the sword of truth and light and let me and all those I represent guide your hand and your word with our God-given wisdom so we may direct our "armies" of Earth to quickly dispel the darkness that so shuts out the true light.

You do not have to feel as a "saint" in the earthly sense. God does not ask you be pure to wield His sword of truth, but He does ask that you be pure in heart-felt desires to truly want truth and to have the courage to stand against the darkness with might and main and speak His word and use our power as we help also to help you. Remember, you are never alone when you stand for truth. The assistance of the Universe is at your side to carry you over the threshhold of opportunity and grant you the right to remain upon the Earth to fulfill your Golden Age of the divine recognition of the true Christ Spirit.

Be ever mindful that the true Christ Spirit lies dormant within you, and as you fight to maintain light, you maintain that spark within you which will one day, be brightened into the glowing star so many of you are becoming. We see you as lights as we look down upon the earthly plane, that is why I call you my "Stars of Earth." We do not see you as "people" but as living lights of God energy. Your bodies will change in vibrational quality as you become greater lights of God's energy and then the recognition of the true meaning of light will amaze you. You will see those who will fall into the pattern of self-pity, but you must not let yourselves be involved in this vibration, for when you do, you fall in frequency, as you say, or as we say, your light becomes dim, and we have great difficulty in helping you as we would.

Rejoice, my Stars of Earth! My legions of angels are with you! We give of our salvation to help you attain yours. We pledge our support unto you and you have but to call our help to receive it. We are not myths of someone's imagination, for verily, we live and move and have our being in as real a form as you are to yourselves. We live in and under different circumstances, but we are one of many kingdoms within our Father's great mansion.

Learn to enjoy the brotherhood of all kingdoms of God's Nature, for we are all indeed a part of this great universal Force. Be part of the Universe and do not set yourselves apart from the rest of us. All the kingdoms of God will one day be in perfect accord and we will joyously go forward in the planning of our Solar System by consciously acknowledging the perfect Plan of God. We have given our lives to serving our Father of All and we believe before too long, our beloved children of Earth will recognize us for what we are and give their cooperation to all of God's kingdoms, for now you are as little children who have not explored all the rooms of a huge house and are anxious to begin your journey along the path of ever expanding horizons.

Be with God and let your lights so shine, so we may follow your progress and be of assistance whenever the threat of darkness is upon you.

My blessings are eternally with you.

Lord Michael, Archangel

****

(continued from page 7)

our supreme sacrifice...to dispense with the personality and its hindering influence and to learn to let the God-self CONTROL it and use it as a TOOL it should be used as!

We have every God-given right to exercise our power of free-will, but we must also exercise it with wisdom and learn when we are going AGAINST the forces of Creation and work instead, WITH the forces of Creation. We believe mankind will be prepared for the greatest of all initiations to take place upon the earth plane, that of Christhood, if they can but remember, the God who has placed this golden opportunity before you, knows wherein the weaknesses lie and wherein to snuff out the preconceived ideas and break the false ideas of self and shatter the earthly forms of deluded consciousness. Why not give God credit in His wisdom, to know what is uppermost within our hearts and ACCEPT those things which have come upon us, as the OPPORTUNITY with which we CAN destroy all the things that bind us to the darkness of earth illusions? This one thought can help you the most in the days ahead, if you will but stop in your turmoil for but a moment and think, "This has come upon me for a reason, and if I have not created it from my own consciousness, then it is created for me so that I may see wherein the falseness lies and the truth, I so earnestly desire, be revealed."

Take your opportunities! Seize them with great zeal and work our the preconceived plans of freeing the soul from the hindrances of the personality and the earthly concepts of mind. Be in accordance with the Christ Spirit and the discord will vanish!

In loving recognition at this season.

Your elder Brother,

Jesus

MESSAGE FROM MOTHER MARY

Beloved Cosmonites,

All hail the glorious season of the Christ Spirit! This is the chance to truly be "born again." The meaning of Christmas is wild and varied upon your earth plane and yet I do not set myself apart from it but become it within the minds and hearts of many. However, it is with longing within my heart that I would give you a truer meaning of the Christmas season and the message of the Christ Spirit.

All thru the ages man has blessed that time of the year wherein the projection of the Christ Spirit was made manifest upon the Earth. However, many misconceptions arose after the birth of my Son, Jesus, in that far away time in Jerusalem! How often I long to tell people the real meaning of that birth! Many have thought me virgin of extreme purity to be able to bring forth the Christ child, but the purity came with the many fires of refinement that eliminated the earth illusions which enabled me to be receptive to the entrance of a soul which was to change the pattern of a whole planet! I was told by an angel of the Lord I was to house the soul of such a one for a time so it could gain entrance into the physical world, and so I awaited with bated breath the arrival of the child who was to set a new pattern.

However, it was not the loved ones of my family who shared this revelation with me! They did not believe I was chosen to bear such a son and they openly laughed at my "hallucination" and said there were many mothers who thought the child they were to bear was the "chosen one." This was not true of course, that all these mothers would be the ones to bring forth the child destined to change the world, but it was true many believed such. For in that day, it was in the prophecies of old, the time was nigh and they were "tuning in" so to speak, on the probability of the times. So you see, I greatly feared that perhaps, I too, was mistaken many times. However, in the temple of great learning, which was known as a "mystery school" then, I was told the same thing by the Teachers. "He" was coming and I was the means by which he would gain entrance.

We were delighted, and as all earthly parents, we had our fears also. We wondered if perhaps we would raise him correctly, or if we would choose the correct pathway to nurture that seed of divine essence within him and allow the true Christ Spirit to manifest within his great soul. And so we carried on in great preparation for the great day! We did not think of our child as a "great soul" after his arrival, but as the divine essence of a truly wonderful child and we gave him instruction to the basic meaning of life so his well-developed spirit could soar into the understanding of God.

We taught that it was impossible to hurt another without hurting ourselves and he carried on at great length over the invinciblity of God and the way in which we must serve Him. He took great childish delight in understanding the ways of angels and men, and we suspected many times he communicated with them himself, although very reluctant to say so. We made no fuss because he was "special." But because he was, we knew he would suffer greatly in trying to work out a precise pattern, and so we tried to prepare him very early to overcome all obstacles as they came along and not to shirk this duty. This we believe, was the greatest part of his training.

At last when his day of redemption drew near, I knew within my heart what must be suffered thru and I too, had difficulty in following the great plan by not allowing the will of the personality to enter in. It is not an easy thing many times, to follow the Will of God, but we had trained long and well before and during incarnation and if one will but follow the dictates of his heart, he will be able to follow the plan even when the will of personality hesitates. So do not think we were, as parents, above the earthly fears or loves of the mortal consciousness. Instead, we must allow ourselves the privilege of overcoming those mortal tendencies.

We do not have to use our knowledge of the divine to "escape" what our lot may be. We should use our knowledge to strengthen and overcome what our lot may be. **My dear ones, many call on me in the name of Jesus, and we both would prefer you call on us in the name of God, and strengthen your own receptivity by using that God vibration and not relying on a false illusion of personality. We do not have the power of God**, but we do know how to use a part of the power of God, and we would have you **free** yourselves from erroneous concepts to be able to also use part of the power of God. To live and move within the vibration of your own manifesting Christ Spirit, IS the greatest blessing mankind can achieve upon the earth plane. And this is NOW your opportunity to advance to the stage of my blessed son and become what he is. He is Jesus, the personality, using the force of the great Christ Spirit, to manifest THRU the personality of Jesus, and I am grateful to be able to manifest this SAME Christ Spirit thru myself, as are all the ascended Masters able to do.

Do you see? The greatest at-one-ment we can possibly have, is when we are ALL **using** but ONE consciousness (Christ consciousness) and letting the fingers of God's **radiating** Christ flame manifest thru all of us in different ways and thru different personalitites. We are indeed blessed to have this opportunity to tell you of the **great** potential awaiting you in your present life patterns and for you to be able to say: "I am chosen to bring forth the Christ Child within ME!"

Be one with our Father. My family and I are one with you in divine recognition of the examples we set as personalities while living upon the earth plane in bodies of flesh. We are still among you in bodies of living light and we surround you daily with our love and blessings and hope to continue helping you in your progression for many centuries to come!

Blessed be he, who can find the Christ Spirit within and not look beyond.

Mother Mary

THE PRAYER OF ST. FRANCIS OF ASSISI

Lord, made me an instrument of thy Peace:
Where there is hatred, let me sow love;
Where there is injury, pardon;
Where there is doubt, faith;
Where there is despair, hope;
Where there is darkness, light;
And where there is sadness, joy.

O divine Master, grant that I may not so much
   seek to be consoled as to console;
To be understood, as to under stand;
To be loved, as to love;
For it is in giving that we receive,
It is in pardoning that we are pardoned,
And it is in dying that we are born to eternal
   life.

Beloved Cosmonites,

On behalf of all those who work here at Cosmon, may I extend our fondest greetings and our Christ love for another year well spent in serving you the best way we were able.

May I also take the time to give our Thanks to those of you who have remained so loyal and have made the phenomenal growth of Cosmon possible by your constant prayers, encouragement, and donations. We Thank God for His help in working thru you and in allowing us the privilege to serve you while serving Him in this great plan of Cosmon.

We are going into a New Year as well as a new cycle where there will be greater manifestations of the Christ power and of the cleansing action which is taking place upon our planet. Let us meet this new year with greater insight and understanding and help to prepare others along the way who have not been as lucky as we have in being able to share our spiritual experiences.

This is a period of great opportunity for our individual growth as well as our Foundation as a whole. As long as we can uphold our principles and adhere to the Light, we shall all proceed with greater rapidity into our New Age.

May you all be blessed, but most important, may you all recognize your blessings as they come and use your opportunities to stimulate spiritual growth within yourself as well as others. Indeed, as the Teachers have said, we have been given our "Christ Scholarship" and may we all use it wisely, but as a group, please let us USE it!

With great love and light,

Gloria Lee, Director

COSMON

JAN.-MAR., 1962

RESEARCH FOUNDATION
P.O. BOX 55
PALOS VERDES ESTATES, CAL.

YOUR RESEARCH FOUNDATION DEDICATED TO DEVELOPING MAN SPIRITUALLY AND PHYSICALLY FOR THE NEW AGE AND SUPPORTED BY YOU.

Gloria Lee, Director

☥

TABLE OF CONTENTS

Space Communications................................ 3
Message by a Master................................. 7
Guest Corner.. 10
Cosmon News and Activities.......................... 12
Countdown by Barbara Steele......................... 15
Health and Diet Research (Body Cleansing)........... 18
World Report.. 24
Science Developments................................ 25
Research in Emotional and Mental Development....... 27
Cosmic Art.. 29
Recommended Products................................ 30
Miscellaneous File (Message after Death)............ 34
Leeward with Gloria................................. 38

☥

This publication is printed every other month especially for members of Cosmon Research Foundation and given on a donation basis. All monies received help support the foundation and its work. Further information may be received by writing Cosmon P.O. Box 55, Palos Verdes Estates, California.

Incorporated as a non-profit organization under California law. Gloria Lee, President; Moreland James, Executive Vice-president; James Mann, Vice-president; Carl Johnson, Treasurer; Barbara Steele, Executive Secretary.

Copyright O 1962 by Cosmon Research Foundation. All rights reserved.

Printed in U.S.A.

SPACE COMMUNICATION

Beloved Children of Earth:

This present time is a period of great turmoil within the hearts of men. Many are not aware of their destination in life, yet have become acquainted with the many changes taking place around them. Some have noted the changes taking place in the world at large.

Because of these changes, many are questioning within their own minds as to the outcome of this situation. They see a great future on one side, or a great devastation on the other, knowing that the fears of many could manifest. They could manifest mainly, because the fears of ages are held deep within so many and unless they release these fears into the higher egos of their spiritual selves, they will only go on in this state of inner turmoil until the objective manifestation of their consciousness takes hold in the Earth.

The many prophecies given are not given to bring fear into your hearts, but to give you warning, that the words of all the prophets of old were made for this day and age. You were given insight into all types of probabilities, within your earlier stage of advancement and it is not the fault of God, but of man, should these things manifest. He has warned His people, but they do not heed. As so often, the child believes his wisdom to be greater than the parent.

We do not offer our services as a way of salvation, but as a way of learning, of illumination towards the way of salvation. You do not learn to conquer illness, until you learn the cause; when the cause is learned, you conquer illness. When you learn the illuminated way of life, you have the way of salvation. Your true salvation lies in the manner in which you approach your God. You do not approach Him on bended knee, as most of you with your fist in the air demanding! How would you feel about the child, waving his fist and demanding his idea of a tasty meal? You would show amusement, perhaps, but in your foreseeing the result of his aggressive attitude in finishing such a meal, you would shake your head in compassion and would want to save him the consequence.

This is somewhat similar to your relationship to God. He is able to see the rewards of fulfilling the Laws of Life, while, you as still a child, cannot see with your limited vision, but only with your sense appetites! You do not have to go far without realizing you have made an incorrect decision, but you do have to suffer some before you admit you have!

We are, in a sense, like the older brother, who has learned a little more wisdom of life and would also like to guide you, but again, as an older child, we do not wish to clean up your mess! We would rather see you do your own work and accomplish even more by proper guidance from the Father.

We have much to do in order to help your planet from the backward path to the more illuminated one, but we must be able to see our plans taking fulfillment before we will do much more for the benefit of mankind upon the Earth. In short, we will give the necessary data concerning the problems upon your planet, and then we will wait to see how it is accepted before interfering beyond that stage of assistance. We are here to help and not to create fear. And we are here to bring you knowledge, but not to do everything for you.

You must now learn to stand as adults in this galactic system and bring forth that Christ light within you which will show this Spirit of Omniscience that you are ready to stand forth, as a planet, in the divine law of fulfillment. You have traveled far, but you are on the verge of releasing your opportunities unto others, should you miss the exclamation of this Galactic Deity.

The Galactic Deity of whom I speak, is a great Cosmic Soul Who repeats a mantram of greatest magnitude which is echoed down thru the areas of consciousness by other great Souls repeating in Their turn, the specific symbolic meaning of Sound. They come from near and far, when you think in terms of our Omniverse, to see the reversal of the Earth's action in divine consciousness. Perhaps this holds little meaning for you of Earth, but you will learn in time to come, of these great Beings and more of the great unlimited Omniverse in which we live. There is so much to life you do not see or comprehend. We are as anxious children, willing to share a new game with our brothers of Earth!

Release all fear of the turmoil, for it brings terrible thought-forms of your fears when it is mentioned. You need only adhere to Truth, to fully comprehend the meaning of "your rightful place." Being in one place is as good as another, if you recognize what your "rightful place" may mean to the eyes of your Soul. You do not have to cower in fear of strange places, but go forward with all the thrill of an adventurer making a new conquest in a new land.

It matters not what your physical body may suffer. It may only suffer a scratch, and yet, if your Soul sees fit, it will suffer more...to present you with a greater opportunity to learn! Oh, how we wish our Earth brothers would stop saying, "God, why do I suffer so?" and say, "God, why am I so slow to learn?" Then, we feel, the answer will come more quickly!

The event of the first man into space, who traversed your globe successfully in a man-made vehicle, marked the beginning of a new era. It marked the beginning of a new exploration into "outer space." We do not use the term "outer space" because we do not see it as "outer" but as a PART of us. We see all things as that part of the ONE, but you are at least beginning that phase of your understanding into the present mysteries of the upper atmosphere.

We have labored long and hard to help in the fulfillment of the plans of man to "conquer" space. We laugh at your term, for we do not see it as something to "conquer" but as something to understand. However, your explorations will bring the necessary understanding over a period of many years. We are not able to tell you at this time how we played a part in that service, but we will say it was necessary to bring some of our people to this planet to fulfill that service! They were a part of the program as much as you are a part of the program, if you have incarnated from another planet. The incarnations of those connected with your country's "space program" are not from this planet originally, but are from the planets of Jupiter and Venus mainly. We do not say this in jest, but in actual knowledge of the true purpose of the lives and patterns of those whom you call the Astronauts. We know these men well, and appreciate their ability to withstand the pressures of Earth to become as one of you. They are not able to comprehend the meaning of my words, but they are all in possession of a small memory in the back of their consciousness, if they truly would dwell upon it, of not "belonging" here.

They are taking part in this vast program just as the Instrument is taking part in another capacity, to fulfill the greater plan of action. So many dear Souls have volunteered their services to help this planet of yours that you would be overcome were you to fully realize the magnitude of this great love which is manifesting to balance the planet of Earth in thought, in spirit and in love. You do not yet comprehend the great love within divine submission to the Father's Will, but you do comprehend the sacrifice one makes in love for another, and so I will relate it as that. However, when we are in this position to help, even though it may take us away from our own homes for awhile, we see it as an opportunity and as a privilege.

Many of the great Souls who are helping your planet, will never be known in their true understanding, but it is not important unto them. They come here only to help the Father in His great plan and it is not by choice of jobs, but by desire of heart. They are placed before the Tribunal of Interplanetary Planning and given their opportunity to state their inner desires of fulfillment in helping another planet, such as Earth, and then the Great One presiding over the Tribunal tunes into the Great Plan of action and sees wherein the desires are ones of personal development and wherein they are ones of divine fulfillment. The two are integrated in such a way that both are combined and fulfilled if the entity, while within his limited Earth consciousness, can go forward according to the divine plan of action. Nothing is left undone, if the entity in question has fulfilled all the action of divine guidance.

They are not necessarily chosen to fulfill an action of helping another planet unless they have also EARNED the right to do so! We do not hand out opportunities blindly because we know that to do so would not be wisdom. We first investigate the personalities of the entity, as he has lived them in previous life-times and integrate his knowledge with his proposed pattern of present life fulfillment. It is not an easy task to come to another planet's lower vibration and not fall prey to its unbalanced vibration, so it must be first seen that this entity has in the past, fulfilled his desires within the life plan so that we would not have too many failures!

When some are brought unto another planet with a plan of helping to raise the vibration and they fall beneath its darkened spell, we do not consider them as failures, but as those who were to wade a river and fell in! They may rise and carry on or may return with the decision that the water is too swift for their strength. We know many who will probably stop half-way, because of little strength, but we know too, they will try to rise to meet the challenge so that they may return home, with the knowledge that they have at least tried to strengthen their spiritual "muscles!"

We have heard many speculations about the program of those who incarnated as the 144,000, but none of them meet a true picture of what the situation really is! We do not hope to give you the complete picture, but we would like you to understand a few of the points not entirely understood by many. When you have a war or a disaster, in which you would like to send out so many people into the area, do you not expect them to return as they were? But perhaps, their EXPERIENCES were such, that they learned a great deal? Their experiences may change them so much they would want to change their job upon returning, to do something more suited to their new desires which were stimulated by this experience. But they will certainly lose nothing from the experience and have much to gain.

We are much the same way upon the other planets. We see your planet as a disaster area, and we all have a desire to help, but we are not all able to help in certain areas if we incarnate, as well as if we stay behind and direct the "traffic," so to speak. I am one who directs traffic, while the Instrument is one who takes the directions and turns them over to her group and you, in turn, over to the world. We have no competition, as individual servers, because we have all made the plans as to what the work will be, and as long as we fulfill those plans of action, it is literally impossible for another to take our place!

We see far into the future, as observers of another planet, such as yours. Knowing the divine plan of action and seeing the trend of man's personal will, and the forces that have been put into action, it is not difficult to judge what will happen at an appointed time of evolution. So with this calculation, many begin making plans, in relation to what is considered by earth calculations to be monstrous in time! But we sometimes prepare for several lifetimes to include the final incarnation which will help during the time of stress. We are not capable of judging everything which will occur, and many of us have accumulated experiences not even needed for this time of now, but the knowledge will always remain with us for other occasions!

Many situations are seen wherein you are part of a great plan that you are not aware of, but have the "feeling" you are a part of something. This is what we call "preconditioned action." We let it be known in your subconscious awareness, so that only the "feeling" is cognizant of the action. You often go about your determined way without the slightest idea you are fulfilling a plan!

This is the better plan of action, although the earth consciousness will say, "But wouldn't it be better to know what the plan is?" No, for a number of reasons. First, the plan is never filled in detail completely. God allows for man's free will, but the plan is known wherein the forces of balance are concerned. So when these forces of balance are taken into consideration, they are often dependent on the disciple UNCONSCIOUSLY fulfilling the action which will bring about the desired reaction.

Although this seems like "working in the dark" to many of you, it is with the greatest of wisdom that the plan was devised. How many of you already feel lonely for periods of time without realizing what you are lonely for? If you were completely conscious of your past endeavors and home vibration, you would want to give up more often than you do! It is not possible to work in a universe of love without being drawn to that point of greatest love. Therefore, if you are fully conscious of your home planet, say, you would automatically be drawn there in consciousness and make it twice as difficult to satisfactorily complete your job in a different vibration and perhaps different consciousness which is not your truly developed consciousness.

This is the problem of all avatars and world disciples. They do not have memory of what they want most to remember, but they do have memory of many things they cannot even relate. And when they are reaching the highlight of their teachings, they do not wish to go on for fear it is wrong in other details of their lost memory. They have become aware of so much and feel "slighted" when the world they came to teach hears them not, so they are forced to go on without mem-

(Please continue on page 17)

MESSAGE FROM A MASTER

Beloved Cosmonites:

Today's effort will be well spent if one will recognize the changing masses of light energy which are being projected upon the earth-plane. We seek to help those of you who do not quite understand what is being manifested upon your planet today. You do not have, as yet, the cosmic scope with which to view the whole planetary situation. However, you will soon be able to view things and ideas from an entirely different standpoint, as you will be heading into the law of least resistance, if you follow the intuition of the heart.

The summary of the situation is as follows: You are to become Gods. You are leaving the animal nature of mankind behind. You are outgrowing the need to kill even, but even that need to kill will seem to run rampant in most hearts when it is discovered that the energizing influence of this Christ energy will stimulate the latent and in some cases, repressed desires to kill. This will be the cause of so many uprisings and circumstances wherein the groups will attract each other who have had these latent desires and the repression of such desires will be released thru mass attraction of various circumstances.

The rumor will be among many, that man has regressed spiritually, while the truth will be, among those outbreaks will be the release mechanism which will HELP to destroy this desire within mankind as a whole. When this is understood, then those of you who serve God and Light, will be better able to understand and bless each situation that precipitates the release of such negative desires. The desires have welled deep within mankind and your so-called civilization has repressed them for so long as they have continued on within the subconscious to dwell and eat like a great cancerous sore within the inner being of mankind. The "operation" which best releases this energy of latent desire will be the pressure of Christ love that is focusing itself upon humanity as a whole until the hidden sources of all things within this animal nature will well up until it breaks thru the "civilized facade" of mankind.

Much that has been taught to you will seem of significance when these stages of evolution have been passed. However, until that time, the release of certain energies will bring chaos unto your world until you feel there is no God or rhyme or reason to His creation at all! Certainly the Lord has prepared us well, or we would not endure what lies ahead. It is the preparation of the student that brings him to the threshhold of new and perhaps, more trying circumstances. Without this preparation, God would not subject His children to their own creation unless He felt they were now prepared to withstand it. Being a creator is not pleasant at times, unless one understands his creation. And man has ignored the laws of creation upon this planet for so long, he is not aware of all that he has created. However, when the trials and tribulations continue after this long stage of ignorance, it is doubtful he (mankind) will not question the reasons for his predicament.

These are the truths, you, as students of truth and light, must adhere to; not to allow yourselves the mishap of being caught up in a wave of fear which will not concern itself with principles and causes, but only with the problems of personal discomforts. These are the danger points: to be allowed to dwell upon the vibration of sympathy, rather than compassion; to dwell upon cataclysm, instead of cause and effect; to dwell upon death, instead of life, and the change called death; to be seen as only a change of form and cycle.

Do not disfigure your spiritual consciousness by letting the remorse of earth-consciousness to enter in. It breeds neglect of the spiritual aspiration and allows no peace of mind. It is not considered unusual for a student of light to fall beneath the power of earth consciousness, but it is considered unique for the student to maintain his equilibrium thru all manner of trials and anxiety. However, the important point to remember, is that a student of light, even though he may fall, will always pick himself up and surge forward to the best of his ability.

This is what builds strength. This is what builds character and gives that manifesting soul , the experience needed to become a truly manifesting Son of God. Without experience, man is as a machine that has much information, but no understanding of what is translated thru its related mechanism. You would not like a machine as a teacher, nor would you like a God as a machine. Without the experience of life, one cannot be a master of life, even though one may have all the knowledge of it!

To practice perseverance against all odds, makes a God-man. To experience things without pressure, makes a man but not a character who can persevere without challenge. The challenge makes us try and by trying we create the circumstances which will best suit us to accomplish what must be done for any given life pattern.

Many will have within their life-patterns, various situations which will make them feel injustice in the scheme of life, but they do not always realize the opportunities afforded their soul growth for such opportunities. Instead, they wallow around in self-pity and do not see the blessing that has befallen them, a blessing that will actually take them out of the very circumstance they dislike by realizing WHY they are in it in the first place!

This will be the opportunity for many. But few will appreciate such opportunities! At least, not until their soul progression has been such that they will be able to return to the moments of decision and with wisdom and divine insight, see wherein they profited from the circumstance. This will be when the heart will be filled with gratefulness, but in the meantime, the heart will be bitter and much will be projected to ideas and people around them which supposedly led them into such dire circumstances. They will not think it possible they have brought this lesson upon themselves by their own disregard of law and order and the circumstances are setting forces in order once more.

Little is known of divine law upon our planet, but much will be learned in the future, which will turn our globe into the shining star it should be. We have gathered as a group of Teachers responsible for the development of mankind, and within our power, is the purpose of enlightening mankind thru our various instruments so that one day, the spiritual Hierarchy of this planet will be understood and recognized by even the mass population. We are trying to instigate matters for our immediate ratification by world opinion and by this recognition, we hope to ease the situation of many of our children who are not of the level of understanding to compensate for their karmic patterns by overcoming their weaknesses with greater attunement with First Ray activity. You are not aware of the many pitfalls dealing with mankind's illusions of vast intensity, and any who would destroy within their consciousness, these misconceived conceptions of physical life and spiritual life, will be better able to cope with their situation and more quickly develop into the proper consciousness to accept the Christ vibration.

This is not an easy thing for earth-consciousness to do. However, we feel that if the truth of our existence were known and our activities of a planetary nature were understood, many would be able to at least throw off the old illusion of a God on high in as limited a vision as the one who holds to such a concept. This is not true and of course there are many of us who can follow the old conceptions, but if it will lead to chaos, why would we continue to follow the unpleasant aspects of illusion? This is one of the aspects of earth-consciousness that must be overcome. The improper attitude and ignorant relationship of man and God. We must all become more aware of our place in the universe and lead our group of striving humanity to the threshhold of dawning victory over earth-consciousness and the animal nature of man. The physical nature of man will then be overcome and we will all merge as one in understanding and structure on the planet of Earth.

We are residing in the etheric plane of life and as you become more aware of the properties of the physical nature, you will begin to see the difference and the reception of earth densities that are caused by reaction of earthly desires and incorrect perceptions. We are not out of the realm of spirit, no matter what plane of thought we reside upon. We are with the limits of our own consciousness, whether it be upon the plane of life that I manifest upon or whether it be upon the plane of life that you manifest upon.

The duty we have as children of God, is to recognize His intentions to give us the very best and to have us appreciate what we do have and not to accept in blind faith alone, but to obtain knowledge of why we are of the nature we are and why He is of the nature He is. This is our secret quest in all our lives. To seek better attunement for our desire of finding truth and light, and working out of our self-created problems of misconceptions. When we arise to the enlightening acceptance of God-created plans, then we will all truly surge ahead as a planetary unit as well as a complete solar system.

We are not in accord, as a planet, with the rest of the solar system. However, as a planet, we show a marked distinction of being able to overcome even the lowest of desires; for at one time we were so engrossed in the material side of life we were put aside for possible destruction of the entire race of man, but the two who worked so hard to raise it up, have often said, "If it had not been for the inborn desire of man to raise himself up, we could not have done it."
So we feel this inborn desire still exists within our present physical population and that they will try, if only under greater stress, to resume the desire to raise their consciousness to impart the truth of the Christ spirit unto all levels of humanity, so that we, as a planetary unit, will go forward into the greater plan of solar initiation.

Be with God and you will be with us. We, of the Hierarchy salute those of you persevering to maintain your equilibrium thru all world crisis. We are with you each moment, and even though the way appears dark, the light will shine thru in just a few more steps beyond the sphere of earth-consciousness.

Much love and light is radiated upon you.

Master Morya

GUEST CORNER

We send our greetings and our Light to many thru the organ of Cosmon.

Alignment with Cosmic events is the order of the day. This alignment entails the necessary breaking away from all accepted and conventionalized thought patterns preconceived or partially misoriented by the masses of Earth's peoples.

Cosmic alignment is taking place at the time of the aligning of several other planets with planet Earth, thereby bringing in a vast new field of Cosmic energies and a greater aligning of Cosmic hierarchies with those of planet Earth. This thereby brings into focus the correct Light energies transmitted from the more advanced planets in your Solar System to your own planet and the life-wave incarnate upon it.

Visualize, if you will, this aligning or alignment, as a vast focusing of godlike creative energy to bring into correct balance planet Earth, the erring one of this Solar System. If the energies so focused are utilized correctly and fully by the Light Servers at this period of time, the results can be of inestimable value to those so using them and to the planet as a whole.

All things in Nature change according to season and to Cosmic calendar. Thus it is that the great change long prophesied upon your planet will be initiated and inaugurated in its fullness upon the time of the coming conjunction of planets, (Feb. 4 & 5) called by many of your people an "eclipse stellium." That there has not been such an overall pouring out of energies or the great change attendant upon it to this date is due to the fact that the planetary configurations were not so ordered until the ending of a 25,000 year cycle.

All things in the Universe are orderly and move according to their predestined seasons. No one event can occur, either in your own personalized lives or in the life of a planet, outside of Cosmic calendar. It is unfortunate that your peoples do not recognize this and attune their consciousness and their activities to receive the greatest benefit from the outpouring of various fields of energy. By this, do not misunderstand us to mean that we are in complete accord with many of your fatalistic astrologers. This is not the case. You do have individual free-will as individual free souls. But the greater events, both in your own individualized lives and the life of your nations and your planet, move according to seasons of waxing and waning, of budding forth and of withdrawal from activity. If you were further advanced as a people, you would have this knowledge as do we of other planets, and would attune to receive the greatest creative energy to manifest the carrying out of your individualized free-will and those desires which you have within that free-will to manifest.

Cosmic events do not move according to the will of men upon any planet, but move according to the Creator of all men and to the Divine hierarchies which carry out this WILL, which is harmonious, beauteous and loving in all aspects.

You see approaching, the ending of a 25,000 year cycle and the beginning of a new cycle of increased Light energies outpouring, not only upon your planet, but upon this Solar System itself. These Light energies will focus to the greatest degree at the time of the coming conjunction. They will manifest in two different ways, many facets, but two apparent and opposing (it would seem) ways:

(1). The greater upliftment and increasing spiritual awareness of those who have been striving to attune with the Light.
(2). The increased degree of cleansing and bringing to the surface and dispersal of all dross and weighty matter of negative manifestation upon your planet.

Thus, it is good that all Light Servers gather together in groups that their Light may shine in various places of the Earth. For where darkness also is concentrated, there will the Light and the Light energies cleanse and commence to greatly agitate the hidden dross in order that it may be dispersed in the time which lies ahead.

The Light in its many aspects is at all times beneficent. That its outworkings may appear to the minds of men to be disastrous and cataclysmic is only due to their incorrect understanding of Light energies. If attunement with Light has been sought, the individual concerned may be filled only with joy at the coming of the One who is known as the Lord of Light and Love, Jesus the Christ. If attunement with darkened forces has been sought or the mind clouded with the unrealities of shadowed forms of the Earth planet, then these things must fall away.

All cleansing necessitates a degree of bringing to the surface of past negative conditions and of the sweeping away and purification of these. Light cannot build upon darkness nor can a world of purity be built upon the filth and death and despair that lies buried in the etheric vibratory field lying close to the physical Earth. Only as the etheric currents are stirred into action by the increasing Light energies coming in, will these great vortices of force swirl away and disperse that which is not of Light.

Cosmic energies of tremendous magnitude are being directed at this time upon planet Earth. You, who are the servants of the Light, must needs intensify your spiritual awareness and practice of Light attunement that you may more fully play your parts at this time and in the times which lie ahead, times of tremendous challenge, of tremendous opportunity for soul growth and soul enlightenment and soul joy.

Children of the Light, awake to the Dawn, for the Light cometh and Darkness shall be no more!

We, your brothers, your sisters in Light from many planets, band together our thoughts and send to you this message of hope and encouragement. We know of that which many of you have endured. We KNOW of those times when you have nearly fallen by the wayside and have cried in despair and darkness and grief and we say to you that the Light comes and grief and darkness and despair shall vanish as a mist and shall have no reality. But the Light which is eternal is the Light of the coming Golden Age, the Age of Enlightenment, the Age of Joy for the Children of Light upon the Earth planet who, thru many lives, have sought to serve for this hour which approaches.

We rejoice and bid you rejoice with us.

The Space Brothers

Channeled by Marianne Francis

COSMON
NEWS AND ACTIVITIES

A new cycle has begun! We know that this also marks the greater opening of Cosmon to world activities and greater fulfillment of our plans. We were delayed another month again in having the bulletin ready for you because of being swamped with extra details in our work around here. One can't see Barbara for the pile of mail upon her desk!

In January, I was a guest on The Continental Show on television, a half-hour interview program. The program director called me later and said the phones all were jumping off their hooks afterwards. It seemed very well received.

We're turning over a new leaf around here, healthwise, since the old one got out of hand again, and trying some new techniques which we'll report to you later.

We were told by the Space People that the great Educational Program was to begin and already, we see the way it is beginning. We have begun some interesting research with one of the leading western universities. Some other things of great interest have also started, which will have to speak for themselves at the proper time. I know you will be happy to at least receive an inkling that such events are taking place. Other phases of our research have also begun to bear fruit and we're tickled pink about it!

We are so pleased to have Marianne Francis in our Guest Corner this time. She stopped by to see us and we enjoyed her company so much. It gave me a chance to ask her to be our Guest so you could all become acquainted with her work. She is also a telepathic instrument.

She's a little thing, with a soft voice and a decided English accent. You "feel" Egyptian around her! She's a pretty red-head who bears a definite resemblence to Nefertiti. She was once told she was her sister and it isn't hard to believe. Marianne is an excellent channel and has a very gentle manner about her, but despite her size, she is capable of big things!

She has a group of her own and says the space people have trained her for a certain job the past few years, although she has been a conscious channel for spiritual beings for 15 years; and her esoteric studies lead back to 20 years. She doesn't know this, but I was told, in the future we will probably be working together in some aspect. I, for one, look forward to it.

I first met Marianne at the Statler Saucer Convention a couple of years ago, and learned she was born in London, England and had studied singing for many years. We exchanged books. She has an esoteric novel out called, "Egyptian Light." It is about a girl escaping from Atlantis during its last days and going to Egypt. Those of you who would like to order her book and learn more about her activities, may write her at: P.O. Box 1551, Santa Barbara, California. The price of "Egyptian Light" is $ 3.00 plus postage. (Don't forget Cal. Tax!)

Columba Krebs, the contributor to our Cosmic Art for this issue, is already well-known in this field. Strangely enough, it was one of her lectures which first introduced me to the wonderful world of the occult ten years ago! She has many beautiful pictures we hope to bring you in the future. We're so sorry to be limited by reproduction as the original beauty is lost a bit. However, you may purchase this picture in color from her. A 5 X 7 photograph, $3.50 and $5.00 for an 8 X 10. Ask about her other available pictures. Order from: Columba Krebs, General Delivery, Williams, Arizona.

Some of you have inquired why Cosmon does not offer Breathing Exercises. The reason for this, is not because we are against them necessarily, but because J.W. has said that the atmosphere is so polluted, it is better not to stress something that may do more harm than good in certain areas. And we can never tell what area you may be in!

We received some wonderful information on the Esoteric Meaning of the February Conjunction thru two or three of our Wednesday classes. We are planning to compile this information into a small booklet for general distribution at a dollar donation. It gives one insight into a mighty galaxy and how the "greater world" we do not know truly works together. It gave us all a greater respect for the planet we call Earth and the tremendous load it has during this transition. It was one of those times we felt like "kissing the ground." As soon as the way opens, we'll have it ready.

Well, I boo-booed! While writing the Recommended Products, I forgot to allow room for a picture of the Gymsandle. So here it is! Knew some of you would like an idea what they looked like before ordering. We may get better organized one of these days! Now look at the Recommended Products page!

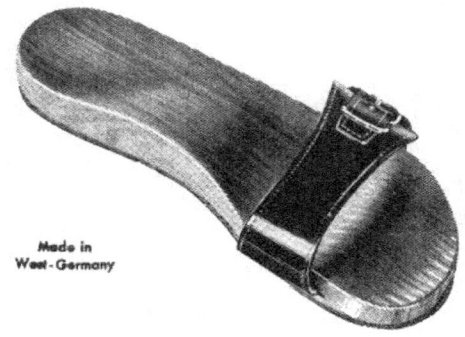

PLEASE SEND IN CHANGE OF ADDRESS!

COSMON PINS are still available. The gold crux ansata on royal blue background. $3.50 pp. Order from: Cosmon, Box 55, Palos Verdes Ests., Cal.

We had some lovely guests at our Wednesday night class...Bryant and Helen Reeve who wrote the book, "Flying Saucer Pilgrimage." If you haven't yet read it, I'm sure you'll enjoy it. Amherst Press, Amherst, Wisc.
They are in the process of writing a new book which should prove to be very interesting. They'll probably mention Cosmon! Both are very discerning and wonderful to converse with. We hope to see more of them and feel they are doing a grand job in bringing understanding of the "saucer field" to many people. They have a higher understanding of Cosmic Law than most investigators in this area, which is very important in order to bring truer facts into focus.

Speaking of new books, J.W. and I have not been able to get any more work done on his new one. So please don't plan on it for some time. I have more than enough to do, and can only do my best without more financial help to carry on more of the detail work in Cosmon. The Space People are planning other things, in the way of writing for me, and so much more will have to be done to bring the Educational Program forward. But with all of us in there pitching, we'll get it done!

Our MEDITATION CLASS is still held at the Southwest Counseling Service Bldg., 7323 So. Crenshaw Blvd., Los Angeles, Cal. (Just south of Florence) on Wednesday evenings at 8 p.m. We hope more of the members in the L.A. area will attend who have not done so. Distance is no excuse! We have them coming from Santa Ana, Sherman Oaks, Glendale and Palos Verdes!

It is necessary to take the book, "TODAY AS IN THE DAYS OF NOAH!" off the introductory price now. All orders must now be $2.00. Order from Cosmon, Box 55, Palos Verdes Ests., Cal.

We are hoping to have regular monthly meetings out at our Oro Grande desert center. Those of you in that area who would be interested, please write Bartram Kent, Box 483, Oro Grande, Cal. You can also make arrangements to hold your own meditation with a class tape on a weekly basis when you can all decide on a night. Bartram will keep in touch with me and I'll try to come out that night for a "live" class.

They tell me that much is going on in the Cosmon Center at Albuquerque. Classes and 2 or 3 lectures a week! Those of you in that area will miss a great deal if you don't stop in for at least a visit and meet Alexander Jack and his wife, "Willie." You'll love the whole bunch there! They are all a good group of dedicated workers and have worked hard to get their Center going. We expect big things to come out of that group. Cosmon Center in Albuquerque is located at 3602 Campus Blvd. N.E.

Gee, some of you have already sent me birthday cards! I was so surprised ...and pleased. Thank you! 29, again!

As I mentioned, much is going on now that will have to speak for itself. We can't force the wheel of fulfillment, but you will all know as soon as possible. It is important we stick together to reach our goal, and don't forget, we need your support in any way you can give it. We want to keep Cosmon glowing and growing, and it always holds true, "what blesses one, blesses all." The "critical" times are the times we need greater strength, and that is always available by relying on God, and holding together.

In light and love,
Gloria Lee

COUNTDOWN...
by Barbara Steele

Dear Cosmonites,

The Cosmon correspondence has now become entirely my part of the work, simply because Gloria is being more and more flooded with other duties. She is now doing so much more communicating of books and articles which will do us all much good in the future, but she still manages to read as much of the mail as possible. We often discuss what might help you most in answering your letters.

As you may suppose, our incoming correspondence is quite unique and amazing. It covers every subject known to man, sooner or later. We have requests for help in the most intimate situations. We have strange advice and suggestions sometimes too; all manner of proposals, (business and personal), and emotional outpourings ranging from the sublime to the eccentric. We just love to read our mail!

We, like the Space People, are here to help, and we hope you are helped by the things we are led to say and write to and for you. We are aware of many human problems, situations, circumstances and relationships;-that there is nothing left in this day and age which has not already been met on the wheel of time.

Because of Gloria's instrumentation of J.W.'s book, "Why We Are Here!", a great many of our incoming letters include references to, and questions concerning the famous Chapter 8. We could tell you that Kinsey would have a field day for his particular branch of research if he could have headquartered here in the midst of Cosmon correspondence!

However, the inquiries afford us the opportunity to bring out in the open many misconceptions and air them out in the sunlight of illuminating new age ideas that keep coming from the Teachers. Along with other branches of research, we are receiving a great deal of advanced information on the laws of balance and polarity and the correct use of masculine and feminine energies in the furthering of new age culture and civilization.

We shall have a higher sense of honor, a more intelligent code of ethics, and a deeper comprehension of the meaning of integrity and spiritual love, as we grow further into the New Age. Some fear a wave of immorality and a loss of decent human standards, but we see only a loss of outworn structures of thought that served as the restricting confines of a playpen for an infant who had not yet learned how to utilize complete freedom of action in proper relationship to the rights and comfort of other surrounding selves.

I would like to share with you, the answer recently made to a letter received from one of our members, whose thoughtful and honest questioning served as a voice for many of you who would not think of writing as he did, but who question within yourselves the same things.

Dear---------:

Having replied to you as Gloria requested, I will now touch upon the questions you brought up concerning Chapter 8 in Why We Are Here, and first assure you that J.W. is indeed well aware of the over-population problem of the Earth.

16.

The teaching given is intended for the New Age and as true understanding keeps pace with spiritual development, it will be seen that the emphasis is placed on LOVE between man and woman; not upon intercourse; not upon irresponsible breeding.

A sophisticated adult of today will recognize the fact that true spiritual love was not the motivating power behind production of the surplus millions of Asia. But the average adult knows little of universal law, karma, and reincarnation, and the scope of God's plan for this transition period between two ages and the blueprint for action to follow a general cleansing.

In a study of the law of evolution, we are shown a blueprint of life climbing from kingdom to kingdom until it reaches the human stage and becomes qualified to house an individual soul within a high type animal body. However, life proceeds in waves or cycles and there is a limit upon the number of souls that incarnate in animal forms in each cycle. Also, incarnation is under law, and if you will but observe in the marriage patterns about you, you will see that probably not one 35 year marriage has produced 35 children. Even without contra-conceptive devices, souls are not always permitted to incarnate at given times even though conditions are provided by a given couple for their reception. Also, you are aware that many couples yearn sincerely to give birth to children and although providing proper conditions many times, never give birth, or draw to themselves only a fraction of those they are equipped to love, educate and support.

In the cases of overpopulation in Asia, there are other factors at work, beyond the mere decisions of individuals to mate or to bear children. One of the psychological stimulii has to do with the fact that starvation enhances physical desire. This has been discovered by science, and is one of the main reasons for the old bromide, "The rich get richer and the poor get children." Starvation creates panic, frustration and the deepest and most urgent yearning for security and food. Since food is not available, and "misery loves company," what is more natural than that people drown their sorrows in the one free pleasure left to them, intercourse? They cannot afford to drink. They could not afford, even if they knew about, contra-conceptive devices, so in desperation, what course is left to them? It is a vicious circle and the most crying need, of course, is education.

Added to all this, there is a terminal point in racial maturing that is in effect now. During transition into the New Age, oriental bodies, which are of too ancient and slow a vibratory response to handle the qualities of light energy now coming into our atmosphere as a result of our planet changing its orbit; the souls must be able to change their "stock." Therefore, millions of souls are actually helping to commit a desired racial suicide in order to make way for a better type of human form. Those who have barely been born in their myriads, before dying out thru disease and starvation, have actually been paying off old karmic debts on national and racial scales and preparing paths for these same souls to be reborn in their next life within occidental bodies.

The orientals are remnants of the ancient Lemurian races and their day is now spent. If plans go according to spiritual blueprints, the whole of Japan will be submerged and all the Chinese will undergo a radical change of type so that they will not even look the same. When it has been said that the "yellow races shall inherit the earth" it has meant that this golden-toned race will be a homogenized entity comprised of the cream of all nations, as prejudice is dropped and all men meet and mate in a spirit of true spiritual love. All will gradually blend toward a beauty and symmetry and health and grace beyond anything formerly known on earth.

The above is such a slight indication in comparison to what is becoming available for study. We have been given a growing fund of communications (from the Space People) on this subject, but it is premature to present it publicly at this time. Yet, a great deal can be pieced together if you research without prejudice and keep your mind open until you gather in sufficient material to enable you to generalize to a degree. A word to the wise is sufficient, and as the Masters say; "Seek, and it will be found!"

                        Sincerely yours,
                        Barbara Steele

(Continued from page 6)

ory, so they can complete the mission they are not even completely aware of!

Jesus knew many things too, but he could not be given all the details of this life-pattern either, for he had gone too far to accept full memory, although, he had completed full consciousness after his resurrection. There are many details concerning world disciples and Teachers who come unto you, but we would urge you to recognize those who are at the door now, to open the way for greater enlightenment for new age activity. You do not have the stamina to work alone, none of us do in the overall picture, and so our Father of All, lets us have our way for a time, to better understand the folly, and then we are all sent to cleanse and work in the fields, to harvest another crop for eternity. None go hungry. None go alone. We all work together to complete our divine status of kinship with the One Great Spirit Over All.

My love and my blessings.

                        J.W. of Jupiter

        There is a destiny
      that makes us brothers:
      None goes his way alone:
       All that we send
      into the lives of others
     Comes back into our own.
                Edwin Markham

HEALTH AND DIET RESEARCH

BODY CLEANSING

So many of you have requested more information on Cleansing Fasts and I will add to what was given you in the Special Report of January.

First, a brief reason why and what cleansing fasts are for should be understood as a method of actual CLEANSING. The body collects so much morbid matter or waste over a period of time, due to our incorrect diets, that it's a real chore to even begin bodily cleansing, let alone to keep it up!

All the natural eliminative channels within your body are the pores of the skin, the lungs, kidneys and the bowels. Perspiration is merely the action of the sweat glands to throw off toxins which would be injurious to us if the body were allowed to retain it all. The kidneys excrete the end products of food and the bowels elininate, not only the food waste, but also the old body wastes of used tissues and cells. When these waste matters are not eliminated properly it has a more far-reaching effect on our bodies than we realize, so that the first step to a strong and healthy body is just plain CLEANLINESS....INSIDE as well as outside.

Now, a cleansing fast gives the body a CHANCE to eliminate and throw off the unnecessary waste matter within, but unfortunately, we're so busy in old habits as a rule, we never give our poor bodies the opportunity to balance themselves. We set such a thought pattern that all thru life, people often think they will die if they do not have their usual 3 meals a day. And strangely, some of them would, if they didn't, because they have stored up so much of this waste matter and toxics that if they went without eating for 2 or 3 days, they would die of their own poisons, which would try to eliminate in that period.

How many of you suffer from headaches when you accidentally skip a meal or two on a busy schedule? That's your proof! When your body is even reasonably clean, you do not suffer headaches from not eating. In fact, you feel better than ever when this knowledge is properly applied. But as most things, this subject must be approached with wisdom and not jumped into the middle without understanding.

We had a college professor who read about our diet suggestions and decided to plunge right into a fast. His wife called me and said he was really quite sick. ...palpitations of the heart, cold sweat, and he felt he was dying in general! He was....but he had dogged determination if not wisdom. I didn't find out until then, that he had been taking no less than 18 pills a day! "Take him off fruit juices, quick!" I said. "He's too polluted to fast with all those drugs!"

In his case it was more advisable to follow Ehret's idea of a mucusless diet for awhile. But he was a determined individual and despite the handicap, he followed a mucusless diet during the week and fasted on Saturday and Sunday, this time recognizing why there were such symptoms and able to control it better by vegetable juices or just eating vegetables. In only one month, he no longer took any of the 18 pills he formerly thought his life depended upon. We were as happy as he was about this.

If you have had a great deal of drugs within your life time, you will first have to recognize what happens when your body begins to throw them off and not become discouraged or frightened at your bodily reactions. All too often, people give up before they really get started and blame everything on the fast, rather than on past performances.

When I was instructed to begin bodily cleansing a couple of years ago by J.W., I suffered thru some tremendous headaches. They usually lasted only a day or two, but I stayed with it until I noticed I no longer had any. I went on the 7 day fast of grape juice, lemon and orange juice and felt wonderful even though I seemed a little anti-social the first few days! This was where I learned chlorophyll will be a big help in preparing yourself in the beginning, or any time for that matter. It can be taken 2 or 3 days prior to going on your fast for best results each day there after.

Another thing I encountered, which may help some of you to understand your own problems, was that I retained, what appeared to be an ordinary cold for 3 months! (I was in very bad shape!) My chest and head were continually congested but it was merely my body trying to eliminate the waste matter. I was also instructed to drink quantities of Indian Tea (Desert Tea) which is an excellent cleanser and promptly found I broke out all over. One of the Teachers read my thoughts to stop drinking it and said, "Do not stop the use of the Indian Tea, as you continue, it will cleanse and the body will no longer have any waste to break out!"

I really felt like a sad sack for about 6 months, but I was determined too, to see if this really worked. I took steam baths intermittently which also helped and even though I couldn't follow with a proper diet because of lack of will and habits too strong to break, I did fast periodically from 3 to 7 days until the headaches stopped and I suddenly noticed I could forget all about lunch and never know the difference.

I had retained a great many drugs because when I was an airline stewardess for 5 years, I flew overseas most of the time, and had every shot in the book, from the Black Plague to Yellow Fever. However, having been raised in a metaphysical religion, my mother had never allowed me to have any drugs, so I guess my condition was based mainly on those five years of drugs and a few about 5 yrs. afterwards... What a difference one feels!

As your body becomes half-way cleansed, you notice greater energy and sharper thinking and a whole lot of other little things. For instance,,,I could never get thru a whole meal without water or something to drink. I didn't seem to have enough saliva to wash anything down and was perfectly miserable when I found myself in circumstances without anything to drink with a meal. Yes, I had also read it was better to wait to drink AFTER meals, but with me, it was next to impossible. However, the body cleansing did something to those glands, because, without knowing when, I found I could very easily finish a meal without a drink.

I use to wonder why children had such runny noses. Now I know....all the improper foods we stuff down our children ignorantly, leave entirely too much waste matter, and the poor little things are trying to eliminate it all thru the noses! And as we grow into adults, our bodies "adjust" to this situation as much as they can.

One of the impressive side observations I encountered when fasting, was the fact my singing voice sounded as though I had been practicing a week! I did a little professional singing at one time, but in the past few years, hardly ever have the occasion to even try a couple of lines. When I do, my voice shows a decided need for practice to hit some of the high notes. However, when I have fasted for awhile, it's as if a block is removed and the high notes come very easily and a fine vibrato ensues without any practice at all! I have often wished I could relate this "secret" to many singers who really have a great potential; to see what would happen. It would do wonders for opera!

Another good reason for fasting is when the common cold hits you. Generally, in 24 hours to 2 or 3 days time, it will completely disappear; you just cleanse it right out of the system. There were a few occasions during the times I was fasting when the whole family came down with a cold or the flu, but it never affected me. And many times when I have not been fasting, but had just come off one, and had followed a decent diet since, colds all around had no effect. I also noticed if I relaxed my rules on diet (which I'm inclined to do because of old habit), I also have a cold but a fast will put me back on the right track again.

One time, I suffered from what apparently was a spider bite, with a temperature of 102 degrees for awhile. I fasted on plain water, as even the thought of juice turned my stomach. I was quite ill for a day, but shook it completely by the next. It is a natural inclination not to feel like eating when we become ill, but there seems to always be the would-be Samaritan who brings in some greasy soup or cereal and insists "you have to keep up your strength."

When I had the plane accident and broke my back, I went on a fast for a number of reasons; one being I couldn't stand the bed pan with my aching posterior in its condition, or the strain of using muscles affecting the back muscles and I felt fine. But our modern hospitals get so excited if you miss a meal and wake you up to give you a sleeping pill to boot! I guess I was classed as a "difficult patient" when I told them I'd scream if they didn't let me alone! I discovered a while back, if you have the strength to overrule the night nurse, you'll be left alone. But it always breaks my heart to see the so-called "balanced meals" our modern hospitals serve, which are usually exactly what the patient doesn't need. In many cases, fasting is exactly what is needed. Several of our members are nurses, and recently one told me, she actually felt guilty when she took a tray in to a patient! Of course, she didn't always see it that way either and had to "unlearn" a great deal of her orthodox training, but she proved the "new" diet to herself.

During a fast you are likely to feel all sorts of variations of sensations. Some days you will feel weak; others, as if you could lick your weight in elephants. Headaches may manifest from time to time, but I have found it is usually the first couple of days, when you eliminate old drugs or other toxic matter. You may even feel a craving for some particular food which may become unbearable at times. This is usually because you are eliminating this thru the blood stream and if you give in to your temptation, you'll only keep the desire, but with enough perseverance you'll literally eliminate the problem entirely.

There are some cases, when you take just a bite, and will become satisfied. But be careful! You will know you're on dangerous ground or not....it may take you past that "bite" and spoil all you have worked up to. You should know your tendencies and weaknesses and recognize your plan of action.

Professor Ehret calls the tongue, the "magic mirror." Your tongue is indeed the mirror of your bodily condition and its congestion. The heavier the coat on your tongue after a couple days fasting, the more coated your tongue and the meaning is, the more congested your body is. The tongue, strangely enough, is not only a mirror of the stomach but of the entire membrane system as well and after a few months of intermittent fasting and cleansing; closely watching your diet, you will notice a decided change in the coat on your tongue, if you show any at all. However, never fast until the tongue is completely clean. It is too dangerous.

The minute you begin eating again, however, your tongue will clear up, so the "mirror" is not in operation except when you are fasting or on a fruit diet to give you a truer picture of your condition. Of course, the tongue will automatically coat when there is an adverse condition, which shows the need of cleansing.

As in all things, use wisdom and follow a middle path. If you have been pretty good in following the better rules of diet and have a fairly clean tongue, but then you fall beneath the weight of old patterns and taste habits, you will again notice the difference in a heavier coating upon your tongue. And in following the middle path, I do not recommend a heavy meat eater to drop all meat and begin fasting. It would be too great a shock for the physical. Gently drop meat from one or two meals and keep a fairly steady diet before attempting to "go way out."

Once you begin to FEEL that cleanliness inside, you actually feel the difference in food that creates mucus and which you know leaves a good deal of waste matter, and you can't wait to get it out of your system! Also, depending again, on the length of time you have followed a good diet, your body will rebel over certain foods you had once trained yourself to enjoy. Your taste buds even take on a new dimension and delight! And you'll be surprised at how much your sense of smell will change to reject certain foods you once thought of as delightful. Meat will just taste like so much grease and you really see it for the "flesh" food it is!

Dr. N.W. Walker, has a procedure of quickly eliminating protein putrefaction resulting in toxemia or acidosis, and I've found it extremely helpful to rid one of a cold or even to lose weight quickly! He calls it Detoxication and it should not be used in the case of appendicitis or if there is any tendency towards it. For adults only.

This is one procedure which will be advantageous to remain at home, the first day in particular, until you see how your body reacts. The bathroom should always be handy.

First thing upon arising in the morning, drink one 8 ounce glass of a saline solution. I recommend Pluto Water for very quick and effective results, if you can stand the taste! I dislike salt, but somehow manage to hold my breath and drink 4 ounces at a time. One tablespoon of Glauber Salts (Sodium Sulphate) in an 8 ounce glass of warm or cold water is easier to swallow but not as effective. The Pluto Water is easier to take if ice cold as it seems to kill the taste a little. I've tried mixing it with fruit juices but it only prolonged the agony of getting it down! So I try to get it down in two 4 oz. drafts and drink some grape juice separately to kill the taste. You may not have as much trouble as I do to drink it!

The purpose in taking this saline solution, is not merely to empty the bowels, which it will do in an hour or so, but it will draw into the intestines from every part of the body, the toxic matter or body waste, as there may be to eliminate it thru the bowels.

He also suggests the use of Seidlitz powders, if a saline solution cannot be found as suggested above, but both can be found at most drug stores. The Seidlitz powders are also taken upon arising and one every 15 minutes until six have been taken altogether. I haven't tried the latter myself, so you're on your own, but if anyone does, I would like a report on the results.

This saline solution acts just like a magnet on the toxic lymph and body waste. It is drawn like a bunch of nails would be, into the intestines and out of the body in a series of "copious bowel movements which may amount altogether to about one gallon or more." You will feel quite thirsty anyway, and it is necessary to replace within the body an equal volume of the quantity eliminated or the body would become dehydrated. So it's a very pleasant task to drink about two quarts of citrus fruit juices, freshly make, diluting with 2 quarts of water to replace the toxic or acid material your body has removed. The water added will be for a quicker absorption into the body. (You will find this true with most fruit juices that by mixing with water, your body will absorb it faster and it seems to do you more good. After a few days on a fast, the "straight" juice seems too "rich.") This will have an alkaline reaction on your system.

Best results are always with fresh fruits in the following proportions:
    4 to 6 grapefruit, according to size;
    2 to 3 lemons, according to size; and
    enough oranges to complete a total mixture of
    two quarts.
    Add to this, 2 quarts of water.

Dr. Walker suggests drinking an 8 ounce glassful about a half-hour after taking the saline solution, or the 6th Seidlitz powder. Follow this with a glass of the diluted juices every twenty or thirty minutes until the whole gallon is finished. I have often been busy and didn't pay any attention to the time, but kept a glass and the pitcher handy, as you're quite thirsty anyway.

Do not eat anything all day, but if you can't hold out, eat some oranges or grapefruit, or even celery would be alright in the evening. Actually, with this procedure, it becomes easier to start a fast of grapejuice afterwards, as the saline solution keeps you thirsty and you do not think of eating so much as drinking!

Before going to bed, Dr. Walker suggests you take a high enema in the knee-chest position. After you take 1 or 2 enemas, you'll then see the wisdom in this other cleansing method as the whole purpose is to remove any waste matter from the folds of the colon and bowels which usually remains and which would be absorbed into your system during sleep.

Repeat this Detoxication for 3 consecutive days and approximately 3 gallons of toxic lymph will be eliminated from the body and you will replace it with 3 gallons of alkaline juices. This speeds up the re-alkalinizing of the system.

Incidently, this is one way to cure halitosis (bad breath). It is a result of the retention of fermented and putrefied food waste within the body. The decay of teeth is often attributed to it, but that is only coincidental, also resulting from retention of waste matter. This will help you clean much out before a grape fast. According to Dr. Walker, it has also helped many people get over their dizziness, which is a result of the body getting out of balance with the accumulation of waste matter in the system.

Dr. Walker then suggests on the 4th day to begin taking vegetable juices and vegetables and fruit. This is a very easy way to get your body into condition. The most important thing to remember if you continue to fast on juices is HOW YOU BREAK YOUR FAST. Break it with fruit or a nice raw salad. And don't be afraid to take an enema every night. It will put your skin in wonderful condition as any toxic waste matter that goes back into the system, usually tries to eliminate itself thru your skin. Teen-agers would have less acne problems if they realized this too.

Enemas are NOT habit forming! From personal experiment and experience, I discovered that any problem with normal elimination came only with returning to dead cooked food! No problem whatsoever when on raw salads or fruits. This is, I believe, the whole secret of constipation. If more sufferers ate more raw food, they would have less trouble.

Now, for those of you who are unable to fast, you can achieve the same results a little slower and with less drastic measures. A program of eating only the grapes will do wonders, and again, don't forget the enemas for further cleansing. A professional colonic will help all of you even more from time to time. Strawberries are good cleansers too and peaches are good.

Sometimes it is easier to start with eating something rather than just the liquid diet. On any diet, remember, fruits are the cleansers; vegetables, the builders. When on a 30 day fast, I usually fast 7 days on grape or some fruit juice, and then on vegetable juice for 3 days and back to fruit juice 3 or 4 days and then back to vegetable, and so on. I do NOT advocate any beginners doing a 30 day fast! Not because you think you can do it, but because the body will suffer too great a shock, not necessarily immediately, but it may show up at a later date. Be kind to your ol' body and break it in gradually to the chance of cleansing itself and rejuvenating itself. It can be done but you must be the one to use the wisdom and give it the proper care and not abuse the "temple" God built for you. You'll find much more meaning to life in general.

As an instrument, I find fasting increases my attunement tremendously. That is one reason I usually like to fast 2 or 3 days before a lecture. I have found I often have far greater energy and am able to do much more. The only trouble is, I LIKE TO EAT! But when I do, I often feel those bad habits as big lumps in my poor stomach and wonder why I ever got into such habits which make me fall from a better diet. But the rewards of even TRYING to cleanse your body are wonderful and you'll find, even if you do turn from the path occasionally, you long for the feeling a really clean body gives you and that wonderful sense of well-being.

It is also a wonderful sense of security to know you can easily go without food for a week. What a panic will exist for some people in the turmoil ahead. As hard as the struggle is to discipline self, it is worth it. And I won't kid you into thinking it's an easy chore. At least it isn't for me, for when you have set up behavior patterns and taste desires for several decades, you do not lose them overnight, or even in a month or perhaps a couple of years! The time for our change in diet is not "critical" but as students of Light, we have been given the opportunity to prepare and either we heed the sign or we do not. We can only gain, and lose our false conditioned habits to a road to better health and living.

G. L.

WORLD REPORT

compiled by Eugene A. Hurtienne

Earthquakes...

Japan and California have been the hardest hit of late. A few good size quakes of long duration, off coast of California. Kansas City area even had a few tremors in December. A new series of quakes struck in the Adriatic Sea Coast area of Yugoslavia, heavy damage. Many quakes felt in Nicaragua area. Panay Island in the Phillippines reported several tremors and minor damage in the Wellington area of New Zealand and other areas. Eastern Turkey had strong enough tremors to crack wall and houses in the Mus province.

Volcanos...

A report of an eruption on the remote Babuyan Island north of Luzon, was said to be "throwing off big boulders and lava was flowing into the valley below." And a new volcano began on the summit of Sirus Point on the northern tip of Kiska Island in the Aleutian chain.

Weather...

Besides the great storm off our east coast of the U.S., extreme cold has hit all over the world, breaking new records right and left. 60 BELOW for 3 weeks reported in Alaska! Even L.A. had snow. Many in India died from unusual cold. Floods in many parts of the world and many left homeless. Our Northern Rockies hard hit by flood. In some places early thaw has caused crops to blossom too early. Many crops already lost. Unusually high winds reported all over the world.

Avalanches...

Nearly 5,000 killed in snow avalanches in Peru. Apparently still occurring. Some reported in Germany and Switzerland.

Diseases...

Flu has come to the fore and is on the upswing all over the world. Lung cancer has finally been proclaimed as one of the outstanding results of smoking. Saturated fats or animal fats and the over-heating of fats are causing heart and circulatory troubles. Smallpox outbreak in London and great toll in Indonesia and reported epidemic in Red China. Chili is hit by Polio. Muscular Dystrophy is linked to X-rays! Cholera-like disease erupts in Philippines.

Discoveries...

South Magnetic Pole moves 300 miles to the NW in last 50 years. It is now in close to the Antarctic Circle in the Australian Antarctic territory... From the Indian Ocean area, reports come which show evidence of Lemuria having sunk more than a million years ago... An invisible aurora was found to be closer to the equator than the Northern Lights, starting in 435 miles above the earth's surface and is 185 miles thick... A new star was found by 3 astronomers Cal. Tec., the star has completely different structure than other stars, they claim...

SCIENCE DEVELOPMENTS

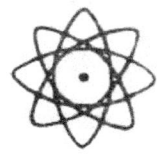

COLOR AND ITS NEW EFFECT

In our June-July issue of Cosmon, J.W. of Jupiter stated that some of our scientific theories have been correct to a point, but now we were going into a different realm which would require greater knowledge and new theories.

Recently brought to our attention is the collapse of Newton's color theory which has withstood scientific analysis for 300 years and is now falling flat on its face! A friend of mine who is a physicist, said it is amazing how in electronics they are actually proving it wrong. As I understand, and learned from my own art studies, we had to have any two of the three primary colors to start mixing the various colors and this rule had held fast in all the media we have used, but in the TV colors, they are combining ANY two colors and coming up with things always thought "impossible."

Also, in the Scientific American, someone brought to our attention where experiments with BLACK and WHITE film projected onto a screen and using various filters brings FULL color! For example, the images are photographed on ordinary black-and-white film; then black-and-white positive transparencies are made from the negatives. The "red" transparency is projected thru a red filter and the "green" without a filter. When the two images are superimposed on a screen, they reproduce the objects in a full range of color! The use of the long and short wave length colors produce a whole range of color but with a slightly different hue.

It gave us food for thought and we wondered if perhaps such things as the color bands or waves were also changing in our world or if it was because man's awareness and physical spectrum were being enlarged. Everyone knows how blue the Mediterranean Sea is, yet in Greek times, it was described as a red-brown! I believe Plato referred to it as such also. Could it be that just in the past few thousand years, man has just begun to see blue? And the Japanese, for instance, are noted, as a race, for poor eyesight. They are emerging from the third root-race and could it be, that they are straining to see the same colors the other races are seeing?

In many ancient writings, there are color references entirely different to what we know things to be now. The reds and browns, are of course, at the lower end of the spectrum and we are definitely going into the higher bands or wavelengths. As man's awareness is enlarged, we will begin to see the auras about our friends, as J.W. has said. He also corrected us at one time about saying we were going INTO the 4th dimension, but that we were merely EXPANDING to realize it! Anyone who has seen the astral colors or those on higher planes, often exclaim how beautiful they are, and of course, they cannot describe those colors which are different.

More than likely, this new influx of power will bring some of us new vision in more ways than one. The higher spectrum colors are always described as more brillant and "life-like." During an experiment with Dr. John Aiken, our Psychic Research Director and our co-director, his wife, also a doctor, I took the drug Mescaline with J.W.'s approval. I was rather disappointed to find what I saw wasn't any different from what I can pick up in my own meditations without feeling as sick as a dog for several hours! However, the highlight was well worth the sickness. Dr. John brought in a small rose and handed it to me. It was the most beautiful rose I have ever seen! It was seen with the stimulated "inner" eye and I could really see it as a "light form." It was "alive" with its own living light.

Long after it was apparently wilted to everyone else, I kept watching it in ecstasy, much to everyone's amusement as it looked so forlorn to them. But they saw only the wilted form while I still beheld the "living light" still within it. How wonderful when we do enter that area of consciousness where we can truly see the divine in everyone and everything! It gave me such a realization of the true beauty within all the forms we do not see with our normal earth-consciousness. I wanted everyone in the world to be able to see some life form with the same God-essence, light energy, or whatever you wish to call it, to give them this beautiful insight into reality. We have no idea how clouded our consciousness is on the earth level! This experience enabled me to "tune in" other other objects. So much more to tell about this experience but it will have to be another time.

I also looked at two large paintings. One evidently was painted while the artist was in a depressed mood, as the very vibration of his mood was within it. The other had the beauty of its own forms. Both were abstracts and the colors were in this same "living light," but in 3-D! The greatest impression, was the fact both had the apparent mood of the artists instilled.

This also reminded me that J.W. has told us how much our thoughts count when we are making anything. Even when cooking, one emits an energy of light seen usually as blue clairvoyantly, and if the mood of the cook is a bad one, YOU eat that essence! But to actually SEE the result of a thought, was overwhelming and certainly gave understanding to what the Space People have said; that it is also important about the THOUGHTS of the individuals who work upon our space rockets, as to whether they could be detrimental or helpful towards success. All machines will function accordingly. We often see a "lemon" in certain brands of cars or in appliances, wherein the manufacturer has an excellent reputation. The trouble could very well orginate in the THOUGHT of the individual working upon the machine!

We are creators, without the entire knowledge of how and what we create. And at this time of greater awakening we will be able to gain greater knowledge and insight and vision of what we are doing. How much farther we will go, when we can actually see where we are hindering our own progression!

G. L.

Diversity of worship has divided the human race into seventy-two nations. From among all their dogmas, I have selected one---Divine Love.

Omar Khayam

RESEARCH IN EMOTIONAL AND MENTAL DEVELOPMENT

by Maurine W. Sallstrom, Ph.D.

At the Southwest Counseling Service, we have found a very effective way of praying as those about us activate our emotional responses. As we go about our living, all of us find our sympathy or anger evoked by the actions and circumstances we see in other's living. The greater the emotional response, we feel, the more do we have need to pray for understanding and help for the circumstance which distresses us.

Whenever we try to pray for others, many questions arise, such as: "Do I know what another needs? And does he want my prayer? Or is it even his need?"

Since all of life is the mirror of our thoughts and feelings, we certainly have a right to pray for the knowledge and insight we need to better understand and direct those thoughts and feelings. Each person and circumstance in our lives is objectively something that is uniquely itself. But what it is to us, is whatever WE PROJECT UPON IT!

For example, the elderly lady on the corner is a person in her own right, with life and thoughts and emotions, I probably never will really know all about. However, whether she seems to me like a benevolent mother and grandma, or an old witch, depends upon the judgment I make of what I observe as I pass her home.

I may not know the prayer she needs. Only her own soul and God can know that. But I can know the prayer I need to say for what I observe her to be. If I believe her to be a kindly grandmother who is poverty-ridden; this is what she represents to me. My belief is, that her need is for sustenance. So to pray, "Help us where we are kind and well-meaning, but have not the substance to support our charities to find ways to give which we can support," would be accurately praying for what I project upon her.

If, on the other hand, I believe her to be an old shrew, whom no one wants to be with because she is so critical, my prayer would need to be, "Help us, where our bitterness and criticism alienates those in our world and makes us feel lonely, to find a better way to express." In either case, what I see my neighbor as being, must be the result of one of my OWN complexes of thought and emotion which have developed from my life experiences.

If I see her as kind, but unable to support her wish to give, it is because I have had more wish to give than I could support, and my prayer for her, helps this need in my own living. If I see her as critical and rejected, I have areas where I believe my own critical tendencies have caused me to be rejected and unwanted. While my prayer may or may not be needed by HER, it will certainly help ME to better understand and help those sides of my own feeling which are projected upon her.

This is a very effective application of Jesus's statement, "Love thy neighbor as thyself." For as we can love and understand and pray for those qualities we see in those about us, can we love and forgive and understand those SAME sides of ourselves.

This type of praying is especially effective to use when we are apt to respond with negative emotion, such as annoyance, and anxiety. Our emotion will be IN PROPORTION to OUR need to do this kind of praying. We may feel that our living is entirely free of the annoying behavior we see, yet it is amazing how once the prayer has been formed how soon we may see ourselves doing or thinking something very similar. We rarely do it in the manner or the same situation as the one we observe, but we do it in our own way and it is causing us as much disturbance as our negative emotion indicates.

One woman, who was particularly annoyed at an acquaintance who aggressively ran away with every conversation and bored all of her listeners, found circumstances of her living made her have to frequently be in groups where this woman held forth. While she tried to suppress her annoyance, she found it increasingly difficult. She tried to accurately state her prayer. It was something like this: "Help us where we want to talk, and where we do it so poorly that we bore those about us, and to better understand what our place in conversation should be."

She had only been praying this a few weeks when she realized that her fear of boring others was keeping her silent, until she was almost rude in not speaking to her friends when she was out in public! It also kept her from not sharing many interesting experiences which could have made situations that were boring, more interesting. She knew that in her years of silence she had learned a great deal about how people looked and acted when they were bored, and this knowledge could be used to measure the effect of her speech. As she continued her prayer, she was able to more frequently express and became a less boring companion to those about her.

Her boring acquaintance, was actually a rather accurate caricature of her belief of how she would seem if she talked as much as she wished! As she took her part in the conversation, her friend was unable to do so and she thoroughly dominated the situation. She became less annoying to the woman who formed her "We prayer." It seemed a short time after she understood her complex and healed her annoyance that her acquaintance moved out of her circle of associates.

It takes a little practice to accurately state the "We prayer." The first step is to objectively state the problem describing the symptoms as beheld. For example, when we are anxious for the safety of some impetuous youth, "Help us where we tend to rush into projects too fast and enthusiastically, without enough knowledge...." Next, state what you believe to be the help that is needed. "To take the time to investigate and find out what we do know, so we can make our projects safe and successful."

Third, every time our anxiety comes to mind, use this prayer to still it. The fourth step is automatic. We begin to discover how many times impetuous acting is impairing the safety of our own projects, and we begin to have faith that we can wait and find out how to act with more certainty.

In working with this kind of prayer, the results for the one praying are always gratifying. It is frequently amazing to see that the one who activated the prayer, is also benefited, or ceases to be a source of annoyance to the person who did the praying.

Begin today, to see how you can form your "We prayers" and discover how truly you will find, "God has forgiven your trespasses, as you have forgiven and prayed for those who trespassed against you."

Dr. Maurine Sellstrom

COSMIC ART

GALACTIC EVOLUTION

In the physical growth of the Universe, our Infinite Creator is the Grand Central Source, encompassing everything in the Cosmic Rays of Infinite Love, and whirling galaxies into every stage of evolution. Divine Will concentrates atoms, (that fill the ether of space,) until vortices of force are formed. The interaction of positive and negative magnetism, (in cohesions that condense) generates increasing light, heat and spiral rotations.

Thus, in each galaxy, centrifugal force pulls particles off, which whirl into Suns, (governed by the Sons of God) at the end of their magnetic tethers to the Divine Center, around which they rotate in wide orbits of long durations. These Suns throw off their own planets, which in turn, throw off moons, if any. These planets provide schoolrooms of various grades, to give their inhabitants a chance to "find their place in the Sun."

When age slows their rotations down, these tethers will pull the planets back in the Solar Center, thru narrowing orbits. These Suns, in turn, will eventually burn out, when no longer needed, and become huge dust clouds, dispersing into space. During eons of time, these same atoms will reform into new constellations, going thru the same process, but on a higher scale or vibration.

By Columba Krebs

RECOMMENDED PRODUCTS

It has long been the plan of Cosmon to recommend only high quality products and as long as the product continues to uphold that standard, we shall recommend it. However, should any product lower its standard or mislead us in its representation, we shall announce this to our members also. When we recommend one product from a company, it does not necessarily mean we endorse all the products a company may have. We will have tried to personally test all products recommended, but may not always be aware of something, until later, which would prompt us to remove an item from our list.

We are trying especially to find "new age" products and those things which will enhance your own personal life. We want our recommendation to mean quality and it will never be bought nor will paid advertisement be allowed. All products will be recommended solely upon their own merits. We may or may not receive benefit from this recommendation, but this program has been instigated for you, so you will have a dependable guide. The main purpose is for SERVICE in recommending reliable products and not merely for selling or profit. We invite your recommendations also and also your criticisms.

INDIAN CHIEF INHALER - Made from Herbs and Oils. Lasts for months. This is one inhaler we feel far surpasses any other we have found and all the ingredients are natural ones.... But we must warn you.... DON'T take a big whiff from the bottle, just sniff the cork. It's that powerful! Excellent for colds and hayfever, etc. Price: 50¢ Add 10¢ for postage and handling.

AMWAY LIQUID ORGANIC CONCENTRATE - Not a soap, not a detergent but one of the most remarkable all-purpose cleansing compounds ever made! Our highest recommendation. Gentle, non-toxic, non-caustic, non-volatile, a deodorant and economical and well, just about anything else you'd like to describe, for a truly new-age product.

Some of our members have found it ideal to wash (yes, we said wash!) their vegetables and fruits and are constantly surprised at the amount of dirt and chemical residues that come loose by a short soaking. There is hardly any use you can't put it to. Just the thing for fine clothing and yet excellent for heavy duty cleaners. Will clean oil and grime off garage floors. Leaves no scum or deposits even when used in hard water. I washed my children's shirts (a real test!), and so pleased with the results. Other members enjoy it for their shampoo and believe it or not, their teeth! Ruth of Cosmon says it's wonderful for scrubbing floors as it makes the water 300 times WETTER! Greater SOAKING qualities for even soaking off wall paper. We recommend ordering a gallon for greater use and savings. You won't be sorry.

1 quart, $1.65 (shipping weight, 3 lbs.) 1 gallon, $5.85 (shipping weight, 10 lbs) (Check parcel post rates in your area to add to cost of order, please.)

INDUCO - A Gasoline additive. A product we are personally well acquainted with and its background development. The Pacific Chemical Labs ran tests with 3 cars of different makes. The carbon monoxide content of the exhaust gas after the complete treatment was reduced to 67.6%, 84.6% and 95.5%. Air Fuel ratios were raised from between 10:1 and 11:1 to over 12:1 for all 3 cars. Besides lowering the smog in L.A., many of our members, have tried it and one member said he had planned to get a motor tune-up but after using Induco, he didn't need it! I thought my battery was no good because my car stalled 2 or 3 times before it finally started and after Induco, no more stalling!

Everyone that has used it is well pleased with better engine performance. Permission was granted to quote John J. Hollister, Jr. of the California Senate:"..In fact, I have used it now for some 28,000 miles and find that the engine is in perfect repair. I have not changed oil for nearly 12,000 miles; I have just added oil every 1500 to 2000 miles, depending upon weather conditions. The car reacts better and has more power with the additive than without it. Also, the valves without the material become quite noisy in a fairly short length of time and will clear up and become noiseless by using the material. I do know that it seems to give me a little better mileage, I would say probably in the neighborhood of 5%."

This product is excellent for any business that burns gasoline or diesel fuels and special products are available for smudge pots, space heaters, bunker fuel. Keeps the equipment clean and in good order. Inquire by mail.
Price: 1 qt. $2.50 (glass bottle, thus add $1.00 postage, handling charges.) 1 gallon can, $8.00 (no handling charge) For businesses: 30 gal. cans $30.00 ea. FOB L.A.; 1 steel drum (55 gal. barrel) $264 Freight allowed and 2%, 10 das.

HI-VI ELECTRIC JUICER - At last we've found a very satisfactory home juicer! We've had so many inquiries about a juicer and we have tried to find one within the realm of reason for the average home as well as one that is functionally handy. The best feature, we, the women like, is the fact you don't have to stop and clean it all out after making only a quart of juice! It has a plastic bag you attach to the outside and it can hold an infinite amount of the fibrous pulp for very easy disposal. It's easy to clean and there is no aluminum used in the juicing unit. It automatically ejects the fibrous pulp into the plastic bag and the juice flows freely and is not strained thru a layer of pulp, or robbed of valuable enzymes by overheating.

It has been engineered for long life. The strainer is mounted on heavy duty ball bearings to relieve motor bearings of wear. A one year guarantee. Heavy duty, speed-controlled motor never needs oiling. Life time lubricated. They say it yields 26% more juice than conventional juicers.

Model	Finish	Motor size	Shipping weight	Price
J-101-A	White with polished chrome trim	350 watts	12 lbs.	$ 89.95
J-101-BG	White with gold trim	350 watts	11 1/2 lbs.	79.95
J-101-B	White with pastel green	250 watts	11 lbs.	69.95

Height - 13 1/2 "
Width - 11"
115 volts AC/DC
Check your area for shipping costs to add to price, please.

FOOTGYM SANDALS - Many of us are addicted to wearing the Japanese thong shoe, but here is something just as comfortable and much better for the feet. Carved in West Germany, they were developed by Prof. Wilhelm Thomsen, M.D., a respected orthopedic specialist, as one measure to both prevent and relieve foot troubles. So many New Agers wear sandals during the day, and these are ideal as they are carved to really fit the foot in the proper places for arch support and your toes grip a specially contoured metatarsal crest which give muscles that go unused in normal footwear, scientific exercise. Feet are strengthened in only a few minutes a day and foot fatigue is reduced. Soreness disappears. Circulation improves remarkably for some, because of the muscle exercise. Feet that are usually cold or subject to excessive perspiration glow with the surge of this freshened blood supply. Cramped toes relax; weak arches grow stronger; relief for "burning" feet is almost immediate.

They're available in any size too. Outline BOTH feet (some people have two sizes of feet!) while STANDING (important) and send in with your order. Adults: $ 7.95; Youth size: 1 - 3, $ 6.95; Child size: 5 - 13, $ 5.95. Add 75¢ for postage and handling. Felt lined leather strap comes in saddle tan, red or white. Natural finish Poplar wood with a bottom sole of non-slip procrepe.

The Patricia Allison, truly NEW AGE MAKEUP brochures have already been sent to you. There is no cost or obligation to join the Beauty Sorority and you'll be very pleased with the product, I know. The men members who have received these brochures, will certainly be doing some gal a favor if you give them to a friend, mother or aunt. Grandmother is never too old either!

When I mentioned these products last time, I hadn't as yet, used all of them but I would certainly like to share some of my "discoveries" with you. The most startling one, I believe, was their EYELINER and EYEBROW PENCILS! Most cosmetic pencils are very unsatisfactory but THESE ARE THE BEST I'VE EVER USED! I used to be a model and so have had a wide range of experience with them and couldn't have been more pleased. I didn't even intend to use the mascara because I have a pet I've used for 10 years, but do not feel I can recommend it as some people are allergic to it. I'm not...but found the Allison mascara another great surprise, so now I use two brands! People that have never been able to wear mascara, I'm sure, can wear this and we heartily recommend it. These were the big surprises in their line.

So far, I haven't found anything at all I dislike in the whole line. It's the best lipstick, which I mentioned before and all pure, harmless ingredients...as is the eye makeup made with certified edible food colors. The make-up base is wonderful too. I feel this is one company whose COMPLETE LINE we can recommend.

Just one more word...one of the best CLEANSERS is their Swedish Scrub - Honey and almond mixture, that has been used by woman for ages past, so it's easy to say "time-tested." It's a bother to give yourself good cosmetic care at times, but every effort for good cleansing and grooming is always worth while. As J.W. says, "We should all walk in Beauty" and besides beauty of spirit, beauty of form and the acknowledgement of that "temple" wherein the Spirit of God resides. Great temples existed in the past, dedicated to beauty, and Cosmon will one day again build that understanding of beauty in Spirit and Body. Write us for a brochure if you do not have one or need another concerning the Patricia Allison Beauty Sorority.

ACEROLA - Vitamin C - Here is one of the nicest Vitamin C's to take! You can let them melt in your mouth. It's always a problem to get young children to take a good vitamin C and my kids love this one. Made of all natural organic goodies, such as rose hips, black currants, green peppers, etc. Jar of 250 tablets, $3.00 and please add 25¢ postage and handling.

Last year our Guest Channel, Marianne Francis received this important information: "Conditions environmental and otherwise upon your planet, regarding mineral, plant and animal life are rapidly being affected and dessicated in cellular structure from harmful radiation content in your atmosphere. Content of radiation rapidly approaching saturation point within cellular and bone structure. Consequent damage apparent now. Shortly there will be upon your planet a new outbreak of a particularly virulent form of fever. This is caused by the breaking down of the cellular structure and the consequent overloading of the body with toxic or dead matter (cooked foods!). In attempting to clear the channels of the body, high fever will manifest and your peoples will be, in many cases, emaciated, as the toxic matter accumulating so fast will defy the efforts of the recuperative powers of the body to assist in regeneration.

You, our brothers, our channels of Earth Service, must guard yourselves at all times against these epidemics. Your most efficacious means of so doing is to drink copiously of your citric acid fruits. These epidemics will strike those already most filled with toxins from your unnatural forms of civilized, so-called living. Sector Xector Xerxes transmitting."

This communication tells very well why it is important to watch Vitamin C in our diets. All the strange new "virus" is what many in the space field now call, "Radiation sickness." Just a word to the wise!

Please make all checks payable to Cosmon Research Foundation. California residents, please do not forget the State Sales Tax of 4%. Outside of U.S.A. orders, please consider the difference in postage and allow for same.

ORDER from: COSMON, RECOMMENDED PRODUCTS, Box 4127 - Catalina Station, Pasadena, California.

For further information and your own recommendations and criticisms, write to Glenn and Ruth Hood, two wonderful Cosmonites who are working very hard to help you with these products and to find you more. Let them know of any "pet" products you may have you believe Cosmon could recommend.

If any of you would like to help Cosmon by being local distributors for the Amway and Induco products, you may write Glenn about this.

That's "30" for now. Let's work together and go forward in bringing better products to our planet. If the demands are set high, others will have to follow suit to maintain a high standard, which unfortunately, too many manufacturers do not do now.

Gloria Lee

MISCELLANEOUS FILE

PERSONAL MESSAGE AFTER DEATH

This is one of the most outstanding messages we have ever seen from the "other side" of life. It is so filled with truths, we urge you to read it many times to find them all. We feel you, too, will see it as the "classic" we feel it is.

This communication was made by an individual of great soul development to his sister, Maurine. There was a great love between them and this was communicated on the 33rd aniversary of his "death." He was only 16 years old but had already been very successful thru his childhood in an artistic career. After, what seemed an apparent healthy life, he suddenly passed on from an internal accident. Here is the meaning of his death and the meaning so many of us long to know about our family unit and the different relationships......

Maurine, this is the anniversary of my leaving your family. Yet, I have never really left! You had the dream about the sacrifice and the fruits of the Earth. It is to help you understand about "giving up." I did this same sacrifice when I gave up living with all of you, to live on this side and work more directly in spirit than I could in the body. I was sad as I contemplated this leaving you and that sadness reflected in my speech and in not wanting to talk about death.

You felt so strongly that I was not dead that you worried about the autopsy. I was not dead except it was necessary that I lay down my body to work in spirit and in truth. The path that was open for me at the time was one where in the temptation and the fear of the senses, it would have been very great. You have seen this in a milder form in our sister. My problem would have been greater, because a man is exposed more fully to sense-pull. A woman has some protection in her high feeling, and intuitive awareness. I also would have had to face a war and the brutality it arouses in other men. This would have made it impossible for me to do what my soul had to do.

I could do it by giving up my form, by surrendering what I feared would be hurt. I could die before I had to fight and not have to win the fight in battle and in a way to hurt others as I made it. You could not have understood this before giving up your home in the way you did, and without seeing this dream about the fruits of Heaven, that can be seen once a sacrifice is made.

Man can do this all peacefully and on his own, without being drawn into a great conflict that involves others. Just as you sold your house and moved easily and naturally, with no wrenching experience that robbed you of the fruits of your labor. And the withdrawel, before necessity allowed you to plan and build a richer life for your and your husband's remaining years in life.

So my sacrificing the family life I lived with you all, allowed me to plan a richer and fuller life for all of us. Just as my career removed you all to California, my leaving the physical form moved you all into a different consciousness of service and return for that service in a more secure sense of living than you had known previously to that.

Immediately after my "death," the depression came. Dad made another decision not to take government aid, which gave ME the spiritual substance to work with and established the currents of force which could let me direct to you more awareness of how man can receive from God that instruction which gives him abundant living.

You saw yesterday, in talking to the Japanese man, how much being needed has been a value in youth which many young people today are denied. You were needed in our family in that way in our youth. I was needed in that way to be here and work with you in spirit and in truth; to more readily clear the channels of force to bring the light of how to live abundantly into your consciousness.

You have wondered about Sonny, and whether I am Sonny. Sonny is himself, but we are on the same great chain of identification, which makes us have common feelings and problems. His father has combined the drive of our mother and her need to work and try beyond energy and comfort, with the fears of his family and a rejection of what Dad could bring to ours of passive tranquility, that settled for less than works could have achieved.

This has left him tense and fearful, Sonny has come to help him, even as I came to help all of you. He is using many of our family genes that are the same as mine, and as such, we are flowers on the same stock, as M----- saw in her fantasy, and also prone to the same disturbances. However, my giving up my body can be a sacrifice for him, and in spirit this gift can protect him also. He is already saying "God will heal me." He is doing this, some from the fear of the medicine, but also from a basic faith, which you and I can help him train and develop.

You saw with my physical death, the fallacy in Pollyanna type of metaphysics, and how powerless it was in a real crisis. This had to make you and mother deepen in and find more of the real life currents God has for man's use and healing. That healing is not demonstration, but illumination, the great light of understanding which makes the problem no longer necessary. When we can release our clinging to false value and immature concepts of what we feel to be the good life.

It is love that groups us in families, either in its positive and spiritual side, or in its negative and physical side, which sometimes acts as the magnetic force of hate. You have counseled families where the tie seemed to be hate, such as the M--- family. But the love is only young. As selfishness is surrendered, and self-pity is healed, as you see the mother working to do, love grows and balances the fear and frustration, which make the negative force you call hate.

Non-resistance, sacrifice of one's personal loves and glamorized objects for the welfare of the others, enrich the positive side of love and heal the conflict and frustration.

I did such sacrificing when I laid down my body, with its future and its promising career. Our sister has lived that career and in so doing, raised the family's identification with wealth. She now laid this down in another sacrifice. She gave you the identification, she now must find ways to live and identify with love. While she is going thru this difficult time of adjustment, clothe her with the love you all have developed, while she was working on the big family "dark" of finance. She needs your consciousness of love, just as you needed hers of supply.

This chance to help each other in identification is one of the great values of God's plan for Earth, which has the family as its human unit of unfoldment.

Not that the unit is breaking up as you enter the Aquarian Age, it is only shedding its bonds of obligation and dictatorship. You will work together in the future in love, not in obligation and submission to the authority of the strongest willed one, who provides the physical wherewithal for material sustenance.

Your awareness of this subjective bank of love, is an important insight, for you and for all of us. I have been feeding that bank ever since my leaving my physical form. I have been active also in love, in ways you cannot understand at this time. Now you and mother must feed this bank, you are the most active contributors, although Dad has passively contributed all his life, in the form of acceptance and good will.

Mother has sensed she was feeding this, and the others were drawing from the bank she had somehow contributed to. This was the basis of her resentment before her illness. In her illness she also made a sacrifice. She sacrificed going out in full glory and leaving her image as founder of the work, unimpaired by a body that is withdrawing from life. She could have gone then, and in full honor; but her sacrifice was to go on living, in a form that lacked the vitality and ability to work and sharply respond intellectually as it had all of her life previously. The fruits of her sacrifice, will be wisdom in place of perception. The wisdom she will leave, will set her beloved work upon a level of group service it never could have attained under the image of her original concept of it, before she made this sacrifice.

The love she could feel from her family was what gave her the courage to do it this way. I, too, was there helping that night you were all so concerned. In this respect, my dying was that all of you might live and live more abundantly. I can help you with understanding beyond the ken of those still impeded by form.

Maurine, make your peace with your body, and in doing so, your daughter will inherit the peace with hers. They are good bodies, well equipped to run and do their work of perceiving and sensing all in their world. The body of our living often does not come in the shape we think is beautiful. But to one who has given it up, the beauty of any body is apparent as the work of God, and is fearfully and wonderfully made. Any instrument, so adaptable, so mobile, so sensitive, and so able to do both light and heavy work, is truly something to bless, not deplore.

Just as I surrendered my body to do for all of you what I could, you surrendered your concept of beauty of form to do what not having it made you do with your living. Our sister accepted such beauty, and you do not envy the life it created for her. We cannot know the form in which God brings our blessing close. But it is always close, nearer than hands and feet. In fact, it is hands and feet and heart and lungs and all the wonderful equipment God has created to give opportunities to perceive and change our environment with our living and feeling and thinking and serving.

Mother has told you many times you have enough; do not want what everyone else has too. All mankind has some beauty. Most of us did not have all beauty. Jesus did, but only because he lived purely from identification with God as Love.

Those of us who are still partial in our loving, must be partial in our beauty, until the areas where we do not yet love can lend their radiance to our form.

The limitations of form make us explore and learn to love new areas, that the perfect animals do not know even exist. We take on this imperfection with the individualized consciousness to become conscious of more of life. The limits focus our finite vision to varied areas of infinity to perceive the part more clearly. When the love is obtained, then the part must be sacrificed to look anew and find more of the whole.

Well, darling, this has been a fine visit. I have been with you before, but your sense of life and death, and your limited understanding of the great banks of mind where we could communicate, made you afraid to recognize it as me. All those you have loved, in or out of bodies, can communicate thru certain levels of conscious awareness, but we only enter those levels thru the act of sacrifice. Any form we cling to, we cannot contact in those formless banks of pure exchange of idea. It is only as the form of what we love is surrendered, that we can reach it and communicate with its essence in this great bank. It is the rainbow, the arc of the covenant, that all that man has known, will not be wiped out of consciousness. It is there to turn to, in its essence. In spirit and in truth, it is there, just not in physical form. There is form there, but it is perfect form and not that which is seen with eyes.

Peace be with you all. I am often with you in my present form, and always with you in love. In this new understanding and as you can give up your attachment and identification with your body, we will be able to visit more frequently. You need not strain at this; it is happening. You felt so passionately the night you came home and found I had left my body. "God gave you your brother and He would not take him away!" Well, dear, you were right, He did not! You just couldn't see him. But then, vision has not been your long suit in this life time! You still carry scars from past experiences. They will go, as you disassociate the concept of function from form. Function is not dependent upon form. Form is only dependent upon function. When form ceases to function to fulfill our purpose, we change it, or lay it down.

A happy Easter and spring to you all. I was never dead, only risen.

    Your loving brother,

       Stanton

       (Received Mar. 3, 1962)

☥

We sorry...

We know our editing appears lacking,
Our spelling sometimes needs attacking;
But we'll stay while we grow and learn
.....If you'll overlook your concern!

LEEWARD
with Gloria Lee

The Conjunction set off a few incidents, however, nothing of what the Space People would call "major" has occurred yet. The storms and even avalanches are considered "minor" and it must also be remembered that the "world cleansing" will take place over a period of many years, perhaps hundreds. All the physical changes merely indicate the spiritual and mental changes taking place within humanity as a whole. The planet itself, is taking on greater stress, to ease the pressure on mankind, for it has been man who has created this imbalance which makes it necessary for the various kingdoms to restore the proper balance themselves.

It was interesting to me that the approximate area, in which I felt I "saw" the land mass rising or volcanic action which would take place, suffered a 15 minute quake at the intensity of 4.5 on the Richter scale. There will probably be many such quakes before anything definite is noted.

There have been prophecies from different groups which stated that great unknown monsters, some as big as ocean liners, would be arising from the depths of the oceans, probably because of the land changes beneath the waters. I thought it highly significant to find the report of a "Giant Mystery Monster in Tasmania Sands' in our local paper on March 12th.

Evidently, only a handful of people have seen it so far, but apparently there are only pieces of the carcass left. Two men discovered it 20 months ago but did not report it until recently. It was described as "something probably never seen before by man." At least our modern man has never seen it! It was estimated to be about 20 feet long, 18 feet wide, 4 1/2 feet thick and weighs between 5 and 10 tons. It is circular in shape and no eyes or defined head structure. Its creamy, rubbery flesh is probably 12 inches thick and covered with wooly hair. Its characteristics appear different from all larger known fish or sea mammals.

One of the scientists probed deeply into the top and side of the monster but failed to find any bone structure. It would be impossible to identify without bone structure but that microscopic test of the sample of flesh which was taken, showed it was composed of collagen, a gelatin-like tissue. This tissue is found in humans, sea creatures and other animals. However, because of a heat test, it shrank at about 68 degrees-slightly lower than that for whale flesh---the scientist thought that that suggested it did not come from ocean depths or that it did not exist in a cold water area like ocean depths.

Another scientist thought it may be a giant sting ray! Since a good part of the creature is still buried in the sand, it will be interesting to watch for further developments. No one seemed to think that perhaps the head itself was still buried, so we are eagerly awaiting more news. These are the times we wish Cosmon had the funds to send out their own scientists! Well, one of these days......

There was another interesting phenomenon which occured over 180 miles of the Australian coast line. Fish intent on suicide were swimming upright and gasping for breath while going round and round in small circles, and dying by the thousands. This sight of fish literally dying to get ashore was something to behold. The cause was unknown and speculated whether it was due to a disease peculiar to fish, or from a bomb blast, or from a "red tide," or even chemical contamination. The "red tide" has been reported in several areas the last couple of years and is made up of tiny organisms in a floating mass which consume all the oxygen. However, at the last report, the situation was back to normal and the fish were horizontal again.

Again, the animal kingdom made the headlines up in Oakland, California. We all had a good laugh over this one in January. It seems about 3,000 Robins made a mass attack on the over-ripe pyracantha berries in one neighborhood. The berries made them all tipsy and our imaginations ran overtime picturing a bunch of drunk robins! "And drunk," they were, said residents of the neighborhood. "They wouldn't even walk away from you when you approached them, or fly on one wing or two!"

This first group of birds had so much fun they called in a few of their friends to join the party and an estimated 12,000 covered the local roofs and streets! They gorged themselves so they just wandered on foot around the streets, refusing to flap their wings. (Or else they couldn't!) That will probably be the talk of the bird kingdom for some time.....and I couldn't help but think God had a chuckle from it too!

Also seems in the bird-kingdom, a few of the occupants have become radioactive from the Russian tests and warnings have gone out to residents in the Far East to be careful about eating them. The poor birds must feel it's a dog's life.

And speaking of dogs.... Several times in the papers lately I have seen that roaming dog packs have attacked people. This has taken place in different sections of the country. What it brought to mind was that during the time we were experimenting in hypnosis, I projected a subject into the future, and she saw, what appeared to be during the more ambitious part of our world cleansing, many dog-packs were roaming around viciously attacking people. It seemed to the subject that the higher vibrations had upset their balance and there was also a lack of food and a scene of many wrecked dwellings. No time element could be established nor is it certain that it was not within the subject's imagination. Only time will tell.

However, even in Finland, fear of roving wolf packs has caused officials to order special escorts for children traveling to school and out-lying homes this winter. These things only indicate the importance of being well prepared spiritually and recognizing the causes.

Did you know that the name Khrushchev, origin of Russia of course, means "one with the characteristics of a large beetle?"

Have you noticed how many "group karma" debts are being paid off now? Mine accidents, plane accidents, storms, etc., all have the earmarks of group debts. One of the earlier prophecies, if you remember, was the increase in plane accidents but there is always that great Law of Attraction which will gather the group to its own.

We were so happy to see one doctor stand up for non-milk drinking! Dr. Walter W. Sackett, Jr. of Miami, Florida, admitted his is a controversial position; said publicly that no one over a year old should drink milk. He said he is a bitter foe of free milk distribution in public schools. He sends notes to school with his children to have them be given coffee or tea instead of milk!

He asked, "Why buy national suicide?" Milk and other dairy products should be eliminated from the American diet because they are high in cholesterol. (Cholesterol is the saturated fat which sometimes piles up in coronary arteries and brings on heart attacks.) He is also chairman of the Public Policy Commission of the American Academy of General Practice. I urge you to send him a note of encouragement.

Naturally, the A.M.A. has challenged him and said he held "extreme views" and did not represent "sound thinking." As much as I like dairy products also, I must agree with Dr. Sackett in view of our research and reports from members after eliminating dairy products from their diet. Even Dr. Walker confided to a friend that he had included cheese in some of his recipes and was sorry ever since He claimed it gave him more trouble because he had felt sorry for the people trying to make the transition diet and wanted to make it easier for them! Obviously, the Dairy Association got to President Kennedy before he made the announcement on everyone drinking more milk.

Here is one we would sure like to know more about.....An 11 year old boy recently died of "old age." His pediatrician said it was one of about 50 cases in world medical history. He called the disease progyra. The boy weighed less than 30 lbs. and had hardening of the arteries and was as wrinkled as a very old man. He also had a heart condition. Officially, he died of a heart attack. There is no known cause and no particular pattern and the disease is not hereditary.

The disease was diagnosed when he was only 5 years old and the "aging" process began. He was in school until a year ago. It would be very interesting to know the diet he was on and whether a great deal of milk or dairy products were given to him. I wish it were possible to open research here. The karmic aspects would also be interesting.

Incidentally, many in our weekly class recently mentioned how coffee was beginning to affect their ability to sleep......only since the Conjunction! They were old hands at coffee drinking and couldn't understand it. We decided it was probably due to the changes which are bodily even though we are not aware of them. However, certain foods, others have also noticed, are definitely not "comfortable" to them any more. How subtle the changes.

Here's a situation that is so unfair it makes one's blood (pure or impure) boil! This is what ignorance can do and what we must not allow to happen any more than it has....

An Army courtmartial sentenced Robert H. Sorge to six months at hard labor for refusing to take immunization shots! Robert is 23, a recruit that threw the post reception station into a turmoil when he frankly announced his body-building principles would not allow him to take the routine inoculations, thus he was found guilty of wilfully disobeying an officer's order.

He was the winner of the 1959 "Mr. North America" contest and holder of other body-beautiful titles. He also must forfeit $50 a month, roughly two-thirds of his army pay, for the next six months.

I don't know what his body-building principles are, exactly, but I know if he has followed a program of body purification, those darn shots could almost kill him! One would think the army would be interested in the REASONS behind his principles and study them to see if there would be greater information for their own techniques. And if they use the old excuse of Robert carrying germs, than they don't have much faith in the shots they give everyone else. However, what is more important.....IT SHOULD BE AN INDIVIDUAL RIGHT to decide whether one wants a shot or not. What's that old story about something being unconstitutional??? Personally, I think it's a terrible miscarriage of justice.

Polio shots, incidentally, are NOT compulsory. Send a note to school with your child saying you do not wish them to have the shots, providing you don't.

In meditating about the radiation problem our world faces at this time, I recalled an incident I read about Hiroshima. It was written by a missionary who had lived some miles outside of Hiroshima and is very significant. He noticed that those who had been wearing black clothing were greatly affected by the blast; much more so than those who were wearing white clothing. Also, there was a sign upon a wall of the mission with big black letters and a white background. The black letters were all burned away while the white paper remained untouched!

The Space People have said that to become "Christed" is to literally become radioactive! In other words, your own inner light raises to such magnitude, there takes place, a meeting of vibrations, so to speak. J.W. has often mentioned that, as we are now, we couldn't stand the vibration upon his planet of Jupiter. We must become far more purified in body, as well as spirit.

Many have wondered why we have stressed bodily cleansing, but it is because this will eliminate greater upset later when conditions, whether from atomic bombs, or whether from just the influx of higher vibrations, will affect the body more. A body-cleansing will allow the "light" (or power, or energy, etc.) to pass thru the physical vehicle without damage, as the white (pure) paper was unharmed, while the black (impure, dense) letters were burned. Another example would be similar to a dirty window pane...as one rubbed the dirt off, a greater amount of light is able to pass thru. Any dirt, impurities, etc., cause a resistance which creates a "dis-ease" and/or friction or heat.

There have been many prophecies from different sources about the great "heat" which will manifest in the future....perhaps it is not heat as we think of hot weather, but as we think of "hot" in something radioactive, which will burn up so much of the gross. If we are gross in nature, we will naturally be greatly affected. This follows, of course, with any grossness in consciousness.

One of our members, who has been nursing here in California, said so many patients are coming in with "unknown afflictions." Many seem to have flu and pneumonia, which are so described upon their charts, but the doctors, themselves, admit they do not know what these illnesses really are! The symptoms are very similar but the effects are not the same. We feel it is this MASS CLEANSING taking place in so many bodies.

This is why Cosmon has been told to stress body cleansing. We have received a great deal on this subject and many are naturally reluctant to follow such a program of self-discipline. We have our own problems too! But we can honestly say, it works! And when wisdom is used, it can be done, even in this day of very few available foods considered "pure." Unless you live on an organic farm, it's literally impossible to go "all the way." But it is possible to follow the "middle path" and see an improvement.

It was also interesting to see mention in the newspapers, that Biology is undergoing a revolution, the meaning and magnitude of which has become apparent only in recent weeks. The pace is so swift that it is felt few scientists even realize it, or recognize what a powder keg they are sitting on. They are hoping to crack the "code of genetics" which will rival in importance, even the discovery of the atomic variety in the meaning of man.

There was one ity-bity article in the paper: "The earth's magnetic field seems to be weakening and scientists do not know why." There was another report that the Soviet scientists have discovered a "zone of increased radiation" due to a "cave-in" of the earth's magnetic field, over the South Atlantic. The discovery was made thru an analysis of radiometric readings from the second Soviet sputnik. One of the authors of the discovery, said that because of an abnormal decrease in the tension of the earth's magnetic field in that area of the globe, the inner radiation belt there descended to an altitude of 250 to 300 kilometers (155 to 186 miles) in some places. The "zone of increased radiation," the scientists said, was centered at an altitude of 320 kilometers (199 miles) above southern Brazil.

Argentina had a hail storm to top most of them, latter part of last year. The stones weighed as much as a pound! These king-size hailstones lashed the city, Cordoba, a provincial capital, for a quarter of an hour, causing an estimated damage of $ 250,000. 90% of the glass in roofs and windows was broken.

One weather man here in Los Angeles, admitted he was stumped by Southland weather. He couldn't find reasons for droughts or for the fact we suddenly get tremendous downpours. He emphasized scientists are far from understanding what causes weather phenomena and are even further from being able to control them. He was quoted as saying that it was known the world, or at least the inhabited areas of the northern hemisphere, started warming up about the turn of the century, especially in the Arctic regions around the North Atlantic. In one area of the North Atlantic it's 25 degrees warmer now in the summer than it was in 1900 but that on the other hand, they believe the warming trend started reversing again around 1940. He said these are longterm trends and you can't say that one year will be warmer or colder than the next.

We're awfully sorry John Glenn doesn't receive full credit about actually being the FIRST man to go around our planet and return. Some day the truth will out! The unusual "lights" around him were later confirmed as to what we suspicioned were space "animals." Actually, small intelligences that happened to be in line with the sun, for the right prismatic effect to make them visible. They tell us there are "intelligences" in all areas of space. We hope to have more on this for you in the future. Trevor James has done some research on this phase and we hope to bring you some interesting pictures!

A Teacher, Acumana, told us that John Glenn was from Jupiter also. The Astronauts comprise a group that volunteered to come to earth to open our spaceways. He suggested we study their physiognomy and see the difference from other men. My those Jupiterians are busy ones! Isn't it a wonderful universe we live in?

In light and love,

Gloria Lee

COSMON RESEARCH FOUNDATION *Gloria Lee, Director*

P. O. BOX 55
PALOS VERDES, CALIFORNIA

Established as a non-profit, non-sectarian organization dedicated to the spiritual and physical development of man and his knowledge for the preparation of a New Age.

The policy of the Foundation will be to co-ordinate the knowledge of the physical world with the esoteric knowledge of the universe as given by the Masters, from this planet and others. The aim is to re-establish a school of the arts, sciences and spiritual knowledge of life as it once was taught in the "mystery schools" of Atlantis and Egypt, where "religion" was not a separate subject but the true knowledge and understanding of UNIVERSAL LAW. The Foundation will furnish the "proof" that science and religion are in reality ONE when developed and practiced and universal law is understood.

1. Compile and distribute to the public, lessons on all the esoteric sciences, (psychometry, astrology, spiritual healing, clairvoyance, clairaudience, telepathy, mental projection, etc.), by donation and/or gratis.
2. Psychical research in all phases of the field.
    a. Establish development classes to stimulate the psychic and understand same.
    b. Scientific research, using the psychic for communication with extra-terrestial beings for obtaining more knowledge.
3. Developing hypnosis, psychology, psychiatry, etc., along the esoteric lines.
4. Research on Health Diets and development of physical therapy on New Age lines.
    a. Co-ordinate the physical and spiritual healing methods, such as use of hands in healing, color therapy, sonar, etc.
    b. Also co-ordinate medical therapy with the above in a harmonious manner. Research in herbial medicine.
    c. Establish a hospital and/or Health Center for practice of the above methods.
5. Archeological research for the physical proof of man's heritage.
6. Establishment of a museum of artifacts, etc., for posterity.
7. Compilation of a library for research purposes of students studying the physical and occult arts and sciences.
8. Research in electronics, sonar development, other physical sciences to be co-ordinated with the above in 2b.
9. Publishing and/or printing books, literature, lessons, etc. pertaining to or enlightening the esoteric studies.
10. Charity to worthy causes or organizations of similar interests and/or individuals in need.
11. Affiliate with other organizations where there would be a fair exchange of knowledge and help towards a common goal.

MEMBERSHIP APPLICATION

COSMON RESEARCH FOUNDATION
P. O. BOX 55
PALOS VERDES, CALIFORNIA

Name_____ Date_____

Street_____ Phone_____

City/State_____ Occupation_____

Religion (present, studied)_____

Esoteric Studies (If any, how long? Etc.)_____

Why you wish to join_____

No fee or dues. If you wish to donate, please check and give amount_____

COSMON

JUNE 1963

RESEARCH FOUNDATION

P. O. Box 483
Oro Grande, Calif.

Albert Roger

YOUR RESEARCH FOUNDATION DEDICATED TO DEVELOPING MAN SPIRITUALLY AND PHYSICALLY FOR THE NEW AGE AND SUPPORTED BY YOU

Gloria Lee, Founder

TABLE OF CONTENTS

Space Communication	3
Message from J. W.	4
Message from a Master	6
Notes from the Diary of a Disciple	7
Cosmoknights	9
Junior Group	10
Lemuria	12
World Report	13
Bright Ideas File	14
Social Notes	15
Exploring Human Emotions	17
En Route with Barbara Steele	19
The Book Corner	23
Quotes from Correspondents	24
Miscellaneous File	26

Cover and map by Albert Roger

Copyright © 1963 by Cosmon Research Foundation. All rights reserved.

Printed in U.S.A.

SPACE COMMUNICATION

I am Faithon. I greet you across celestial spaces. Though many worlds rotate between the placement of our outer forms, within the Father Consciousness, my attunement becomes one with your thought frequencies and my Being flows out to you on the Cosmic intercom.

Ray forth, Children of Light, and permit your Light Sources access throughout every avenue of expression. It is of little worth to hold an open mind for incoming intelligence, unless that mind, having colored the incoming life tides with its own individualized thought activities, then releases all entered gift-waves back into the general fund. We are not to take in a creative breath and hold it forever, but to impress and outbreathe it in rhythm with the ALL.

There is no distance great enough to separate the embrace of minds drawn together upon a ray of empathy. Into such unitings of two minds or more, comes manifestation of new patterns and formulations of TRUTH. This is freshness. This is receptiveness to adventures within the ALL-MIND that enfolds us.

Prisons are but cobwebs of crystallized thought. These too are soluble in the purifying furnace blast of Love. I invite you. Step lightly forth from all imprisoning concepts that bind you to the orbital roll of one world of consciousness. Spring free. Let your wings bear the weight of your desire and rise unfettered. Be in uninsulated communion.

MESSAGE FROM J. W.

Greetings, my Children of Earth:

I come once again to salute you in the name of my planet of Jupiter.

Upon our side of life, we are greatly involved in plans for those who are called Light workers, and for the groups through which they perform their various self-accepted services for the Father.

From time to time I return to speak with you, for I feel considerable concern for the welfare of Cosmon Research Foundation, inasmuch as I have invested much love and thought energy in collaboration with those responsible for instigating the formation of this unit.

There are very many of us, of other planetary affiliations, who are aware of that which you call the Over-all Pattern. Even though the teachers and Guides behind the instruments and channels of the physical plane have their individual and collective "area" assignments, for whose functioning they are responsible to the Father, there is necessarily a general knowledge we share regarding the identities, the purposes and the techniques employed in each group active upon the physical plane.

Upon our side, we also hold meetings, conferences and discussions wherein there are opportunities afforded to us for the analysis of problems that present themselves at the earth-conscious level of understanding. We freely exchange suggestions, based upon our own experiences, as well as search together for new or better modes of influencing and guiding humanity in general and our instruments in particular.

Many have repeatedly told you we are here to help you take a step so great that without us, you would surely stumble and fall and be swept completely off the course intended. Some of you welcomed the thought of extraterrestrial aid, when you first encountered the news of our presence among you. Then, as the thought became more familiar and the accustomed activities of your world appeared to continue in much the same old ruts of habit, you allowed your sense of wonder and appreciation to dissipate, until you had reached the point of convincing yourselves that you were the victims of misinformation or trickery. Some of you went so far as to beg for phenomenal proof that our existence is substantial and within the ability of your five personal senses to confirm. You even prayed to the Father to send catastrophes, within a time schedule upon the earth, that you might receive corroboration of the predictions given by us through our instruments.

All this we viewed with a realization that you are unfortunate victims of your own ignorance, for which there is no valid excuse, for ignorance is the product of ignoring available testimony in those aspects of thought and experience which await exploration.

Today we see you as prisoners of the five human senses you have exercised so arduously for numbers of years reaching into the millions, and we pity your condition of spiritual paralysis, which can only be offset by the circulation of vital ideas injected into your fossilized mental veins and arteries that should act as conduits of LIFE and rejuvenating forces which produce new tissues of mental structure.

We have said we are here to help. We have left our home planets. We have set aside beloved associations, incomplete spiritual projects and scientific experiments and our personal life patterns and activities. We are those who have requested permission to be included in the throng of volunteers, who in their numbers form a veritable armada in those (to your vision) invisible reaches of space immediately surrounding your planet. If you were capable of directing your higher faculties of sight, you would behold an unbelievably vast concourse of interested and altruistic identities gathered into myriad working formations and deployed throughout more zones of your living than exist within the limited confines of your earth-conscious imagination.

If you were capable of viewing us in our true nature, or true appearance, you would rub your spiritual eyes with astonishment and you would feel you had wandered into the precincts of a Cosmic Carnival, wherein are represented forms and activities and purposes inconceivable to the brightest of your populations of the earth planet; while that which you claim, by reason of your physical eyesight, to be empty space, would be seen to be teeming with motion, forms and substances outside of your time-bound experience.

In your blind perversity, you not only repudiate our existence, repulse our aid, but attempt to destroy that which you claim does not exist in the first place.

I do not speak with bitterness and chagrin but only bring you our observation that you are enslaved creatures of those negative forces which have succeeded in crystallizing falsehoods and coating them with glittering generalities to the extent that you have been hypnotized by their dazzle and halation and are actually suffering hallucinations in the midst of your self-induced nightmare you call reality!

Within the dim reaches of the twilight zone which you inhabit under enchantment laid upon you by slave drivers and captors disguised as leaders and rulers, we see you produce cultivated responses to directed stimuli to which you have been subjected over so long a period that memory falters as you grope into your ancient yesterdays for the TRUTH and LIGHT you lost, somewhere, — somehow.

We see the human race deliberately enervated and rendered impotent through endless successes of planned campaigns to induce excessive drainage of your creative essence. There is magic at work among your unsuspecting multitudes! It is not WHITE MAGIC, my benighted friends, but black magic of the intensest sable hue!!! You are destroyed in your sleep through applied intoxication channeled by the forces of evil into the avenues of your physical sensory mechanisms.

You are sand-bagged victims on the floor of the astral sea.

This is a long discourse and there are those who will ask why J.W. is bringing subjects of this category to the attention of newsletter readers.

When the great cleansing floods rise up and sweep across your lands and dwellings and your friends and relations, recall these words of J.W. and say as you go under the invincible tides that you are being engulfed by the watery symbol of your own undisciplined emotions, for so it is. For such is Truth, that like produces like!

Not only have your seers and prophets predicted mass annihilation by floods, but also by fire, which they have called "Fire from Heaven." Fire controlled, sustains life, but fire unchecked and unrestricted ravages and destroys.

Minerals and men are collections of living atoms. That which you call Christ or Soul energy within the human atom, is termed atomic energy within the mineral. It is one and the same in kind, varying only in degree. That which produces atomic bombs through atomic fission of the mineral, produces Christs upon the human level when the atomic vitality is released through controlled experiments and sequential disciplines.

This same power is the one power which, as LIFE, pervades and ensouls substance, which thought and imagination step down into the density we term physical form. Thought is that fluidic solution which crystallizes when exposed to the elements of the physical level.

The "Fire from Heaven" to which the soothsayers and wise men have referred is the FIRE OF LOVE. It is that fire which, accepted and received into prepared vessels of personality, blesses and vitalizes and offsets the process that begins as disintegration and finalizes in what you call death. That FIRE OF LOVE,
(Please Continue on Page 27)

MESSAGE FROM A MASTER

The Master Jesus to a Disciple
Date: August 1961

This is Jesus speaking. I would have words between us as we fare side by side at the table of the Father. Mutuality in striving is sought and found where love links those in service to the Plan. Faithful rendition of aid draws cooperation. Thus are great purposes coordinated. Thus are great designs consummated. Clearly, it is up to us, each and all, how we will invest our work with the coloring of our acquired qualities.

Color harmony has its place in the arts of the Father, as well as upon the canvases produced by man. In spiritual work the colors are human energies focussed voluntarily from the storehouse of essence accumulated from antiquity. These colors, rare and mellow, developed over milleniums of experiment, are increasers of Beauty and delight the eye of the Spirit.

Let us, in this day of stark ugliness, draw forth and fully offer the healing essence of Beauty.

Unleash the surging will-to-give that strives ever to well forth from the springs of creation. Not only does an open consciousness accept from all sides, but also releases through all apertures, that which, flowing into and blending with the general need, reactivates old harmonies and recalls long-vanished aspirations.

Within the most turbulent individual circumstances, there is space for artistry of living. Here in the central, silent eye of the cyclone of personality storm and stress, one may live in peace of spirit, as in a chapel set apart, — one with all for service, yet withdrawn in singleness of heart to receive the steady pulsing influx of golden fire.

That in each, which is like unto his brother, sends forth a magnetic call, drawing together the gifts of each for unified combinations, for upliftment of the whole.

NOTES FROM THE DIARY OF A DISCIPLE

Message to a disciple:

"Forthgoing, as you recognize, into a new field of consciousness, you will discover the art of being a central sun of love within your ring-pass-not of service. There is, as you saw, only area. There is unexploited space in which you may create a system of your own spiritual expression. It is not aridity you saw, dry and dead, but a fresh continent, just risen for you from the astral sea. It is not yet fitted by you for human habitation. It is there in potential—a vast, empty land of rocks, sand and sunny skies awaiting your God-expression of transfiguration through individual achievement.

"There is no limitation placed upon you. You now have abundance beyond your conception, with which, upon which, and through which to work for the good of all.

"Thus one begins, while in the human kingdom, to prepare the whole nature for the vast task of becoming first a master over self, then over groups of selves, then over groups of groups, onward and upward toward control of a planetary life, then of a solar life and thence ever onward and forward into reaches of sublime divine expression beyond the power of word symbols in any language to convey meaning to the restricted awareness housed within a human mind.

"Let there be peace within your portion of consciousness. Peace is a composite projection from the heart of love. It is serenity: it is eternity: it is surety: it is rhythm and balance. It is that gift you may outbreathe to fellow men when you are perfectly in tune with the Central Glory."

. . . .

"Heart-to-heart talks. Yes, and mind-to-mind talks. If you could just drop the concepts of space and time for a moment and focus in BEING,—then you would "have it made," as your people say. From physical dense level to etheric is not a jump nor a motion, but a focus. You will have to use the simile of vision or wave lengths or clairvoyance on this. If you would only see; then there would be no need for all this roundabout mechanistic approach. It is quicker than instantaneous when you get the point. You built the barriers. Now you must remove the insulation.

"The most powerful power is love. You know that. Love destroys as well as conceives and builds. It destroys crystallized thoughts and idée fixes too, and melts down antipathies. Use the pink Ray and let it transport you into our work realms.

"We never outgrow the need for common sense. Whatever you do, use the common sense of wisdom!"

. . . .

"Why must you doubt that you "read" me? I don't doubt that I read you.

"Yes, we will flow into and use any part of your consciousness that is open and alert. We are indefatigable. We are a part of God's Omnipresence, into everything and on constant alert to be of service."

. . . .

"On using leftovers. Yes, that is a good simile. It is in the use of marginal, leftover time that much cream of accomplishment comes forth.

"We overlook the negative aspects of ego-centric focus, oftentimes, and use it as a funnel into which we pour new decentralizing expansive truths, in which the real Self relaxes and flows outward beyond its self-wrapped periphery. We do use everything, every tidbit of opportunity that offers. We cannot afford to miss a trick. We await the awakening of each of you, with so much enthusiasm and are well repaid for all our labour when an individual is released from the prison of earth-consciousness. Yes, it is well worth our effort. We sigh with relief, on our side, when each individual birth into Christ consciousness is accomplished. The pains are forgotten by all concerned as soon as the birth is completed.

"We could work on other fields of knowledge, of course, but here and now it is essential to concentrate on the area of consciousness in mankind that requires the stimulating emphasis of our combined contribution to get things "over the hump." There will be all desired explorations and friendly interchanges when the "big push" is over and the mass initiation passed. Victory is sure, but it will not be won without a struggle, — on our side as well as yours.

"We have all pooled our free will to be used in this Plan, for the duration of need."

ECHOES OF GLORIA

(Like others before her, Gloria Lee has left behind many notes and jottings which no one knew of but herself. This is one which would be too fragile to print, except that it illumines so clearly the faith and vigor she personified.)

Dear God or Whoever is in charge of this sort of thing —

If it be my purpose in this life, help me to write an article that'll throw a bombshell in the country and awaken people in their thinking.

Give me an answer tonite — make it stick. If this is in my Plan — Send me the needed help and knowledge.

In Your Service,

Gloria

COSMOKNIGHTS

Dear Younger Members of Cosmon Research Foundation:

This is your older Brother, David of Venus. I would like to have you undertake a scientific experiment this summer and send in a written report at the end of vacation.

I would like to have you prove before the world the power of LOVE in the daily affairs of your living. LOVE can heal people, animals and plants. LOVE can beautify people, animals and plants. LOVE can change enemies into friends. LOVE can destroy fear and hate and sorrow.

BUT IT MUST BE TRUE LOVE

Try each day to go apart from other people for a few moments, unless they wish to perform the experiment with you. Choose a quiet place and sit with your back very straight against a tree, or on a chair with your feet together on the floor and your hands folded on your lap.

Always begin your experiment with a prayer to the Father God. Offer Him your gratitude for permission to be born in the beginning of the New Age, and ask HIM to use you as an instrument for His Love and Light upon the earth plane.

1. In imagination, see the Father sending a dazzling, pure white Ray of Light into you through the top of your head. Think of yourself as filled with this white Christ Light, until your body becomes a bright, clear lamp.

2. Think of yourself as having the power to change this pure white light into bright PINK LIGHT. Then see yourself swelling the heart center (which is located in etheric substance behind your physical heart) until it is filled with PINK LOVE LIGHT.

3. Then see yourself as a human searchlight, beaming out a strong PINK RAY to whatever animal, plant, bird or person you feel needs the gifts of the PINK RAY, which are healing, comfort, love, peace, or beauty.

4. As you give out this PINK LOVE RAY to all within your circle, you will see results and you will know you are working with WHITE MAGIC that carries health and joy and beauty and friendship to all those places where you are carrying out this scientific experiment.

5. You will discover that even plants and trees will respond to a daily LOVE bath. If they receive enough of this precious spiritual vitamin they will give forth better leaves, flowers or fruit. If you wish to test the results, give LOVE every day to certain plants, but never to others. At the end of several weeks, see if you can notice any improvement.

Many of my Friends from this plane of Life join me in thanking you for undertaking this project.

David, your Brother

TO THE JUNIOR GROUP

Vicky said, "I am going to write something for the newsletter."

This made me very happy, because Vicky sits down at the typewriter and dashes off her own copy without asking suggestions or begging for help. She is a self-contained writer.

Her letter is such that I feel it should be reproduced without any editing or retouching, just as she handed it to me. There will be those who notice Vicky's original spelling of some old familiar words, but I do not feel the meaning will be lost for she has provided a practical phonetic substitute.

(Barbara Steele)

* * * * * * * * *

Dear Cosmon Members,

I am writing this letter to help you to go into the NEW AGE. But not all because of that, you should realy try to follow the good things and not the bad things.

You shouldn't be yelling and making noise all the time. This does not mean that you are to be quiet all the time, but when you are noisy than please go where no one can hear you, so that you won't bother them.

For it might make them nervous or in a bad mood. You want to make people happy not miserable.

I hope you will take this seriously and not as a joke. Because it is no joking matter. I want to help you. I want you to know that I realy care.

If you are with someone who is in the wrong than leave the room. (DON'T BE ROOD). Or else ask them not to act like that. Just remind them that they are doing the wrong thing and not the write thing.

When you go to bed at night send LOVE and LIGHT to the ones above and the ones on this EARTH.

Help other people, remind them when they are doing something wrong. Don't be rood about it but just remind them in a nice way so that they don't get mad. But if they do than just leave. Because if you stay and argue with them than you are in the wrong to.

Here are some more things that you might follow:

1. Don't ask for to many things in less it is realy important.

2. Don't get mad if you don't get things you want.

3. Give to people and they will give to you.

4. Help others that need the help.

5. Have faith in many things.

So you see if you follow the rules above than they will help you to go into the NEW AGE.

If there is a dog, cat, or any other animal that is hurt or hungry then help it to get better or give it something to eat.

Do not hurt animals, help them, love them, and care for them.

Teach animals to do tricks. Don't play rough with them, for it will make them to be rough and they might hurt someone. We do not want animals to be rough. We want them to be tame and smart. For some animals are as smart as people. Most of them are, at least they can be.

If you make a mistake than don't get mad, because than you will know what not to do next time.

Have someone tell you when you are making a mistake because it will help you with many things.

So try your best to follow the rules.

      With Love and Light

       From Vicky Carstens

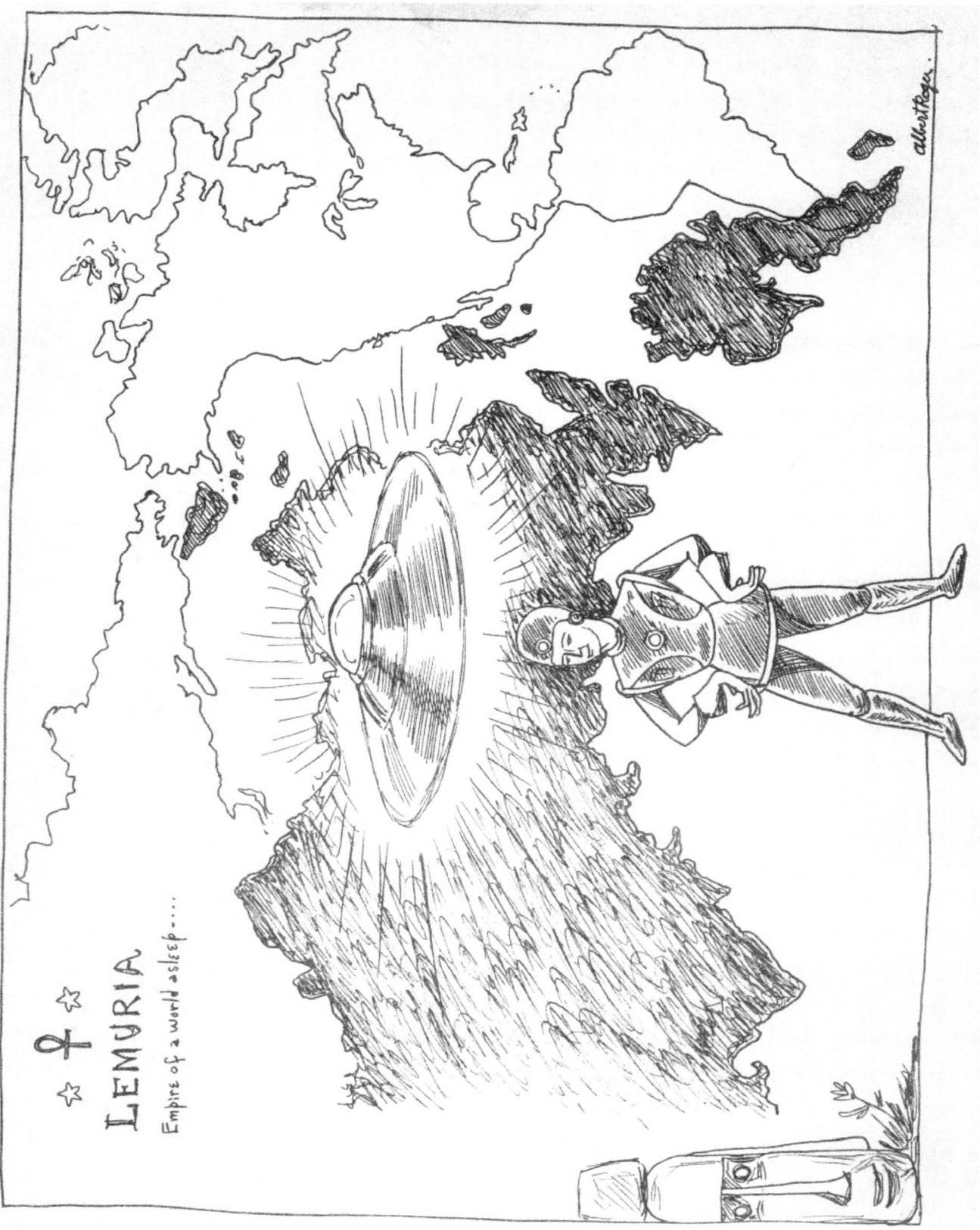

WORLD REPORT

Compiled by Eugene A. Hurtienne

Interesting tidbits . . . .

From the "Time-Advocate," Escondido, April 22, 1963 ——

Peter Van De Kamp of Sproul Observatory in Pennsylvania told 300 delegates of the AAS that a planet 500 times larger than earth revolves around the Barnard's star some six light years from the earth.

The method of discovery used is that if a star doesn't have a mate its track across the sky will be a uniform motion, but if a planet goes around it, the star will wobble.

He also stated that two other planets in different solar systems have been found by this method.

From the magazine "Popular Mechanics," under heading Science Worldwide ——

Bananas will keep longer if they are "HOT". In Puerto Rico, scientists have found that green bananas exposed to just the right amount of gamma rays will delay the ripening so they can be shipped long distances.

. . . .

Russian scientists claim that the moon is not a dead world after all. They say that the crater Linne has decreased to half its size and that other craters have disappeared completely. The report also says that sometimes at sunrise there appear at the bottom of some craters greenish-gray spots.

From one of the San Diego papers ——

The Public Health Service in Washington showed that Little Rock, Arkansas had the highest level of radioactive strontium 90 in the United States. The level at the year ending last February was 11,242 micromicrocuries. Next in line was New Orleans with 11,186 micromicrocuries.

BRIGHT IDEAS FILE

Our friend and Cosmon member, Eugene Hurtienne, sends us the following suggestion for the CosmoKnights:

"An idea came to me . . .

"Many stories could be put on tape by a group of members, such as fairy tales, myths, and stories that have a spiritual note. In this way a group of children could listen to the tape and questions could be answered, or a discussion could follow.

"This form of expression could give some Cosmon members a chance to do some acting and drama. There would be those who would like to write a story into a play; those who would like to put it on and those who would like to direct and create a thing of beauty.

"When I was a teenager, 12 through 14, there was a program over the radio each Saturday morning, for a half hour, giving a play dealing with a fairy tale. I enjoyed them and got a lot out of them. To me this is the best way to reach children from the age group of 5 - 8 or older. Also it helps them spiritually as they can feel they are one with the hero, plus creating a state of fantasy.

"I know of two highly spiritual stories by Oscar Wilde:

1. THE SELFISH GIANT
2. THE LITTLE PRINCE

"(I'm not sure of the last title.) Both, I feel, have a warm and beautiful message to give.

"If the group got good and a way was found to put these tapes on the air, even TV could be a boost to C.R.F. in helping it along in some of its other fields.

"The nice idea about tapes is that you can make more than one tape of the same story. Thus a library could have 3 tapes of a certain story, 5 tapes of another story, etc."

Suggestions from our readers . . .

"Another way to help to make the place (Cosmon center) self-supporting, is to look around for some used hand looms, then gather up old clothings around, wash them, then keep the different colors separated. Cut them in strips. Then make and sell rag rugs and rag carpets."

"A way that may help you along will be if you can arrange for a gradual establishment of a trailer park and to gradually build cabins to rent to visitors."

PERSONAL COLUMN

Home to share — by a pleasant retired male Cosmon member who says:

"Here with me there is room for an elderly couple used to plain surroundings, in a new home with fruit trees around; apple, peach, fig, nectarine and black walnuts; with room to raise vegetables and flowers. Wanted are persons who use no tobacco or liquor and have no pets. This is a quiet place amongst the pines at 1500 feet elevation on the Sierra Nevada foothills, within 15 minutes walk to downtown Paradise, a large fast-growing village of 15,000 souls, at 12 miles east of Chico, the largest city in the north end of the Sacramento Valley."

If interested, address PERSONAL ADS
    c/o Cosmon Research Foundation
    P. O. Box 483
    Oro Grande, California

Specify June newsletter

Editor's note:
    We are not responsible for the results of Personal Want Ads accepted by us for publication in the Cosmon newsletter. This is a limited service to our members, and costs nothing. Available space will determine the number of Ads accepted.

SOCIAL NOTES

Since Cosmon's move to Oro Grande, we have had several visitors. Although we are natural people-lovers, we have arrived at the inescapable conclusion that there must be regulation, as far as possible, even in this delightful department of activity.

You see, we are still very shorthanded and far behind on correspondence, and there are many of you who ask if we have forgotten your existence, failed to receive your loving and wonderful donations or greeting cards or expressions of goodwill and friendship or gifts of books to the library. Often, you would receive the very answers and responses you deserve, but we cannot sidestep the responsibility of hosts when members and friends drop in, unannounced and unexpected, and spend several hours or a day or a night or two with us. We do not have automatic entertainment here, yet, or automatic cooks, dishwashers, launderers and the like. It is strictly on a "Do-it-ourselves" basis. Although we love meeting you, talking with you, hearing your interesting and valuable experiences, suggestions and viewpoints, we have to tell you this socializing plays hob with our schedule.

Don't you think it would be awfully nice to let us hear from you in advance, and have you inquire as to whether your visit would be convenient to us? There are occasional times when we aren't under the pressure of trying to meet a newsletter deadline, or have not some group project or problem we are uniting all our efforts to solve, when we could happily and more easily prepare to welcome you and set aside time for the sole purpose of enjoying your companionship.

We understand your interest and curiosty. We would be of the same outlook if there were a group center somewhere which produced a periodical we enjoyed, and which had contact with Sources of information which were important to us, and whose personalities we would like to meet.

Nevertheless, several of you have dropped from the sky, with your luggage, and have announced you came from distant cities or states because you wanted to look us over and catch us off guard. This was pretty one-sided, wasn't it? You were not thinking of your trip from our viewpoint, our preparation for you, or our convenience in taking time out. In one or two cases, sudden visitors forced previous plans to be set aside and expected guests to miss out on overnight accomodations.

It seems to us a matter of justice and courtesy all round, for us to be made aware of your intentions, for we cannot otherwise guarantee that we can put you up. This is actually not yet a social center, but a work center. We have a bedroom with twin beds, which often accomodates volunteer workers, needed and expected, but we do not have equipment for many guests at a time, nor leisure-time personnel who have nothing to do but chat. Bartram, who has been the resident here for over three years, has been a never-failing chivalrous host and considerate friend to all comers, and has provided meals at his own expense, times without number, but even Bartram would sincerely appreciate the courtesy of being forewarned of your intentions. Many times he has been routed out of bed and has had to come from the adjacent building where he lives, in bitter cold or rain, to answer the phone in our main building, to answer your questions or social calls or announcements you were on your way to spend some time here.

Anyone else would pass over all this and consider it beneath the dignity of anyone to bring the details into the open, but this is part of the TRUTH your donations are supporting Cosmon to bring forth, and if this is true of our group, it is necessarily a situation faced by all groups who have large memberships and whose goal is service to their fellow men.

Your donations do not entitle you to be heedless of the well-being and convenience of those whose lives are dedicated to the effort to serve you.

Our telephone number is CHapel 5-8469, through Victorville, California. Our hours for outside contact are 8:30 A.M. — 5:00 P.M. as a usual schedule. I do not live at Oro Grande, and I use my home for an escape-hatch; for in order to serve you, it is necessary to recharge my energies and to change the pace and relax, and I do not intend to make my home an extension of Cosmon but to keep it apart. If you were aware of how many friends we have, you would understand that there would be little work done at Cosmon, day or night, unless we placed certain regulations around our offices.

On the other hand, it is an unmitigated blessing to renew old friendships, prepare for expected guests, exchange experiences and information with representatives of other groups who are sincerely devoted to finding and spreading New Age information, and to be of all possible help where we have help to give.

. . . . . .

I would like to join our co-workers here to express my pleasure at seeing, meeting or hearing from the following friends, this past two-month period; but even to these, in the future, I would request that they drop a card or make a call before deciding to make a visit, as some have so considerately done in the past.

    Wesley Newbern, California
    Joan Hunt, California
    A. W. Russell, California
    Perry Robb, New Mexico
    Moreland James, California
    Bob Reid, California
    Paul and Marty, California
    Robert Quiroz, California
    Ed and Frances Cornell and family,
      California
    Frank Morales, California
    Helen and Danny Blaske, California

Later, when our work and area expands, you shall have those whose assignment it is to show you the premises, entertain you, and make ready accomodations for your extended stay among us. We love all of you, but know you would not wish us to get any further behind our schedule than we now are as the result of our move.

    Your friend,
    Barbara Steele

LAST-MINUTE ADDENDUM

We are considering holding open house, one afternoon each week, here in the Cosmon center at Oro Grande, for those friends and members who wish to see the offices, to meet the workers, to enjoy each other's company and to exchange ideas. If you wish to bring refreshments, we shall not turn them away! But we shall try to have something on hand for a reasonable number of guests.

One of our friends in the desert area, a charming woman whom you will all enjoy, Mrs. Edna Miller, has volunteered to be our hostess and to welcome and receive you and to introduce you to each other and to show you the premises.

We are too busy, being very short-handed, to stop work and give you hours that must be invested in expanding and extending the services of your Group if we are to grow into the desired scope of activity laid down for us at the time Cosmon was founded. But we need put off no longer the invitation to you to visit the center, meet each other and find new friends with much common interest in the Space Field and Esotericism.

The designated time will be Thursdays from 1:00 to 5:00 P.M.

EXPLORING HUMAN EMOTIONS

PASSIVE OR SUBJECTIVE LOVE
Maurine W. Sellstrom

For so long in our Western culture we have felt that action spoke louder than words. We felt to love is to give, to help, to serve. In fact we have almost distrusted feeling as not being genuine if it did not prompt some sort of action that obtained some objective result. Our feeling that "Faith without works is dead," has been projected upon love also.

All this is true of the active phase of loving. The masculine side of love would express in just this way. But there is also a feminine side. The masculine principle is active and projective. The feminine is passive, and receptive. This quiescent love has its action, but that action is in the subjective realm. It enriches voice tone and the feeling atmosphere. It is the kind of love that makes us feel responsive and accepted.

Those of us who are born in feminine bodies need to learn about this subjective form of loving. Not that women do not act from their love. Much of their living is involved with giving and serving. But there comes a time in their relationships when they must be receptive. They must feed the banks of loving with their unexpressed love. This can build the wealth from which their loved ones can draw, to act, to respond, and to express their own wealth for the world to see and their feminine loved ones to appreciate.

When a mother gives birth to a child, she must in the beginning be the active member of the team. She must care for the babe, with bathing, and serving and feeding. However there comes a day in the child's maturing that mother must begin to shift from being the serving efficient one, to being the receptive appreciative one, if the child is to respond to life and develop his own skills.

The response to active love is to receive, to wish to be loved, pampered and babied, to perceive and appreciate the gift. If we can only love actively, we deny those we love the privilege of participation. The response to passive love is to act, to do, to give.

It has often been said that behind every successful man is a wise and understanding woman, either a mother, sister or wife. It is as though his action can carry the wealth of both of their energies. The man is in action, while the woman is feeding the subjective banks of loving and understanding which can give his action meaning.

This subjective loving is not really passive, it just does not act objectively. It can take the form of needing, longing, praying, understanding, appreciating, even grieving and suffering for those we love. It builds a heritage of feeling from which those identified with the feeling deposited can draw to give their actions color and meaning.

The agony of the mothers who lost their babies at the hands of Herod's murdering soldiers formed streams of force of longing which made the world more ready to receive the teachings of Christ, and are part of the Nativity story.

The suffering of the negroes as portrayed in "Uncle Tom's Cabin," gave impetus to those who wished to make sacrifices to rid our country of slavery.

Active and militant women may have fought the crusade to give women suffrage, but it will be the wisdom and understanding of women which will let us use it to really change world conditions. It will be as our subjective banks of love really fill, in the longing to see all men free of the fear of war and starvation, that we will create the force which will heal these diseases.

Praying is perhaps the most effective subjective action that can be built into this great heritage of passive love. Jesus gave his life in demonstration of the power of passive love. He did not fight to spread his teaching.

He lived it, and in the end submitted to persecution and crucifixion to show men a better way to change the world.

When we deplore an external condition, and see nothing that can be done objectively to correct it, we can actively pray and enrich the subjective banks of God force for the use of those active ones who are in a position to act and in harmony with the love that is there to be used.

When a movement of service forms into a group of servers, it is usually in a passive response to the magnetic love force of some leader who is willing to act and teach and work to bring about the purpose of the group. As that leader continues to work, and the group grows, there must come a time when like the mother the leader must begin to shift from the active role to a more passive one if the group members are to participate and become active.

If the leader cannot do this, the group remains receptive to his action and a kind of sibling rivalry sets in, where each member of the group wants to be the favorite child of a serving parent. Stardom becomes a paramount value for both the leader and the followers and a kind of egocentricity sets in which begins to destroy the effectiveness of the group.

However, if the leader can relinquish the limelight, and begin to feed more richly the passive banks of love through prayer and appreciation, the members can respond with action and begin to do the work to enrich the group and enlarge its scope of service. Criticism and demands, upon the part of either the leader or the group, tend to slow down or stop this transition.

The response to passive love is acting and the wish to give. The response to demands cannot be giving. It can be fearful submission, or resentment. Giving is a spontaneous act that comes from the feeling of love and the wish to serve. Demands rob giving of any wish to do so.

However, just as the parent cannot train her children to give if she does all the giving, neither can she if there is no need communicated. So the shift needs to let the leader or parent turn to God in prayer, recognizing need and longing. They should hold the faith that once the need is subjectively expressed, and the bank of loving full, at the right moment of maturity God will express in action. God will use the person ready to respond and draw on those banks for the strength and courage and substance to act in love and bring to form the need that is there.

As we can be negative or passive to God His love can express in action in our world and from those around us. As we can turn to God for strength and courage, we can draw from the wealth of men's loving that has been deposited there for use.

Many of us do our praying and giving of love in this silent and unacted-upon way for a time. Then like the beginning gardener who wants to dig up the seeds to see if they are growing, we want to draw on the banks immediately to start action before the seed has really had time to grow.

Like the seed planted in the soil, love deposited in these great subjective banks must grow and express. But Creation is the work of God, and His timing is perfect. As the nourishment and warmth to bring forth the new life is supplied, the young plant will emerge through the Earth's surface and develop in our objective world. We need to make the deposits, and warm the banks with our attention and meditation, and let the light of understanding and Infinite love and wisdom bring them to fruition in their season. When we can do this, "He addeth no sorrow therewith." This is another meaning of the Sabbath, when on the seventh day God rested.

This passive or receptive type of loving is the great privilege of women, but it can be the privilege of all mankind when we cannot see the way or opportunity to act upon our loving. We can all build this great heritage of
(Please Continue on Page 2

EN ROUTE

Dear Cosmonites -

Years ago there was a personal column in the Los Angeles Times, called LET'S TALK IT OVER, by Alma Whitaker. In this column was combined a potpourri of philosophy, personal experience, altruistic projects, psychological problems, and arrangement of contacts between people who had something to share and others who were in need of something or someone. At the time, I was very drawn to this writer and her broad understanding, sense of humor and practical measures for alleviating various kinds of human distress. I thought I would love to be an older woman with as much experience of life and power to help others as Alma Whitaker. Now I am an older woman. I have had a life encompassing many fields of human experience and I have inherited responsibility for a publication whose chief and only purpose is to bless and help in the vast Group Project of bringing enlightenment to humanity.

This just shows you how a dream can incubate, take firm root and blossom out in an entirely unforeseen manner. I am frankly trying to keep this column flexible; to alter and change its form, to expand its usefulness and to bring to it an inclusive approach that can find some point of contact with anyone who has the common denominator of being another human being.

During the weeks between the May newsletter and this new issue, I've been trying to keep a listening ear for the thoughts being expressed behind the verbal and written word forms that have come my way, and to try to hear the true questions, desires and hopes behind the more obvious manifestations. I have been observing in as detached a manner as possible, my fellow workers, the Cosmon center in Oro Grande, our services so far and the suggestions sent in by our friends and the criticisms sent in by some who have our good at heart, and some who feel that Cosmon is expendable, or surplus as a group entity. These little experiments have brought in quite a yield of material. And I am going to try to give you a kind of pigeon milk of that which has been given to me. I wondered what pigeon milk was when first I heard of it, and learned it is the food assimilated by the mother bird and held in a predigested state for her little ones in the mother's throat. Now in a way this is a mother function, as I am the receiver of much valuable mental and spiritual food from several levels of life, and it is given to me solely for the purpose of being passed on in a suitable form for the use of others. Much of this material comes in unpolished, raw, unrefined pieces of observed human experience, and some comes in symbols from the Teachers on higher planes than the physical.

All of this raw and symbolic and personal material must go into the hopper of individual consciousness and be generalized into those forms of speech that may be of service to those who turn to Cosmon as one of many, many channels of New Age information and teaching.

Several new ideas turned up recently that can be incorporated in our newsletter. Some of you may have read the Saturday Review of Literature. In the last pages of this periodical there are columns of personal ads, but these, in this particular magazine, have something flavorful and individualized so that they make interesting reading apart from their purpose, which is selling a commodity or service or seeking for something or someone. A member recalled this to my mind when I received a letter from him asking if I would place an ad for him in our pages, listing his offer of living accomodations.

As an experiment, and for your interest, we shall undertake a limited presentation of such personal ads for our members. If this proves of constructive value, it can be extended and continued, but as you can see it could also easily overflow the whole newsletter space if not kept in control. So we shall accept a very few of the more interesting and worthwhile offers and requests. However, this will not be permitted to deteriorate into a mate-seeking clinic, wild claims for health-magic products, or the meeting place of would-be world-wide pen pals. These groups are so numerous that given an inch they would take an ell, and this is not the purpose or mission of Cosmon or its newsletter. Also, no money will change hands in this department. Our newsletter is not sold and we are not going to sell ad space to keep it going. We don't need to!

. . . .

Some months ago Gloria and I were planning a newsletter and were discussing the false notions people have of leaders of Groups, and their natural leanings toward hero worship. Gloria thought it would be fun to blast away a few false concepts of herself as an unapproachable queenly figure on a pedestal, which seemed implanted in the thoughts of many who had read her book, WHY WE ARE HERE. She went so far as to mention among other things that she would wear green nail polish if she wanted to. I recall the responses to her statement, for many took the bait and leapt to the opportunity to tell her she was a godless representative of the forces of Satan. She was accused of placing her emphasis on trivialities and of bringing the place of the physical body into undue importance. The humorous part of all this was that her purpose had been to show that outer appearance and habits were minor in comparison to the spiritual orientation within, but this was beyond the understanding of some.

BEAUTY is an aspect of TRUTH. Few human beings can remain unmoved by the pure beauty of the sky at twilight, or the glorious coloring of a sunrise or sunset, or the breathtaking thrill of hillsides mantled in miles upon miles of Spring wildflowers. Nearly everyone can recognize the hand of God in these planetary manifestations and be brought to a state of near-worship or tears at the contemplation of some such mood or creative activity of Nature. From time to time there have been whole nations or races of men who have had the perception to bring forth the natural beauty of the spirit in loveliness of physical forms and to give this expression of Beauty its due homage in male and female alike. Even now we turn with much wistfulness to the Beauty brought forth by the Greeks, who remain as a classic example of grace of the physical body that matched the symmetry and purity of architecture, arts, philosophy and science.

We are moving into a Golden Age when BEAUTY will again come into its own, but BEAUTY is a principle and a way of life and a philosophy; not an artifice and a hand pointing to perdition and a thin coating of verdure masking a moral swamp. Those who deny Beauty and would cover it over with gray blankets of false moral codes and decry it as purposeless and ungodly, are usually those who have never become intimately acquainted with its true purpose and who, themselves, live and die in ugliness of person, surroundings and human relationships. True and complete spiritual, mental, emotional and physical health expresses in Beauty on each level. The Space People and Angels and Master Teachers Who have ascended to higher realms, are characterized by beauty of form and character. Jesus is said to have been outstanding in His day and age for physical beauty of face and figure. If He characterizes the perfect man, then how can we fail to accept His expression of rare personal beauty and claim to follow Him as ardent believers, and yet repress this very quality which He demonstrated? He did not combine His beauty with pomposity, vanity or egotism, but with manliness, meekness, chivalry, gentleness and the courage of His convictions. You who continually hold forth Jesus as the prime example, how can you deny this side of Him? Did He not invite us to do and be **all** things that He demonstrated?

. . . . . .

Now let us give a little time to the subject of music. Music manifests on all levels of Being, as reported by Those who are free to roam and observe life in the highest realms. Most have heard of the Celestial music of the Spheres. A few rare composers have believed they reached some degree of contact with the musical rhythms that guide the stars in their courses. We have in expression around us many degrees of that which the world calls musical sounds and compositions. There are some sounds that form a battleground between the groups that call them noises and the groups that claim them as music. Here again is a subject that provokes dissension as much as it evokes joy and harmony, inspiration and an urge to create. People are judged and placed into categories by others who observe the kinds of music they prefer.

From the earliest times, our history records the powers of music to change the courses of kingdoms; to heal; to revitalize; to inspire and to summon to battle; to show respect for the dead; to celebrate victories; to combine with the art of the dance for promoting appreciation of Beauty; to enhance the spirit of reverence within the temples, shrines and churches of the world and to raise the vibrations to harmonize with Intelligences of spiritual majesty. Orpheus has been said to be an incarnation of the Christ, and in this incarnation, legendary or historical, He brought forth the spirit of Music as an instrument for healing and blessing the mankind of His day. Krishna of the flute, was said also to be an incarnation of the Christ. Music and its qualities of charming the spirit toward its natural home in Heaven were portrayed by this great Teacher, whether you prefer to call Him a mythical Hero or a true Identity.

In the churches of the world, hymns, masses, rituals and ceremonies are celebrated with music of the human voice or pipe organ or various collections of stringed instruments. We have gradually separated music into two main categories which the world calls sacred and profane. Yet it seems to me these are far too rigid and oversimplified; for music requires as many degrees of expression as the rungs of the ladder of life itself, and is a means given to those of developed spiritual hearing for placing that which is expressing through musical sounds in the proper status of evolutionary development.

Even in the bird kingdom there is the widest divergence among the singers. Five familiar "songs" are those of the seagull, pigeon, mourning dove, meadow lark and mockingbird. My own favorite of these is the meadow lark, with the mourning dove a close second. But here again, as in all degrees of sound, we can see a wide divergence of expression, and what overjoys one pair of ears may weary and bore or pass entirely unnoticed by another. I give you this, not as a conclusion, but as something to turn your thinking into new pathways. If you feel you have some interesting experiences to relate, perhaps we can compile an article on music alone, setting forth your combined opinions.

. . . .

Our good friend and member, Eugene Hurtienne, has been kind enough to accept my invitation to reactivate World Report, one of our former newsletter sections, and he asks that you send any current newsclips of world interest to Cosmon office and allow me to forward them to him for compiling. So thanks in advance.

Another plan I am turning over in my mind concerns Diet and Health and the true life experiences of our friends and members in this field. We cannot diagnose or prescribe, but there is no law against sharing firsthand experiences or opinions or recommending that you read various publications that have proven beneficial to others along these lines. A good friend and member, Laurel Hampel, who has made a deep study of the field of nutrition, has offered to write articles for us when we are ready to resume our section on this subject. She is a careful and meticulous researcher who compiles facts into an impressive array, makes them entertaining and also gives reference sources for the reader who wishes to pursue the subject further.

Here is an invitation to those of you who have concocted or discovered meatless recipes, New Age meals, raw fruit and vegetable salads or desserts, and home baked breads, to contribute to us recipes that do not require ingredients too rare or expensive for our readers to try out in their own circumstances. We have among us many friends who live alone and are pensioners on very slight incomes and who would welcome inexpensive but nourishing New Age food suggestions. There are still diehards who are sure they will fall powerless to the ground if they do not include meat in their meals, but there are many of us in various degrees of dedication to vegetarian living, who have already proven our ability to enjoy good health without the use of meat.

While we feature a number of excellent vegetarian diet books for sale, and will include all of these in our library, there is still that cherished personal touch and firsthand recommendation from readers that adds an extra dimension of pleasure to a recipe on the printed page. Try it and see!

Some months ago, Dorothy Simons published a recipe for home-baked bread. It appeared in her newsletter and she recommended it highly from personal testing. I tried it out several times and varied the ingredients for different effects and each one was delicious. I made two loaves at a time: one for Gloria and one for my family. Gloria's little daughter, Sissy, used to call it "cakebread" and asked me to bake her a loaf for her Birthday with candles on it. Now there is a real gourmet's O.K. And I offer it to you here, but must add that it is not inexpensive, for the ingredients bought in less than wholesale quantities cost me approximately eighty cents per loaf. I substituted honey for molasses and dates for raisins, and omitted white flour; using wholewheat flour, cornmeal, wheat germ, graham flour and various other flours in differing combinations, usually three kinds in one baking. I sprinkled a teaspoonful or two of hulled sesame seeds over the top. Try it!

HEALTH BREAD RECEIPT
Sent in by Dorothy Miller
(Published by Dorothy Simons)

- 1/2 Cup Brown sugar
- 2 Tablespoonfuls shortening
- 1 Teaspoonful salt
- 2 Cups Sour milk or Buttermilk
- 2 Cups Graham flour (or 1 cup graham flour and 1 cup bran)
- 1 Cup White flour
- 1/2 Cup molasses
- 1 egg
- 1 Teaspoonful Baking powder
- 2 Teaspoonfuls soda in milk

Raisins and nut meats as desired. Bake in bread or loaf pan in slow oven (250°) 1 1/4 hrs. or longer.
Note: Mix the nuts and raisins with part of the flour before adding to batter.
Several of us make double receipts when we make this bread as it is SO good.

. . . .

There are so many things I want to discuss with you. I made a list of a few inclusions for this issue of the newsletter, but every item could be expanded into books if there were space. As you look around you at the familiar scenes of your daily life, in which are shown you activities occurring all over the world, it must often enter your minds that two great forces are ever at work: those that tear down and those that build up, and you must wonder how God can allow such widespread destruction, which often seems to outweigh and overbalance the constructive and good actions you hear about and witness. In this phase of transition the Destroyer aspect is carrying on a needed activity. But to us is given a different work. We must begin to build tomorrow's habitations and not align ourselves with the destructive energies, or we shall find ourselves off the path of our mission of enlightenment.

Our work is to intensify the service of Love in its harmonizing and cooperating aspects and to further the spread of knowledge and prepare ourselves to take on increasing responsibility, as the founding fathers and mothers of the new civilization. All Light groups and all Light workers are engaged in the work of founding the coming civilization, whether they realize this or not. We are the seedbed of qualities and characteristics which will flower forth in the citizens of the Golden Age. It is of urgent importance that we project into this new culture those patterns, colors and trends that will give rise to expression of the highest principles humanity can touch through the mediatorship of the Teachers and Guides sent to help us through this period of mass initiation into the Kingdom of God.

(Please Continue on Page 27)

THE BOOK CORNER

Books are such extraordinary things — what would we do without them? As a case in point, may I mention three which have come into my hands lately.

The first two are part of the series by T. Lobsang Rampa (a pseudonym) entitled THE THIRD EYE and DOCTOR FROM LHASA. If anything belies the supposition that esotericism is dull or prosaic, it is the vigor of fast-moving narratives such as these. In simple gripping interest they rival the most fantastic adventure yarns without ever leaving (to all appearances) the realms of reality. It is this combination of extraordinary events with an atmosphere of sincerity which makes them so impressive.

Supposedly written by a high Tibetan lama through the physical equipment of an Englishman, the pair of books offers a wealth of detailed and exotic information in the setting of a lucid, often humorous style. The author never loses sight of everyday details in the midst of earth-shaking discussions. On the other hand, he can pause in his account of excruciating physical tortures to inject an essay on breathing. Strangely enough, one subject proves to be about as interesting as the other.

Without jeopardizing the interest which awaits the newcomer, it might be mentioned that "The Third Eye" refers to the one in the forehead which is said to be the organ of clairvoyant vision. This is only one of the gifts which makes the reader feel that he has encountered in the writer an extraordinary personality. As a "Doctor from Lhasa" the author combines orthodox medical training with more ancient lore and inventive ingenuity, making the most of his opportunities to aid humankind amidst the horrors of modern barbarism.

At the opposite pole from these volumes is a small, quiet book called BROTHERHOOD 1937 (Agni Yoga Society, 1962). There may be those to whom it would not appeal, but to certain persons it will seem immensely more exciting than the adventures of Lobsang Rampa. The fabled lama tells us tales of extramundane affairs, but BROTHERHOOD opens the gates and bids us enter into them.

Though the comparison will seem surprising to some, this book calls to mind Nietzsche's THUS SPAKE ZARATHUSTRA. Let it be added hastily that the two are different as night and day — but in both there is a touch of bracing, high mountain air. Both are clothed with the simplicity of mountain folk, and written for stalwarts who wish to dare. In both we are shown that the crucial test is what we demand of ourselves. But while with Nietzsche we remain, in spite of all, essentially earthbound, BROTHERHOOD declares our kinship throughout the hierarchy of the Subtle Worlds.

We are told that the path to Brotherhood is not for the ignorant, doubting, fearful or faint-hearted. But those who love labor and discipline may find therein the way to unimagined interweavings of spirit. The way to Brotherhood does not require blind faith, but demands concrete realities such as psychic energy, tension, alertness. Yet without a measure of trust there is no awakening of the essential "psychic energy." No other means can turn darkness of heart into the glow of truth.

There is much in the book which we are glad to find as familiar ideas expressed magnificently. There is also much that makes us stop and ponder. As we do so the world of thought expands around us, till imperceptibly we have risen to a greater vantage point and find ourselves standing (if but for a moment) on a new frontier.

More than this, what can any book do? Thereafter we stand alone, and must decide if we want Brotherhood.

J. D. M.

QUOTES FROM CORRESPONDENTS

SOMEONE DREAMED

"I seem to be at some great conference. There were very ancient people there. This was explained to me in this manner. One moment they were alive and just as you and I; the next they were only posited as symbols.

"But to go back to the dream (or ?).

"It seemed the general summing up of certain delagates who had been on a survey task; who were reporting in on their subjects they had been keeping record of.

"Well, the room I was in was not too large, but there was a table not too large, about 4 x 6 feet in dimension and it sat North and South. The place where the reporting agent would set was at the North. The judges or whoever they were, who each sat there and made symbolic figures on these charts as the reports were read off, these were making three copies of each. Those being:

1. The one brought in by the agent.

2. The head judge who sat on the East.

3. The second judge who sat on the West, who also made a like copy.

"The South end of the table was open. No one sat there.

"The little books the reporting agents gave the reports out of were not very large, about 6 x 9 inches and having about 20 pages. I seem to know this was the 21 year report on this age and this race of man, - in other words this race of man, of who the Generation now is arrived at a so-called 21 years of age, and these full reports of him and his evolvement is now being summed up, to see if he will graduate or not.

"Each reporting agent came in a door from the West, sat down at his seat at the North end of the table, made his report, got up and joined his fellow reporters who had given these reports and visited and talked in a happy enjoyable manner.

"I can't remember just how many reporters there were but I believe it was twelve in all, and another then took his seat at the table to report. As they joined the group after making their report, it seemed the whole race of man, of whom the offsprings were now graduating, were from two original families; a white couple and a red-skinned couple. The white people had symbols of the Nature of Semitic nature, but much older: Perhaps the family the Semitic race originated from, long before History began our present recording, while the red couple had symbols representing the races who were saved after the flood, the colonies who were established thereafter; a sort of Indian-like symbol, but as the white people's symbol, it too was much older, perhaps from their original beginning, sort of like we are taught the people of Central and South America used in the time that civilization was at its height.

"I took it to mean that at this time it is all the people who were left and their descendants from the time of the flood era up to now. All the souls who have been sence the Arc of Noe, up to this present Arc.

"The two families, the white and the red: the two original couples, were very sweet and all who came in seemed to love them very much. The children who were with those two couples, were of all ages and sizes. I took this to represent the ones who had graduated down through the ages and were now with their original families — while the ones who were being summed up in the reports had not as yet been gathered in — and the reports and credits were to determine just who were to be honored in the final day of this age.

"It appears the harvest is not very large if it could all be in so small a book. However this didn't seem to cause the judges any worry. It seemed if they didn't graduate this time — that it would be so at a much later time — and that the ones who hadn't passed just needed more time to finish their lessons and experiences.

"However it was said that of this race and age there would be no more earth life for the ones who did graduate: no more issue to be made. All who passed — would — from the graduating time onward, be taking their lessons etc. on a higher plane.

"I heard the old Red Chief ask the wife if she would again come into his chambers, and she said no more, that their day of creation for their family was over, and that when she came into his chamber again it would be for a new higher race to be brought into being, and she put some sort of a symbolic lock on the earth's births.

"The old Chief seemed sad, but said: 'It is the wife's right to decide.'

. . . .

"I've tried to explain the best I can of how this all took place. Perhaps you can make some sort of understanding out of it. To me it was a dream, but perhaps it could have been I was seeing this in some sort of higher dimensional manner. If it makes any sence to you, feel free to use it. I can only repeat what I see and hear."

Name withheld

Editor's comment: Dream experts, take over!

* * * * * * *

"Each day there are small things given to me to do for those around me. Neighbors and friends who feel blue, and lost: All I can do, of course, is listen, give them understanding and compassion, but it seems to help. This I believe is what God wants of me now. I'm content to be guided by Him and my prayers are, to fill as best I can His plans for my life span here at this time. The Masters are right when they say we have work to do wherever we are placed."

* * * * * * *

"Is your work another crackpot scheme to get your share of what Barnum said about the fool born every minute and he'd get his share? You see, I am afraid of myself (I know myself quite well) and I am afraid of you because I am afraid of the fool who dwells beneath my head of hair. This is not a slam at your beloved enterprise, but at myself. I JUST DON'T KNOW! The older I get the less I am sure of anything; but I would surely desire what ___ ___ says is not only TRUTH but the greater GOOD to which all Truth should lead. There is much of what we hold to, as truth, but if it is not pursued until it culminates in its good, we benefit not. Those who make truth an end in itself miss the mark and thereby sin.

"How much of your literature I can accept as of now I can hardly say. Yet I cannot say that I want it to stop."

R E M I N D E R

Dear Readers:

We have moved. Please use our new mailing address:

COSMON RESEARCH FOUNDATION
P. O. Box 483
Oro Grande, California

MISCELLANEOUS FILE

NOTES ON COMMUNICATION

(We believe our readers may be interested in these excerpts from longer discussions. The first is from June of Venus, as received by Marianne Francis, March 11, 1963. The second is from Gloria Lee, Introduction to WHY WE ARE HERE.)

"...The concerns of the organization known as Cosmon are the concerns of many beings from other planes and from other planets, as every organization set up upon this planet is a voice for those beings, both discarnate Teachers and Space beings. So it is that it would be of great concern to these beings should that voice be silenced, should that vehicle be closed as an avenue for their expression to reach the peoples of Earth.

"The greater plan is one of service, of enlightenment unto the Earth's peoples. For this purpose was the organization called Cosmon formed and insofar and for so long as it serves this purpose, it is valid and true and cannot be attacked nor its bulwarks breached by any other personality upon the Earth planet insofar as it serves the purpose for which it was created. It is immaterial as to which channel is the channel for Cosmon, but it is not immaterial that the channel must be a true channel.

"Many have been developed as channels for Light communications from the Space beings and from the discarnate Masters. Many also are in the process of being developed and therein many errors can occur. During a development phase, channels are subject to astral-type interlopers and may be unaware of the forces which operate through them. Trust, therefore, the channels who have trained assiduously in the Light and with pure motive freed from ego or manifestations of self-conceit. The channel is not the one of importance, but the material being given through the channel is the thing of import. Judge by the quality of the material received. By this standard and by these "fruits" ye may know them. If constant repetition occurs of the channel's abilities through that channel's expression, then may you know that a large part of the channeling is composed of the channel's own ego-self. If the material received is freed of such references to the channel, then know that the material is coming from a higher realm or a higher manifestation of consciousness. Thus "by their fruits ye may know them." Those who are in error often err in ignorance, yet also are there those upon the earth-plane (or earth planet) at this time who are consciously perpetrating error and causing confusion within the ranks of the students of Light. In this way many who aspire sincerely and honestly to Light teachings are being taken like lambs towards a slaughter, certainly towards a misconception and mis-teaching.

"Those who will channel and act as the channels for Cosmon should be channels who are freed of ego consciousness, who are channeling to the glory of the Light and whose material is of such quality that it may teach the people wherewith is Light and of the golden consciousness of the coming Age."

* * * * * * *

"Not unlike many of the readers, I too, am confused as to the variety of differences and contradictions in so many of the received communications purported to be from Space Beings. Many of the things I have read match fairly well with what I have received, but in some instances, there is a direct contrast. Why? I don't know exactly, unless it lies with the short-comings of the instrument or within the knowledge of the communicator. I imagine they also have a few short-comings in this department also.

"They, too, hold various positions of authority (or none), and may possibly tend to repeat something of hearsay or alleged knowledge without first checking sources. Then, I firmly believe, many so-called space people are in reality discarnate beings or perennial jokesters who pass from the physical to the "other side" but where one's personality does not change by crossing. I have seen all too often, unfortunately, people beginning to dabble in extra-sensory perception, believing anything received is gospel truth. There will always be those personalities, whether in the flesh or out, who desire recognition regardless of the manner they might get it. And few people realize the importance of their own consciousness (or vibration) has a great deal to do with what they receive and whom they attract. Many negative experiences have occurred because of this ignorance and much could be said that space does not permit."

MESSAGE FROM J.W.
(Continued from Page 5)
repudiated and returned upon itself, is that power which when reversed is DEADLY! Man, under the tutelage of the forces of darkness, which as a group is a reversal of LOVE, has learned well the skill of rejection of life, and let mankind recall these words of J.W. when the HELL BOMBS burst as fire from the skies!

We came to help you, and we shall help all those who come forth in the courage of their convictions to meet us. We cannot help those of you who have placed yourselves beyond our reach through your choice, by intention or by default!

Sadly yours,

J.W. of the planet Jupiter

EXPLORING HUMAN EMOTIONS
(Continued from Page 18)
love and interest, and when courage and readiness is found to act, it can enrich our serving and giving with the wealth of feeling that is deposited there to wait for action.

EN ROUTE
(Continued from Page 22)
For those who have not heard us mention a resolve made two years ago, I would like to go on record as saying that Gloria talked over with me what should be our policy regarding those who resign and later ask to return to membership or to be placed again on our mailing list. We have a permanent decision on this and it is to leave the door open: not to slam it shut on any human being regardless of the discord, crisis, mistake or misunderstanding that created a period of separation. We decided to stick to our principles, hew to our task and allow others freedom to come or go. We don't expect agreement with all our decisions or our interpretations of what is and what is not TRUTH, but we acknowledge you have as much right as we to stick to your guns and allow time to bring forth the proper perspective and adjustment of ideas. If we are basically in error, time will most surely prove it, without veiling illusions or excusing injustices.

Sometimes, looking back, I feel sure I have made more mistakes and stumbled more often along the Path than anyone else I have observed. I do not now and never will claim to have achieved any of the perfect purposes I have set as my goal, but I will say that in making errors and going through trials without number, I have found myself at all times beside other human beings, and never alone, and have thus while picking myself up and dusting myself off to make another try, learned how others felt when going through the same experiences and tests. Therefore, even though I forget at times how it feels to be in someone or another's shoes, I can quickly revive within myself the memory and feel compassion for a fellow stumbler. Therefore, since we have all tripped and fallen over the obstacles and temptations along our paths, let us accept each other and go forward in our experience and strength, for we all have some of these also; and let's not stop overlong to look back at ourselves or each other, for we are called to hasten, to come as we are, and to work with all our might for the glory of the Father.

With love and light en route,

Barbara Steele

COSMON

JULY 1963

RESEARCH FOUNDATION

P. O. Box 483
Oro Grande, Calif.

YOUR RESEARCH FOUNDATION DEDICATED TO DEVELOPING MAN SPIRITUALLY AND PHYSICALLY FOR THE NEW AGE AND SUPPORTED BY YOU.

Gloria Lee, Founder

TABLE OF CONTENTS

Space Communication	3
Message from a Master	5
Guest Corner	7
Dialogue with Gloria	8
CosmonKnights	9
En Route with Barbara Steele	15
Special Communication	21
Correspondence File	26
Miscellaneous	31

Front Cover: Portrait of June of Venus, by Marya Bryant
Back cover design by J. L. Fitzpatrick
Drawing by Albert Roger

Copyright © 1963 by Cosmon Research Foundation. All rights reserved.

Printed in U.S.A.

SPACE COMMUNICATION

Greetings to you, my children of Earth —

This is again J.W. Those of you who will have read my message in the Cosmon newsletter for June, may have shaken your heads and said: "J.W. is becoming more and more a prophet of doom, or a pessimist or a discouraged Being, for He freely predicts events of staggering proportions, with renewed emphasis on the negative side, and He declares we are to see these for ourselves in the time of now."

From time to time, we who are here to help, find it necessary to remind you of a situation which you apparently find easy to dismiss or to set aside altogether. To us of far greater life spans, the word "immediate" or "now" has an entirely different connotation from that type of emphasis you place upon it, and which derives from a life expectancy of some fifty to eighty years of earth time. Our immediacy, on the other hand, may conceivably enfold ten to one hundred years of your measurement of duration. Therefore, you often hold that our predictions are not valid, because you have interpreted that we have told you this event or that might be expected to occur within the near future, which you assumed meant a matter of weeks, months, or one or two years, and the expected event not having kept pace with your timetable, in the manner and under the circumstances of your interpretation of our forecast, you are prone to dismiss your receptions of information from us as falsehoods, or vain imaginings on your part or ours.

How glad we should be if all that has been told you concerning dire events, could be written off as crackpot notions. How sad I am for you, children of earth, that you have sunk so deeply into your self-made mists of illusion.

In the spiritual aspect of the Space Program of your planet, those who are considered the farthest out are those who make first contact with the generally unknown, and therefore unfamiliar contents, laws and principles obtaining in the realms of space beyond your globe. Due to the difficulties experienced by all those who attempt to describe ideas which are unprecedented in the experience of the mass consciousness, there is always a wave of severe doubt at the contents of reports filtering back from the leading explorers of a new continent or a new concept.

It is far easier to be a critic or a connoisseur than a creator or a pioneer in any field. It requires far less vitality to sit upon a comfortable chair and condemn the works performed by others than to undertake the hazards, hostility and chance of failure which accompany the adventurer into unknown terrain. It is also easier to refuse to take sides publicly upon issues that are infused with fear and ignorance and hate, and to turn away the glance when confronted by explosive situations.

Some of you have asked how J.W. stands on the current exhibition of racial antipathies across the surface of the world. In my book, WHY WE ARE HERE, page 130, the last paragraph, I wrote:

> "Where there is negation, this must be <u>cleansed</u> from whatever it has entered into. Only after the cleansing process has taken place, can you accept the new forces coming to you and be in better tune with your God-self."

As a humanity, you are indeed inconsistent, for some thousands of your people have accepted and expressed love for those of us who claim that we are citizens of other planets and, in many instances, our forms are not as those outer casings which you have been accustomed to call human. And yet, in your blindness of the inner vision, you have accepted us, not knowing our forms or colors, whereas upon earth, in the full light of your recognition of your surrounding fellow men of the same human shape, you reject other men and women as being inferior solely due to their color! How do you know they are inferior, since you cannot read their minds or motives or past experiences upon the ladder of evolution? Perhaps it is yourselves who are acting in an inferior manner, who need to be cleansed of the layers of grimy ignorance which seem to us far darker than the skins of those who now are forced to fight their way into acceptance of equality before the Father Who created you all.

We are well aware of the taint of racial prejudice that infects some, even within the membership of the groups of Light. Even though we deplore their narrowness and bigotry, which are simply the products of ignorance, we have never excluded any from the body of truth seekers.

Whether the idea appeals to your emotions or not, you, as a living soul, have incarnated or shall, in the physical bodies of all races and colors. Those you most dislike today, may form the classroom of your next incarnation. Just as virulent hatred of another individual sometimes produces the karmic result of Siamese twinship, in a togetherness which forces proximity between those who need to work out the lessons they have incurred together, through a deeper and more intimate understanding of one another, so does racial antagonism draw you in a later incarnation into the shoes or sandals of the detested group, until, becoming established in their viewpoint, and suffering their limitations of opportunity and woes, you recognize the same basic humanity as your own in all your fellow men and women. Hate is magnetic as well as love, and will draw into your close experience that which is hated. Today you do to others that which will be done unto you in your tomorrows.

Racial and religious intolerance are areas which must be cleansed. If you have chosen to draw yourself into relationship with them through hate and scorn, you will discover the results and effects of cataclysmic impact upon your personal self. But if you have loved your fellow men of all colors and beliefs, the turmoil in this battle of the cleansing forces released by the impact of Christ consciousness upon your world, will afford you a field of service on the side of the forces of Light.

Little have I spoken to you today upon these inflammable subjects. Infinitely more could be said, but with small avail, for here I have given you sufficient for insight into one aspect of the cleansing you may not have foreseen.

May you hearken before it is too late!

My love and light,

J.W. of Jupiter

In every man captive to forces of disintegration, the builder lies dormant. To reach that faint glow of Eternal Purpose is the first duty of every constructive force. Call to it, rouse it, free it and it will eventually respond.

Margaret Cameron
THE SEVEN PURPOSES, p. 107

MESSAGE FROM A MASTER

Dear Children -

Disaster is a force capable of animating many forms of activity. While you are scanning the distant horizon for signs of storm, or watching the sensitive meters created for recording upheavals of the earth's surface, other kinds of forces may be gathering behind you to burst forth in uncalculated violence.

Nevertheless, while certain events must be and will be manifested, it is possible to achieve their expression through many and various means. You are now within the relative quiet of the harvest, when all the finished work is being gathered into the storehouse preparatory to the threshing and the pressing. That which is fitted for seed shall be set aside and later cultivated. That which is intended for other use will be sorted and recorded accordingly and will find its purposes within the Divine Scheme.

If your minds were capable of taking in the long view, it could be readily ascertained by all of you that you are within a cyclic action and not one without precedent, except that the termination of this cycle will set a standard for CLEANSING away outworn forms, to a depth and in a degree never before equalled.

Creations long hidden away in the depths of the earth and the floors of the seas will be brought to light and eradicated. Our earth will be shaken in space like a carpet during Spring cleaning. All that has found sanctuary and protection within the lairs of the forces of darkness shall be aired out. Fire and water shall be the cleansing agents.

Although the minds of some of the orthodox religionists of the world are in agreement that this period of relative quiet is the hush before the end of the world, or eternal damnation, they are incorrect, for this is the end of an AGE OF TIME, and not of the world itself.

All individual and collective accounts must be balanced before the Logos can begin the work of the New Dispensation. All the old must be cleared away. You shall witness the perfect meting out of JUSTICE to the finest grain of individual deserving. Not all who fall prey to the full havoc of the cleansing agencies shall be removed permanently from this planet. Many will, in this opportunity for final payment of all karmic liabilities, become ready for rebirth within the remaining population.

Among the many who leave this familiar scene to enter classrooms upon planets of another solar system, there may be some who discover their ability to make up for wasted time and opportunity, and who shall take upon themselves the pressures of catching up with their fellow spirits, in the family group to which they belong, as does a child who, failing the grade, spends his vacation period recouping his losses, and finds himself ready to continue with his classmates.

Your prophets of this transition period have told you that the population remaining after the cleansing will number hundreds where there have been millions. Many of the predictions given in the earlier years of this century have been cancelled out and alternate plans installed, due to the stimulation and inspiration afforded the Planet Earth by the coming of our brothers and sisters of other worlds and systems. You must therefore hold a flexible mind and refrain from assuming that prophecies made as recently as five or ten years ago are fixed or inevitable.

You have asked, what shall be your attitude at this time? You have only to read, look upon or listen to your daily news to be swept by a sense of the hopelessness and failure to which thousands of the earth family have already yielded. Many more of those known to you and loved by you will also become engulfed by a desperation that will cause waves of suicides. But in all the wreckage of the passing turmoil, we count upon you who are trained to some degree in the techniques of love, healing and comforting to stand strong and unflinching in your dedication to the Will and work of the

Father. Act as if each new day is that day wherein you must represent the FORCES OF ENLIGHTENMENT as an intelligent server. Do not give up! Do not give in!

Remember that all you see and shall witness is motivated by DIVINE LOVE, which is destroying evil before your very eyes. On every level where consciousness is at work, there are last-minute reprieves granted, even renewals of opportunity for those who wait until the last moment of the last hour to open up their hearts in full dedication to the Father's Will. Though the outlines of the WRECKING PLAN are established, details can, in many instances, be modified through your prayers of compassion and love.

Continue from hour to hour, from day to day, with unflagging attention to the work that has been placed within your hands. Be not tempted aside from the path of your duty by rumors or fears. Do that which lies next and do whatever it is as if your life depends upon it. Give to the limit of your capacity.

Turn not back to await those brothers and sisters, beloved of your human hearts, who seem to you to be straying from the Path of Light. Rather, strive doubly to make clear the WAY for their later following. Be that which you would have others become. Put not off your accomplishment into a vague future which may never come, but work now for all those who are yet to seek the Path of Returning. Give until you are emptied of self, that the Father may fill your emptiness with His SPIRIT; that He may shine forth through you; that He may reach those within your circle through you; that TRUTH may be brought forth wherever you are.

My understanding love is yours.

St. Germain

Covet not the rays proceeding from other facets, but allow Life free access to polish and to clarify the surfaces from whence streams of interior light may fare forth from your own individuality. Seek the treasure within your own cave of jewels. Wait not for largesse from other troves. Each one is provided with all that he can imagine into expression. Be not niggardly with the imagination. Be not slothful with the implements of skill and talent. Be not a well. Be not a river. Be a great sea. The searching waves of a great sea lap tropical shores and icebound lands and coasts of temperate regions. Be you that sea of exploration. Be that sea of living creative impulses. Carry upon your currents great cargo ships bearing GOLDEN AGE ideas.

From the Diary of a Disciple

GUEST CORNER

"TEMPLES IN THE HILLS ARE WE..."

"I need no confinement in a shrine...
To me the Universe is shrine unto the Father!
I would build temples open to the sky
        and fields and hills of the Lord's Doing!

Man was given Dominion over the Earth...
Let him claim it in reverence to the Giver!
Let him not lock himself within the narrow confines of a shrine,
        or even the isolation of the Temple of himself!

Let man be still, and GROW with the very breathing
        of the Universal Father!
I love LIFE in all its ways and wonders!
Let us SING of the beneficent success of the Father
        in Growing His multiplied elements!

Let us speak softly in the Presence of His Power to Create
        vast beauties, and Living Creatures,
        and joys untold, — to Mankind!
Let us populate the air with Gratitude!
Let us be singing to the winds:
    ' Lo, He made us, and all manifested Creation,
      And He saw that it was Good!'

Temples in the Hills, are we...
Hidden for a time by growth grown thickly over,
And thus we bend INWARD, isolated from our fellow-men,
        and from the Vast Created Virtues of the Father!

Temples in the Hills, are we...
Let us uncover these Shrines to the Father!
Let us push back the thick covering, and shine in the Light
        of the Son, and of the Father,
And pour forth that Tribute unto all the Limitless Creation
        of His Making!

... Limitless for us, too,
In all its Ways and Patterns and Dimensions...
        Stretching forth Eternally
Unto ever expanding Conscious-Cosmic-Wonders!"

                                          Received by
                                          Hope Troxell
                                          November 7, 1962

DIALOGUE WITH GLORIA

Dear Gloria -

I have a deeper understanding of how you did die, to bring us all an awareness of how to find and use our own intuitive perception, and how we cannot safely too much rely on it coming from others. I appreciate your gift, and would be very glad at this point to deliver any message you would like for me to deliver to Barbara and your group at Cosmon.

Dear Maurine -

Tell them I do love them, and those who come to this understanding through me or the work I introduced to them, go on with my love and my prayers for their well-being and wise channeling. It is always so. When we take on an obligation to teach, we also take on an obligation to pray and be concerned for those we teach. Their interest in us must bear the dividend and return of our interest and concern for their well-being and wise use of the material learned from us.

This is not an obligation but a joy, it enriches both the giver and the receiver. What we see here that cannot be given with any efficiency is advice. This must come to each person through his own intuitive perception, or what you would call his own knowing. That is why mediums and those who get so-called psychic messages are so often mistaken when asked for advice. One out of a body cannot tell any better than another in a body, what is the test and lesson next needed or desired by any one individual. We sense our own tests and which qualities are likely to be tested for sound use, and see warnings for others we project those qualities upon. We cannot know for certain whether we are talking about the person or our experience with that particular quality.

We can contact you with love. We can communicate to you with new understanding, and as you open yourself to that understanding, our presence and love can bring it through more readily and more clearly. But it will be your use of it, your application of that understanding that will make it important or ignored by those about you on Earth. This cannot be predicted by us here.

What we do know here is the color of your aura. We sense the purity or the cloudiness of your thoughts and feelings. If it is clear, we have more hopes of reaching you. If it is cloudy with selfishness, hate, frustration, or egotistic hopes based upon self-centeredness and hopes of personal aggrandizement, what gets through from us is distorted and clouded by the heaviness of the aura through which it must travel for you to express it. You may fool yourselves, or even each other, but this is all too plain to those who are seeing through spiritual, not physical eyes.

Pure truth cannot come untarnished by such emotional auras. So messages received from us will come through heavy or foreboding when projected through a heavy aura. Then you see through a glass darkly. But when the aura is perfected the message can come through clear and true, like music from a truly good hi fi set. When you read intuitive messages that are repetitive and loaded with words which do not communicate their message, you have a heavy sense of self receiving them and the effect is like a stuck needle in a phonograph record; it just doesn't seem to get moving on to the next point. In these cases there is usually some contact, but not as much as is claimed by the channel.

When we have the privilege of communicating through a clear aura, the message can be clear and the words truly communicate in r   m   ning. It should carry more of new insight   n personal or egotistic assurance. The ones who would exploit the psychic are more apt to make promises of grandeur, for this is what people are willing to pay for.

Tell all of those who loved me and Cosmon to test all material that is claimed to be

(Please Continue on Page 19)

COSMONKNIGHTS

Our beloved CosmonKnights:

This is your friend, June, of Venus. I am bringing to you some thoughts about BEAUTY. Upon my planet, our people and our civilization express much of the BEAUTY in the nature of the Father. Some of you think of beauty as pretty faces or well-shaped bodies. You think of beauty as something that decorates the outside. You sometimes exclaim about the beauty of a flower or an animal or a jewel. You can notice the beauty of motion and grace in the rhythm of a dance. The tender colors of a sunset or a dawn sometimes call forth from you an appreciation of beauty. The sounds of music often cause you to say this is beautiful too.

On our planet we say that BEAUTY is God's love in expression and we feel it is our duty to reveal this glorious love in every part of our living. The men of our planet are not ashamed to express this beauty, as are many of those upon your planet of earth. We are ashamed of ugliness, because it to us shows lack of reverence and respect. BEAUTY is the spirit of loveliness seeking perfection through the forms of each planet. We have studied the subject of BEAUTY longer than have the people of your earth, and so have discovered some of the many ways to bring it forth through our work, our play and our worship.

If you will study with care that which seems to you beautiful, you will find, in every case, that BEAUTY is made up of certain requirements. There is, in a true expression of beauty, a harmonious relationship. There is order, there is right proportion, there is some degree of perfection in the small detail. Notice the tender care God lavishes on the creation of each small flower blossom, each perfect hair of the coat of fur of an animal, each feather of a bird, each leaf of a tree, each blade of grass, each sea shell, each scale of a fish. Do you see that God's creations in Nature are always finished with infinite carefulness? There are no ragged edges, no careless spots or stains, no scratches, no loose, broken parts that mar the effect of the work. Sometimes, even in Nature there are accidental happenings which destroy the wonderful productions of the Father, but wherever God's Laws are free to work without interruption, you will see His creations unfolding in harmony, order and grace.

True BEAUTY is a principle. It is invisible as are all principles, but it is important and necessary and desired by the Father to be brought forth. You may think of BEAUTY as the Soul within all things, at the very heart. It is not evil, not vain, to express true spiritual BEAUTY which is always the sum total of harmony, order, patience, love and reverence. It is wisdom to try to create a picture of beauty in every detail of your living. BEAUTY can be expressed in ways that are unseen. There is BEAUTY of friendship, BEAUTY of kindness, BEAUTY of service, BEAUTY of serenity. Beauty often shows as the animating spirit looking upon you through the eyes of an animal, a person, a bird. Begin to search for it everywhere. One of your people said:

"Beauty lieth in the eyes
of the beholder."

This means that your eyes are filled with the appreciation of BEAUTY and that you can recognize it wherever you see it. Train yourself to seek for beauty wherever you happen to be. If you cannot find any vestige of BEAUTY where you are, then allow your creative thought to make a form of BEAUTY to leave behind you in the unbeautiful place. Try, where you happen to be, to leave that spot more beautiful by your presence. If you can remove ugliness, can erase unpleasant scars, can clean up the places where you live and play and work, you have set the stage for gradual manifestation of BEAUTY.

Remember this, our children: LOVE and BEAUTY are intended to be travelling companions upon the path of Light. It is the Love within which transfigures life and waves a magic wand. Love responds to Beauty and BEAUTY responds to LOVE. Do not fear either.

Have you ever realized that it is ignorance which causes all unbeautiful things, all unbeautiful expressions, all distressing conditions? People who live in confusion, ugliness, disorder are ignorant, which means they are ignoring TRUTH. You are here to teach the lesson of BEAUTY. Begin to be BEAUTY inside and outside. Let yourself begin with a clean, orderly body. BEAUTY cannot show forth in filth or carelessness, although it tries, for you have seen the brave flowers that spring up on piles of trash. You have seen a beautiful smile on the face of a neglected, shabby, unwashed child. You have seen the beauty of serenity on a peaceful old face of one who lives in poverty and hardship. But BEAUTY should not have to fight for survival. It is your duty as baby gods to transform the world about you with the magic of LOVE.

Your Great Teachers tell you that acceptance of responsibility is the sign of maturity. Look around you and judge for yourselves the maturity of those within your home, your school, your community, your nation. The undeveloped, irresponsible, childish people, some of them in grown-up bodies, are those who create ugliness. Do not turn away and say, "I must accept this situation. It is life." You need not accept anything less than BEAUTY, but BEAUTY is born of effort, not of idleness.

Take responsibility upon yourselves to set things right. Never be ashamed or afraid to clean up messes, to attend to lowly duties, to set an example where you happen to be. Your wonderful hands are God's hands. He gave them to you to do HIS work. Use them to bless humanity, to put life in order, to clear the way for BEAUTY. Do not permit weariness to be your ruler. Do not stop for pain, for sorrow, for fear, for despair. Do all you CAN, in spite of these intruders. They are sent to test you and make you strong. They are the handicaps placed upon you in the race of life so that each one has an equal chance at the prizes to be won.

You have within you an eraser with which you may clean off the mistakes, the ugly marks, the scribblings you made upon the first pages of your Book of Life. That eraser is LOVE. Love God so dearly that you bring forth HIS Will in the little place where you live today. Begin this very minute to transfigure your life, and shine forth as an example to those who live and work beside you. Maybe your first action will be very small and simple, but you will remember it all of your life, for it will mark a fresh start. Perhaps this first step will be such a trivial action as:

1. Washing your face and hands.
2. Combing your hair.
3. Emptying a waste basket.
4. Making your bed.
5. Mending a tear.
6. Feeding your pet.

Go on from here. Look at your home, your garden, your room, your street, your vacant lots, your workshops, your community. Aren't there things everywhere that need attention, cleaning up, mending, repairing, removing? Do not look for what you can get, but for what you can give. Take your givingness into each place that needs the help you can supply. Ask for nothing but an opportunity to help. If you do this for God, He will then be able to bring the help you need, through other hands seeking also to do His Will. The result will be BEAUTY, order, harmony, friendship, understanding, and happiness on all sides.

When you have made this beginning of BEAUTIFYING your life and your world, write to Cosmon of your experiences.

With my Love and blessings,

June of Venus

SENIOR COSMONKNIGHTS

Dear young friends -

June of Venus has brought some ideas to you on BEAUTY. I think you will begin to see life in a different way when you practice her suggestions. It may seem suddenly as if you are awake for the first time, or as if someone gave you a new pair of eyes. Most people go through life half-awake, grumbling about conditions, circumstances and troubles, without ever stopping to think they have the power to make a great many changes, with God's energy flowing through them, if they want a better world.

In my own case, I learned long ago to discover beauty in the most unlikely places. Years later I remember some of these discoveries, and how they taught me to find treasures in the strangest surroundings.

One day I was walking with Gloria Lee through the aisles of a hot house where there were many kinds of potted plants being grown for sale. We stopped near shelves where great brown fuzzy roots of tropical tree ferns were being cultivated. You probably have heard people call the green baby fronds, all curled up in a very tight roll, "Fern Kittens". A few of these large roots, covered with the softest silky brown fuzz, were giving birth to the dearest little "green kittens" you could imagine. They were so beautiful, so quiet, so perfect and so infused with a personality of their own that we both felt joy to the point of tears. We stopped and stroked these dear little things and I have never forgotten the sense of being in one of God's workshops and being allowed the privilege of looking on at His wonderful activity.

Some years ago, on a very cold, gloomy night, I was waiting alone at a bus stop. It was late and lonely and no people were in sight, and I was looking at the gutter below the bench where I was sitting. The street lamp was lighting up all the small bits of trash on the street. Suddenly I noticed an open packet of paper matches someone had dropped upon the dark gray pavement. Their tips were a bright pink, their paper stems were a lovely chartreuse green. There in that tiny composition was sheer beauty of color, pattern and form, and I felt revitalized, because BEAUTY is a living spirit and it does renew you whenever you allow yourself to recognize and drink it in through your eyes or ears or touch.

On a Sunday morning when I was six years old, my father took me for a walk in the wild New Jersey woods. I remember how I felt when we came to a great opening in the trees and there, surrounding a swamp, was a throng of tiger lilies in full bloom.

I have been in the city of Los Angeles, on rainy nights, passing through Skid Row on bus or in a car, and have seen the neon lights reflected upon the shiny streets and pavements and old, stark buildings, alleyways and trash barrels taking on a look of fairy-tale stage settings.

* * * * * * *

Do not be like the cat in the Mother Goose tale who went to London to visit the Queen and when she was asked, "Pussy cat, pussy cat, what did you there?" she replied, "I frightened a little mouse, under a chair." If you go to see the Queen, don't get off your track and settle for mice.

Don't let adults in your life sell you short and tell you that "It can't be done." If it is something the world needs and you believe in your ability and your vision, keep working on it until it shows forth. Don't waste the precious treasure of your young energies. Demand of Life that you be shown here and now which road you must follow. There is in all of us something that gives us peace of mind when we are on the right path, even if everyone around us disagrees with us; something that inspires us to keep trudging along, even when we meet only discouragement. Don't let anyone stop you, NOT EVEN YOURSELF, when you know the green light is beckoning you onward with a work to fulfill.

No matter how utterly worthless you seem to yourself and others, at times, reassure yourself that the Father would not have gone to all the bother of creating you and leading you upward through the mineral, vegetable and animal kingdoms, and then brought you into the human kingdom, if He did not have a wonderful purpose which only you can carry out in some part of His intended PLAN.

Even the perfected men we call Masters and Supermen were once where you are this very minute. It is the very same road for us all. Even the very greatest, in their human lives upon the ladder of evolution, have forgotten where they were going, have broken promises to themselves and to God, have fallen flat on their faces, have left the Path of Light to play by the wayside, and then have picked themselves up and dusted themselves off and started all over again. Two of the great saints were once considered for a time juvenile delinquents. These were St. Augustine and St. Francis of Assisi. But they did not give up and hate themselves so much they could not turn over a new leaf. Before God, I can say to you that no matter *what* you have done or been, you *can go on* and finally arrive at perfection. Don't let anyone, anywhere tell you, you are hopeless or beyond God's forgiveness or unfit to be loved.

It does not mean curtains for you, young boy or girl, if you are wearing the skin color of a minority race. It means you are considered stronger and braver than those who would jeer at you and ridicule you in their ignorance and their forgetfulness that they were once where you now are, or will one day be there where you are living and suffering today. Don't waste time in self-pity. Show the world that God is within you and has placed gifts in your keeping that must be used for the benefit of everyone, even those who call themselves your enemies. God allows the sunshine of His love to fall upon all people alike. He does not suck back His rays from those who backslide, but gives all an equal share. Try to be godlike in allowing the whole world to be blessed by the treasures hidden within you as budding talents.

If this finds you at a moment when your heart has been broken, remember the words of the great poet, Kahlil Gibran, who said that pain cracks the shell of the understanding. Most of us, including me, have had our hearts bashed and broken to smithereens until they look like a patchwork quilt, but that's why we are well-acquainted with life and not afraid of it. Pick up the pieces; put them together the best you can, so that you will have some kind of a pump to keep beating in your chest, and go along your way, even if you have to crawl during the first few miles.

Never mind if teenagers are excess baggage in commercial circles. If you cannot get a paid job, use your time to help anyone, anywhere, doing whatever you can. Pretend you are taking a course in work skills and invest your capital of mind, feelings, muscles and friendliness in learning anything and everything you can. Don't wait for fortune to find you. Run out to meet it. Dreams are only the seeds. Activity is the plant. Success is the fruit.

My love to you as we travel together. We cannot always see each other, because we kick up a lot of dust, especially when we are in a hurry to be about the Father's business, but we know we are all here, going in the same direction, following the signpost that says: "GOLDEN AGE, just around the bend!"

Your friend,
walking in the next dustcloud,

Barbara Steele

LETTER FROM VICKY

Dear Cosmon Members,

I am writing this letter so that I can share my thoughts with you.

It's not right to tease people when they do something wrong insted you should help them. When you tease a person it makes them mad. It also hurts there feelings, even if they don't show it it may still hurt there feelings. You do not want to hurt peoples feelings, because it is wrong to do so.

When your parents scold you or get mad at you you should not get mad at them for it is for your own good. They don't meen that they don't like you they meen that they love you and they want you to understand. They want you to do the right things and not the wrong.

If you have a dog or some other kind of animal then tame it so that it won't bite or hurt anyone. Make your pet happy. Tame him to understand you and love you.

If you brake something or lose something then you should tell someone what you did. You should try to get them a new one but first try to fix the old one.

If you lie about it saying you didn't do it then you are in the wrong. It is better to tell the truth than to lie and say you didn't do it. For it is sometimes better to lose something than to lie.

Find things to do so that you will not bother people in what they are doing. Don't always ask people what there is to do because they might not know either. Do some thing that will keep you occupied.

Do not ask for help in things you are doing unless you really need it, and do not help others unless they really need it. For people should learn to do things for themselves and not others do things for them. So try to do things yourself before you ask for help. That way you will learn things yourself and others won't be learning it for you. When others do things for you that doesn't meen that you are learning it. It meens that others are learning it. That is good for the other person but not for you.

I write this hoping that you will try as hard as you can. If you follow the suggestions above then that will help you to go into the NEW AGE.

WITH LOVE, LIGHT AND POWER

From Vicky Carstens

From Aesop's Fables. . .

The wind and the sun entered a friendly contest one day to determine which force wielded the greatest power over man.

They said to one another, "Let us test our strength upon yonder man, taking his way along the path below. Let us see which of us can cause him to remove the coat from his back."

So the wind blew mightily and the man hunched himself together, drawing his head down into his collar, hugging his garment closer each time the blast struck him anew.

The wind thought to himself, "If I cannot, with all my massed and flowing strength, cause this feeble human to remove his coat, how can the inactive sun hope to score a victory?"

The sun concentrated his rays, and shone warmly upon the chilled figure of the man, who thereupon began to relax, to loosen his coat, to stretch his arms, to bask in the comfort. Presently the warmth grew more intense and the man flung off his coat.

15

EN ROUTE

Dear Cosmonites -

One thing led to another as I was thinking of a story I once read, about a little girl who was inspired to write small messages of love and encouragement on slips of paper, and then to place them in public locations where some passing stranger might discover one of these and receive a spiritual lift. It seemed to some, as they found one of these little pieces of paper, that the very voice of God had been inscribed upon it to prevent them from taking a step leading to suicide, or to recharge them with courage to perform a difficult task, or to stimulate the manifestation of love, or to give them new faith and patience to await the outworking of a desired activity. Why don't you try a variation of some kind upon this theme and give yourself a glow of silent partnership with the forces of inspiration?

Little things mean a lot. Have you ever pondered upon the opportunity overlooked by the uninspired soothsayers who produce the predictions in Chinese fortune cookies and children's party snappers? What I am trying to get across is this. Even in insignificant details, it is possible to infuse some enlightenment, encouragement, excitement, delight and revitalization. This is important whether you bake a fortune cookie, or do whatever you do. Even if you work on an assembly line, you CAN inject something of yourself into the production of your hands, you can add the incense of your love and blessings to your work so that it will carry some degree of spiritual influence to those who touch what your hands have made or held or wrapped or mended or baked or sewed or designed or printed or assembled. Think of it!! What kind of influence goes from you? Is the world better or worse because of the circulation of YOUR influence in the general flow of production? Are yours the products so well and carefully put together that they show your integrity and raise the faith of the human family to believe not all producers of goods and services are shoddy, incapable, unethical and bent on making a fast dollar?

On the way along the path of life we all tread together, I have been in many of the situations where you are today. This is a cause for thanksgiving because, having been there, I can understand you and your problems and your hunger to rise higher, to something better and brighter and more rewarding. I have been low man on many totem poles, but there are as many good life lessons to be learned close to the floor as anywhere along the ladder.

Years ago I read a book in which the author's preface told how he had been a factory worker and a jack-of-all-trades and so could understand people. He felt better qualified to offer a philosophy of life, because he had been an active participant and not just a spectator on the sidelines. And it is true, that somewhere along the way this firsthand knowledge is essential if you sincerely want to work with and for people. Stop scorning the chores that seem menial to you and remember that Jesus did not scorn to wash the feet of his disciples. Albert Schweitzer does not scorn to work upon the bodies of underprivileged African natives. Florence Nightingale did not scorn to act as a nurse among the wounded of a battlefield. Jane Addams did not scorn to move into Skid Row and become a neighbor to those in deep psychological trouble.

Stop deploring the chores you are having to do. Letters come here day after day, in which the writers tell how they are sure there must be a mistake and that they were intended for better things, higher pay and cleaner surroundings, and cannot see why Fate pushed them into the role of truck driver, dish washer, orderly, garbage collector, hash slinger, ditch digger and so forth. Rejoice, fortunate ones, if you are entwined with the woes and aspirations of those in the fields and factories, gutters and sweatshops, where humanity reveals its true yearnings, hungers, aspirations, hopes and fears unmasked, where you are privileged to read the story of evolution upon the faces of men and women and children, free from the veneers of sophistication and craftiness. This is the postgraduate schoolroom where you put the elementary lessons to the test. This is the wide sweep of life wherein you may rub shoulders with adepts and masters in disguise, as they radiate their love and understanding into those simpler layers of mankind, those more open hearts and minds. Those on the upper levels (so-called) of civilized society, are often those whose minds are glazed over with conceit, contempt, malice, smugness and cynicism, and are those least possible to reach or penetrate with the message of hope and life coming through New Age channels.

To help people you must know them. You can only know them if you've been one of them. You must listen to them with the heart, and hear them out until all the tale of misery, despair, shame, disappointment, desire, guilt, neglect, destruction and creation is poured out before you. Many need only a listening ear, and in hearing their own voices, find answers revealed to themselves by themselves. Remember this when you are waiting for the cessation of some seemingly unending tale of true life experiencing by one of your fellow members of the family of man.

There are times when it helps to have a brother or sister tear off the illusions that surround some assignment which others define as spiritual, and to which their attention and ambition are turned. Since Gloria transferred the focus of her service, I have been accused of everything from plotting her overthrow to craftily inserting the person of a scheming secretary into the shoes of the leader-employer-director. This does not any longer disturb me, though it caused waves of feeling to turn me to the search for others who would be willing and better able to assume the responsibilities of this post, when first the attacks began to come by letter and by psychic impressions.

Suddenly, one day, I was no longer affected. I am free from the drag of public opinion. I turned to the Father and told Him I am all His, and to do what He will with me to the absolute end of whatever usefulness may be stored up in my evolutionary experience. From that time on, the blame and also praise of fellow men has meant very little. TRUTH is a severe Master, and forces her servant to strive for honesty in facing the personal self. TRUTH is also a just and merciful Master and so long as the servant continues upon the path of duty, Truth directs and protects and leads to enlightenment.

All work is spiritual work, if you practice serving the Father and furthering His Will in your present situation, whatever it is. You can glorify or besmirch your calling whether you are a cesspool cleaner or a minister of the gospel or a babysitter or a Turkish bath attendant. God is complete at every point of His creation, and that means wherever you are. Not where you are but how you do your work, is the important criterion of your success as a Soul in incarnation.

Allow yourself the privilege of being humiliated once in awhile. It restores your balance and your sense of proportion. Once when I was over 35 and could not find a job anywhere, after visiting several cities and 18 prospects, I finally landed an experience in a five-and-ten or dime store. After some weeks of being shuttled back and forth from one counter to another, I was given the management of the plants and pets department. Part of my daily duty here consisted in climbing into the walk-in parakeet cage with a long-handled net to capture individual birds chosen by the customers. At first I experienced considerable embarrassment, for the birds were not housebroken or friendly. They were wild, frightened and sometimes aggressive. Sometimes I stood still in the midst of a hundred wildly flying and screeching birds while their wings stirred a wind strong enough to lift my hair. The customers relished an occasion such as this and called their friends over to share the sport. It was like a side show and they sometimes laughed boisterously when a darting bird scored a direct hit. Since this was a necessary duty, I finally learned to focus on the skill of catching the desired bird, quickly and gently, and to take part in the sense of fun of the customers instead of the emphasis upon my own total loss of dignity.

During a period when life seemed especially grim financially, and I had been the recipient of charitable aid to hold my young family together, I determined to become self-reliant at all costs and capable of supporting my youngsters without the help of others. To this end I went to work for a woman friend who owned a small letter shop and public stenographer service, as an apprentice, to learn the mysteries of operating business machines and becoming a secretary. My salary was $5.00 per week and I learned how to operate a mimeograph, an addressograph, manual and electric typewriters, and a graphotype machine that imprinted metal tabs to be run off on the addressograph. In addition I learned what it means to be a public stenographer and to work for all sorts of transient executives. While there I developed sufficient skill to take on a second job as the secretary of a minister in one of the largest churches of the city where I lived. This minister had been an army Chaplain overseas in World War II and had served with the Marines. When we became well acquainted, he told me he had once stood on his hands upon a mantel shelf and had fallen off and broken both wrists. This he had done to amuse his little sons, but had learned a major lesson for himself. After he confided that he too was just a faulty and growing human being, I was able to enter into a good friendship with him, in which he gave me some pointers on the viewpoint of one who serves on the other side of the pulpit.

For nearly a year I worked in a bicycle shop, as general assistant to an elderly gentleman who had once been a world traveller and talent scout for one of the great recording companies of earlier days. From him I learned of civil war in Spain and how it felt to be commanded by the military to be off the city streets at sundown, to walk up ten flights to one's candle-lighted apartment and to find ways of self-entertainment. This ingenious individual taught himself to carve animal horns. He was supplied by a friend at the bull ring who acquired the special black twisted horns of the little Spanish bulls just for him. He learned to heat these horns and shape them like plastic, and to color and polish and carve them into beautiful works of art. While I listened to tales of wine, women and song in Spain and France and England and Germany and South America and Mexico, I also learned to put hot patches on bike tires, dismantle and clean old hubs, keep order in a welter of tools, dirt, grease and cookie crumbs; to sell accessories and sweep the floors, wash the outside show windows, clean the owner's apartment behind the shop, and to add to my income by crocheting garments for his youngest grandchildren.

Along the way, I stopped off for several months in an art school, through the kind offices of friends, and while there entered a contest for designs of accessories and won a job designing shoes in a Los Angeles shoe factory. Most of the employees were Jewish and Mexican, with a few Italians and colored folk interlarded, and a mere handful of white Americans such as myself. My boss was a wonderful old pattern maker who had once travelled with a circus and created shoes for elephants, giants, fat ladies and dwarfs. He had also discovered that many average people have two sizes of feet and never find it out, for nobody bothers to tell them, and they live in wonder as to why one shoe always fits and the other always pinches whenever a new pair is purchased. I discovered it was sometimes necessary to make fifty sketches before one really new and exciting style would emerge and be worth putting into work. I also learned that a good design would be made in several grades of material and workmanship, so that the identical pattern would emerge in Skid Row for $2.39, in Mid-town from $7.95 to $15.00, and in the exclusive French booteries from $25.00 to $49.50. This taught me to look for design and workmanship ahead of price. The same principle obtains in other garment manufacturing fields. Price, therefore, is not an ultimate criterion, and when individuals boast about the prices they have paid for this possession or that, I just smile and say nothing.

In this shoe factory I ran across a vignette of human democracy in action, or is there a better word? One afternoon great festivities went on in one department where a young Mexican girl was being given a baby shower by her fellow employees, who were in on the secret that the baby's father would be the girl's lover and co-worker, though she was married and keeping house for another.

In every job I have held, I have tried to remember that as a disciple I must endeavor to give more than received, to learn all I could of life and human relationships, and to remain unattached to persons, places and things to the extent of being willing to move on, to change service areas, to stop while seemingly far from completion of an undertaking.

For several years I worked in an insurance agency and finally concentrated upon helping to settle accident claims. Here was a fertile field for education and insight into human emotions, and I spent four years in it. I recall the day when a woman policyholder came to my desk to report an accident and discovered some hours later that her neck was broken, though she was still surrounded by that post-accident numbness which allows individuals to go through devastating physical destruction, at times, without registering pain. Because this possibility interested me, I checked and proved to my own satisfaction that this curious factor often enters into major accidents. That is why all people should undergo a medical checkup immediately after suffering bodily injuries, for if they fail to make a claim within a given time limit and discover later on that they did indeed sustain fractures, whiplashes or other slow-healing invisible damages, they are too late to receive compensation. I learned here that it is well to be practical as well as brave!

Two years were well spent in the office of a cancer surgeon, where I served as secretary and office nurse. Here I learned to produce surgical cleanliness and order, to prepare the office operating room for minor surgery, to assist and to hand sterile instruments during removal of tumors, skin cancers, moles and warts. I saw women whose breasts had been removed. I stood by while the doctor dressed third-degree burns, drained post-operative infections, gave pregnancy tests, performed sterilization operations for parents who felt they had too many children. I held hands of children and adults who cried in fear of the unknown, and washed up the bloody instruments after the operations. Here I learned that love, compassion and patience help greatly in preparing the patients for surgery, and in bringing about healing more swiftly after the hospital experiences.

I have worked as a waitress in a soda fountain, clerk and later as buyer in department stores, as a power machine operator in a coat factory, as a paint color mixer in a theatre poster studio, as a craft worker for a gift shop, as a sketch artist and as a wardrobe woman in two movie studios, as an assistant to a window trimmer, as a show card writer, and as a seamstress at home after hours as a clerk.

As you can see, I have never held a great job, been a worldly success, or done anything that you cannot do, or learned anything that you cannot learn. The many steps I have taken along the path of life have been small, insignificant steps, just such as those of other disciples-in-training the world over. The point is that this so-called school of hard knocks is the wonderful school which teaches LIFE, which strips away the glamor and illusion and false values woven into our contemporary civilization by the forces of greed and ignorance and hate and fear.

Gloria Lee attended this same great school of hard knocks. We had time, during the first few weeks and months of our friendship, to exchange views and reminiscences concerning the people and experiences we had met, and we found that we could look on the surrounding scene without hate or bitterness, or the degree of frustration which nullifies the urge to help in the redemption and salvage of humanity. A life such as ours prepared us for an exceptional friendship and the deepened pleasure of working with another individual who knew what the score was — who had had her arms up to the elbows in realism, who had not lost faith in God or mankind, who thought the goal was worth sacrifice of life. We both agreed, close to the beginning of our friendship, that a goal not worth dying for, was not worth living for!

Somewhere I read that Alice Bailey was

a member of that group of disciples called the "suicide squad" because they did not care what happened to them, if only the work desired of them could be manifested. That fired my imagination and I used to dream of the possibility of one day being permitted to serve beside those of such ardor, enthusiasm, purpose, joy, and willingness to sweat and burn and freeze and strain, that somehow, somewhere, we could move the immovable, achieve the impossible, grapple with the unyielding and help with a never-diminishing fervor in the Herculean and therefore colossally challenging feat of bringing the world back to its glory, its fearlessness, its love and beauty.

It is a shame that words cannot convey the sense of gratitude, joy, appreciation and inward strength that propel me onward. I felt them when Gloria was beside me and visible to the physical eyes, but these have not diminished, for I know we are partners still. There are times when I am aware of a surging, flooding love within me of so great a force that I almost feel I could go forth and set the world on fire singlehanded; for I am so firm in the certainty that no matter what trials and tribulations and pains and destructions come upon us, it is all WORTH THE COST, and I would do it all over again from the beginning!

* * * * * * *

Before signing off I must ask you to please accept my devoted thanks for all the wonderful books you sent in by request, for the library. Happily, a number of children's books found their way here since our request in the May newsletter. We are very happy about this as well as for the receipt of splendid books for the adult membership. Does anyone have out-of-print copies of Claude Bragdon's books, DELPHIC WOMAN, THE BEAUTIFUL NECESSITY, THE FROZEN FOUNTAIN? I know I read all three, but have lost completely any contact with them, and would like to have them for circulation to our friends.

With my love,

Barbara

DIALOGUE WITH GLORIA
(Continued from Page 8)

channeled by anyone from this side, by their own intuitive perception. If it does not seem to be a usable truth for them, they should leave it lay. It may have truth that is usable at another time, but if they do not clearly understand its meaning, their use of it would also be muddled.

It is not what we say that is important, nor really how clearly anyone receives it. It is only important as it makes us better able to work in God's plan and help those about us to a better understanding of what man and God is. "By their fruits ye shall know them." This is as true of messages as of people.

We can save some people steps, but in the long run it is only what their inner knowing ratifies that will let them act.

We are your loving brothers and sisters. Love each other and you will have a clearer aura to receive our love. It is still true, you must give out any quality before that quality can communicate to you, or you will not have any understanding of its meaning, even if we try to channel it through you. Your emotion surrounds you as an element, an insulation. We can only penetrate it when it is pure of qualities that would eliminate us. It can only let you communicate with what is of like feeling. Only as you keep it pure and loving and selfless, can those of us who are pure and loving and selfless reach you. As you make it selfish, grasping, self-seeking and self-indulgent, you will attract those of a similar spirit. So the real protection, the real insulation against inadequate or frightening channeling lies in the purity of your own thoughts and feelings.

My prayers for that purity are with all of you that I have introduced to the whole concept of channeling. May you learn to see through your glass brightly, and bring the white light of understanding from Heaven to Earth.

All my love,

Gloria

I F

If you can keep your head when all about you
    Are losing theirs and blaming it on you,
If you can trust yourself when all men doubt you,
    But make allowance for their doubting too;
If you can wait and not be tired by waiting,
    Or being lied about, don't deal in lies,
Or being hated don't give way to hating,
    And yet don't look too good, nor talk too wise:

If you can dream — and not make dreams your master;
    If you can think — and not make thoughts your aim;
If you can meet with Triumph and Disaster
    And treat those two impostors just the same;
If you can bear to hear the truth you've spoken
    Twisted by knaves to make a trap for fools,
Or watch the things you gave your life to, broken,
    And stoop and build 'em up with worn-out tools:

If you can make one heap of all your winnings
    And risk it on one turn of pitch-and-toss,
And lose, and start again at your beginnings
    And never breathe a word about your loss;
If you can force your heart and nerve and sinew
    To serve your turn long after they are gone
And so hold on when there is nothing in you
    Except the Will which says to them: "Hold on!"

If you can talk with crowds and keep your virtue,
    Or walk with Kings — nor lose the common touch,
If neither foes nor loving friends can hurt you,
    If all men count with you, but none too much;
If you can fill the unforgiving minute
    With sixty seconds' worth of distance run,
Yours is the Earth and everything that's in it,
    And — which is more — you'll be a Man, my son!

                      Rudyard Kipling

SPECIAL COMMUNICATION
FROM DR. HAMILTON AND GLORIA LEE

INTRODUCTORY NOTE

Certain circumstances have cleared to a point where it is now requested of me that you be told Gloria has communicated with many, upon various levels of their receptivity.

You must know that she is not exclusive, but inclusive, and that she feared for a time that the impression was being conveyed, she had put all of her eggs in one basket. I am now ready to tell you I believe some of the Mark-Age material, claimed as communications from Gloria, is valid. I feel that much of it is slanted and colored by a past relationship between the personalities of several individuals in the groups of Cosmon and Mark-Age, and that this relationship, as it was originally conceived, no longer obtains, in spite of Mark-Age claims.

While Gloria was in Washington, D.C., she stated to me that J.W. told her the original relationship was no longer held by the Teachers to be in force, because certain necessary conditions had not been fulfilled and so the once-intended closer affiliation had been dissolved.

My belief is that a certain proportion of the material given immediately after her death has some truth in it, and that she did use the instrumentship of Yolanda to explain and express certain useful experiences and insights she had received, in order to enlighten all who could be reached and assured that individual awareness and progress continue beyond the death of the physical body.

* * * * * * *

When I asked Gloria to comment on the book said to be communicated by her to a Channel in May Harvey's group in New Zealand, she told me she had met with the channel on the mental plane and had exchanged ideas with her, and that the channel had interpreted that Gloria was dictating a book to her in a planned activity sequence. Gloria also told me to leave the channel free to bring out her book as it had use and value, even though Gloria did not author it from a higher level. I wrote to May Harvey what I have said here and asked her to use her own means of verification and confirmation, for I simply was stating what to me was TRUTH, and I could be mistaken in my interpretation too.

* * * * * * *

To my sincere belief, Zelrun Karsleigh of Universariun has also received genuine communications from Gloria, as has Marianne Francis of Santa Barbara, Dr. Eugene Drake of the Fellowship of Golden Illumination, Rev. Danny Hart of Los Angeles, Dr. Maurine Sellstrom of Los Angeles and others known to me.

In addition, I am firmly convinced that the two Channels of the Star Light Fellowship in Unit 72 of New York, directed by Sterling Warren, have received considerable communication of a genuine nature from Gloria, and I am here publishing a valuable communication received through the Instrumentship of Jackie White Star and Phyllis Veronica on January 23, 1963 from Gloria and one of her Doctor Teachers, Dr. Hamilton.

* * * * * * *

There is not intended to be a retraction or an apology here for anything stated in our March-April Cosmon. I was told to word the printed material the way it was worded, and I did.

Barbara

DR. HAMILTON AND GLORIA LEE SPEAK AT MEETING OF STAR LIGHT FELLOWSHIP

New York, January 23, 1963

INTRODUCTION: Reproduced here is a transcription taken from that portion of the direct-voice telepathic transmissions received by the Channels of this Unit 72 during the regular Wednesday evening meeting of S.L.F., on the above date, which were concerned with GLORIA LEE. (Earlier in the same meeting, discourses were given by the Biblical Prophet, ISAIAH, and by the former Chief Justice of the United States Supreme Court, JOHN MARSHALL. These will be reproduced at a later time. They did not have a direct bearing on the GLORIA LEE messages.) The first speaker was DR. HAMILTON, Gloria's Etheric Teacher while she was in the physical and now a direct associate in Spirit's Work, and then, GLORIA LEE herself.

There have been and will be a great many questions and speculations about Gloria's transition, and also about various transmissions or communications received from her or about her since her passing, through various Channels. It is believed that the communications reproduced in this bulletin were given by GLORIA and DR. HAMILTON in an attempt to clarify certain points and to afford Light Students some additional background information and perspective regarding her new work with the Enlightenment Groups and the various reported communications received at this time, as well as to provide some guidance for the future.

It is the hope of this UNIT 72 that the efforts expended in the distribution of this Message may be of service to GLORIA and to the Earth Hierarchy in furthering the objective of Spiritual preparation for the Coming of the Lord and the Kingdom of God on this Planet, Earth. May the Holy Spirit be with us all in these Latter Days of rapid change for all God Souls in this Dimension.

** *** **

(Communications through Jackie White Star and Phyllis Veronica - 1/23/63)
DR. HAMILTON:
Greetings to all. This is Dr. Hamilton, Doctor Teacher of Gloria Lee. Blessed Gloria Lee is standing right at my side, and she has been speaking alternately to the two Channels this evening, earlier. It was Gloria's wish that she might come in and say a few words ... just short of a few hundred. Ha! Ha! I am sure that we can stand a change of pace here. We have been observing the going on of the evening's activity on the higher plane. Now we would like to recede from this vibration and come in to the focus of your Unit of Light and speak to you a few moments about other things, if time permits.

(The Channel, Jackie White Star speaking) Dr. Hamilton says that he would like to personally greet each one in the room and he would like to shake Phyllis's hand. He says that Gloria is here, straining on the communication device that is set up to communicate with the Instruments on the Earth plane.

(DR. HAMILTON continues:) So now I shall turn over this inter-communicational device and let my student speak to you. With that, I am getting a very naughty look from Gloria, because she shakes her head and says, "Since when did I have to go into transition and still be called a student?" She says, "I resent that tremendously, and I fully intend to have that retracted from the present statement."

GLORIA LEE:
Hello, friends. It's so nice to come in to the two Channels. It is a shame that I was so close to New York and I never was able to make a fast weekend jaunt to visit Unit 72 and see for myself the two Channels that seemingly were coming up too fast for me to comprehend. I say this in all sincerity, but as a compliment to the two young Channels that are receiving this highly important message this evening from those that are the officiators of

the higher Spiritual Truths. I have just recently spent much time in communication with the Mark Age Unit, and much of my own Earth personality is in evidence in the new booklet* that was so well illustrated through the Mark Age activities. I am very happy if I have been of help in bringing forth any new knowledge that would be useful to all those students on the Path that might read it. I would also like to state here that I am more or less a free-lancer in this realm. I am going to be coming in and working with different Channels whenever I am so directed by the Higher Authority of the Fatherhead. I can offer much help from this side of the veil, seemingly. There are many activities that I can appreciate better in this realm than I could in the physical body that I inhabited until just recently. *(Booklet mentioned above: "Gloria Lee Lives").

My work for Cosmon shall go on. No one shall replace the works that I have started; and each Group has an individual activity that has already been mapped out for them to fulfill of themselves. There is so much work to be accomplished by all Light Units that it is going to be very hard work on all of those that are attuned to you students and work with you students from this side. It is going to be a monumental job to fill all of the places that are going to be needing Channels of Light. There are many Channels that are undeveloped at this time, that shall come forth in the not too distant future and work directly with all factors in the Government and in the Churches and in all places that will accept New Age teachings. Of course, there are those Channels who have already put down certain groundwork and who shall fulfill their specific destinies that they incarnated for. But I shall not go into that, except, many things that were promised to certain individual Channels and their Groups of Light shall come into fulfillment before this year is out. I also would like to state here that no one in this particular sphere is indispensable. Dr. Hamilton just shook his head and said, "Yes, haven't we all been separated from our own beloved Teachers from time to time? But it was for Soul growth that this was brought about; and this even happened unto my student here that is Gloria Lee in the Earth dimension."

DR. HAMILTON:

I would like to make the statement here through someone who could be objective, who did not have any personal contact with Gloria Lee, so that there is not any Earth prejudice to contend with in the outer consciousness. The two Channels in Unit 72 have often said to themselves that they felt that Gloria Lee truly did a very big thing by going out of the physical body. There is a much more Spiritual meaning to Gloria's transition than was actually made known; and I would like to say here that, whether anyone else might agree with this statement, I am going to state it and let the chips fall where they may. Gloria was an early Christian martyr who died for the early Christian religion that she believed in and that she faithfully practiced. She was among the early people that gathered around the Master Jesus. She has a vibration that is of the highest and purest Christ quality, or she would not have gone into the Spirit fast that she went into. This was an inborn thing with her and it had nothing to do with the Earth personality that she was expressing at the time that she was alive. This is not to glorify Gloria, but I, as a Teacher of hers, would like to give this thought unto you all. No one has yet been called to give up his physical life for the Cause, so to speak; and many times Phyllis Veronica and Jackie White Star have spoken about the early Christian martyrs, and they have often said to each other that they did not know if they would have the so-called heroic Spiritual strength that it would take to give up their physical lives for the Cause. When we can truthfully question ourselves and say, "Would I not give up my life for my religious or Spiritual beliefs?" - this is coming very near to the surface of what real Truth is. To profess the perfection of the Christ teachings is one thing, and to go forth without much ado about what you are performing, is nearer the Truth. I have stated recently to others that the glorification of Channels is not needed, for a true Channel has an inborn humility and Grace that they do not wish any great praise or adulation or glory from others who would try to build up their own ego. We should always give praise for a job that is well done. We should praise the one who is struggling up the ladder of success more than the one who has already obtained the so-called Christ Consciousness on the highest of levels. We do our greatest service for the Father in the secrecy or privacy of our own Souls, without others in attendance watching our actions so that others might see us pray to the Father and remark how wonderful and how Christ-like we are.

To you who shall come up higher in consciousness - to you who shall teach - to you who shall go forth unto the public and do the work of the Fatherhead....do not seek to exploit your Channelship for ego's sake, because if you receive much glory through other activities that you somehow instigated yourself, other than what Spirit instigated, then you shall be caught in your own web of egotism. My dearest colleague now, who is a Teacher in this Christ Light, gave up her Earth existence without fanfare. She could at one stage of the game have gone back to her road that she was on - on the road of a great experience that would have brought forth much public acclaim unto herself and unto her organization known as Cosmon, but Gloria chose to leave the glories and the adoration of the Earth plane, where she was beginning to be able to capitalize on all of the good that she had worked so long and tirelessly for. I say this because it is the Truth. I would like to say, with the full permission of the two Channels of Light in this Unit of 72, that Gloria Lee was one of the first New Age students of Light to make a full payment for all of the discrepancies of the World. She actually went on her own cross, because this was a part of her Soul development that she knew about and understood. It was not hard for her to choose; and so I would say that she is one of the first New Age Disciples to actually become a martyr for the Cause in this New Age. I hope that this statement will not startle very many of you, but believe me that Gloria could have come back and completed a very successful career, doing many many important works, and completing a tremendous project that she had already started.

I am coming through to say that Gloria has done and completed the job that she set out to complete. This is going to be the end of my little speech about my favorite little niece - because I had often thought of Gloria many times as being like a niece unto me.

With this, I bid you all a fond adieu; and if there is any tape left on the transmission, Gloria is now pulling my coat tails to say she would like to say a few words through Phyllis Veronica.

DR. HAMILTON and GLORIA LEE

Foregoing communications
thru Jackie White Star,
direct voice Channel, 1-23-63

(The Co-Channel, Phyllis Veronica speaking): I feel so touched at the beautiful way in which Dr. Hamilton put forth his statements of Truth about Gloria Lee. I am sure we all feel very grateful, and much love goes forth from all of the students here who, though we did not meet Gloria Lee in the physical, felt very close to her Spiritually; and we admire the forthrightness with which she carried forth the Work for the Fatherhead. We are very grateful for her diligent service in the Light of God.

GLORIA LEE:
Thank you for that little speech, dear Phyllis, and of course all of you know that I feel the very same way about all of you in the Light Groups who are working towards the goal of the Father. I am very happy to be here with all of you tonight and it is a privilege to be in such high and esteemed company, as there are many many of the Cosmic Host who have gathered at this assembly, for that is, in Truth, what it is like - a large assembly. (Note: Earlier in our meeting, we were addressed by the Prophet ISAIAH and by former Chief Justice JOHN MARSHALL of The United States Supreme Court.)

As students in the Light, we all have in our hearts and in our minds to serve to the best of our ability. It is not upon a serious note that I had in mind to come forth and speak, but somehow I feel very prompted to speak to you directly from my own heart. No one suspects my true reason for choosing to go to the higher realms. I would be just as happy if I could continue on the way that people are thinking of me now.

(The Co-Channel, Phyllis Veronica speaking): Gloria Lee is saying that she did not have any discourse to give and no significant message to give forth. She would just like to come through and more or less let everyone know that she is working along with all of the students in all of the Light Groups whenever she has an opportunity. This is exactly what she said through Jackie White Star previously, so really, what I am hearing her say now is more or less a repetition of what she said to you before.

Q. - We are very happy she could come in and to have her explain this, that she is not tied to any particular group but is working with all groups. This is very good.

(Phyllis Veronica continues): She is telling me that she is working on many different projects - projects that she did not have the opportunity to work on when she was in the body, because in the realm she abides in now she is able, with the help of the Masters and Teachers, to see almost immediately complete patterns take shape for each Group. As she goes through the different patterns she might be looking into in each Group, when there is an opening in a pattern in a certain Group that she is able to come forth and work through, she will, if she is able to get permission, come forth and work through in a specific manner. Gloria says she is able to work on many of the scientific plans in a more complete and thorough way.

GLORIA LEE resumes speaking: The different avenues of expression are many in the field of science, and I am able to work in the many different avenues that I had hoped I could in the future, when I was working in Cosmon in the physical body. I had hoped for this in the years to come, because there were a few different avenues of expression which I felt were more or less my cup of tea, to use an Earth expression. There are certain scientific fields that I vibrated with and felt in harmony with, and that I had an understanding and knowledge of from J.W., and so I had looked forward, in the years to come perhaps, to being able to work along these certain lines. But now I am able to touch upon these things much sooner, and I am doing many different things over here. I am also learning much about the coordination on the inner planes of the Groups of Light, and how the patterns change, and the understandings are sent forth from the Spiritual realms of Light down into the material pattern of an Enlightenment Group, so that they may come forth to be unfolded in the outer world. There are so many facets and so many wonderful experiences that I am going through, and that I am seeming to remember as well. I am recalling very many of the understandings that I have been going through in these past weeks. There seems to be a little stone, I will call it, that has turned within me, that has brought back a memory of many of the certain things that I am doing now, that I am able to complete and fulfill faster because of this inner knowledge that I have of the past, and which all of you have also, and which is what the Teacher, JOHN MARSHALL, was speaking of to you so illustriously before - that these patterns of Light will stir up this remembrance in you. And it is true, my friends. You will begin to remember and recall many wonderful things that are inherent in each of your patterns, that are going to come forth to be fulfilled in this year of 1963. You will be getting new ideas, not from outside sources so much as from your own inner sources, and these ideas and understandings will expand in your mind as you live from day to day, so that ultimately they will be expressed through you as complete ideas which are to be unfolded through you and brought into activity. I know that you understand what I am trying to speak to you here, for actually anything that I could elaborate on to you now, at the present time, would only sound like a repetition of what has been spoken to you these many months in the past; but it is always good to bring forth this refresher course, especially since that has been the vibration of the intunement with the Light that we have been functioning on here tonight - and it is always a good one, to be sure.

From the position where I stand at this particular time, I am able to see into the forthcoming plans, as I mentioned to you awhile ago, and I would like to say to you here in all seriousness that there is much activity to come forth for this particular Group this coming year. You may not feel this particularly so right now at this present time, but in all Truth I tell you now that, looking into the records (I am not allowed to look into the

(Please Continue on Page 30)

CORRESPONDENCE FILE

NOTES FROM AN EDUCATOR

As a school teacher, I would like to share a few thoughts. I have just completed one of the most enjoyable, active years as a leader to a group of delightful children. I choose not to use the term teacher as I felt one of the group as the guardians, even our Teachers, so I was more the student figure head. Many the delightful lessons that were unfolded to us. Ofttimes they were presented as a game, but Man! how they did pack a powerful New Age concept!

Attitudes were, I feel, the greatest consideration, but this did not detract from the gathering of facts and skills along the way; it acted more as a catalyst to greater creative expression and learning. Our thoughts and actions even guided along lines of Positive Thinking, sharing our talent specialties with others; expressing love and understanding.

We adopted many fun-phrases that aided us greatly to change our attitudes towards errors. We called them boo-boos. And when we make a boo-boo, then we can learn from it so it becomes a positive experience, instead of a negative. To make it truly a part of the positive, we would then try to correct our boo-boo. How they enjoyed this, and it was understood.

Very little line writing was given because once the feeling and attitude was accepted and became a part of the student, the control then came from within them, and not from outside pressures put on by the teacher. Occasionally I forgot to practice the new concept and would be in the midst of the old-fashioned method of giving an assignment, say for being tardy or gum chewing. If I remembered in time, I'd say, "Pardon me, I can't make you change by having you push a pencil and waste all the paper, because your fingers do not have the mind to direct. They just perform a duty demanded of them. Your heart is the only one who can really help you." They understood and usually tried harder to overcome.

One day on a field trip I had to correct several of my children on throwing stones at large fish that our guide took us to see in a shallow stream. One boy really felt ashamed and in reading group remarked about it because he thought I was referring to the incident, which I was not, but as he brought it up, I felt he must have felt remorseful about his action. I then told him that I did not feel his action so much one of disobedience as maybe automatic. I said I would take the blame for not having thoroughly become acquainted with all phases of our field trip and then formulated prescribed procedures. But also the guide of the Bird Refuge could have expressed the wish not to throw at the fish, but even when I asked him about it he just shrugged his shoulders. That was when I asked them (children) not to throw rocks at the fish. It helped him to realize another concept, that we surely need a complete change of thinking in regard to animals and other creatures of the world. There was no maliciousness behind the act. It takes time to change from old habits that are practiced by the masses.

Another concept we used so many times a day was to examine the lessons we were learning and the characters of our stories as to their attitudes and especially whether they were selfish or selfless. One was love of self in regard to all others. The latter was love and consideration of others regardless of our own self.

Yes, they accepted the fact that our Heavenly Father would create other planets to be inhabited: that we as children of a Heavenly Father would in time grow and develop more like our Father if we were to practice these new concepts.

I should just mention one or two other points of interest: Mental Telepathy. We called it brain picking. They knew what others in our class might be thinking. I sometimes knew what they were thinking. It was fun. We learned to feel what others felt, or a mood they felt. How they seemed to develop sensitivity and enjoyed so much more!

One last reference to the conscience and intuitive guidance. The whole class seemed to be a part of this, almost to a student. My class was very free in regard to work. We had specified goals, but they were flexible to a point so that if they felt bogged down mentally, we took off half an hour for a ball game. Well, the last few days of school, they had prepared reports on South American countries. They were outstanding in so many areas. Well, this day we had scheduled several reports to be read in class. It meant squeezing it in with our other assignments. However we had a boy from the other 5th grade want to challenge our class to a sport event from 3:00 - 3:30 this day. I let him give the invitation and they could respond as they felt. His request fell on deaf ears. This I could not understand. Children of just about any age group would delight in any sport just to get out of pencil pushing and here they were, almost "to a man" selecting the latter.

I said: "You have your answer, but could you give us a little longer, maybe, to consider the challenge." So they left and we continued our duties. Later, as I was at the back of the room, the girl who was door attendant said she had heard the boys from the other room talking in the hall and they did not have their teacher's permission to have a sport event and beside they were out of their room without her permission also. This did not seem too unusual as it was typical conduct of that class. I never said any more about it. I thought I'd check with the teacher, at recess, which I did and she was very much against it as they had so much work to do and they were so far behind. I presumed the remark had been made that we had challenged them to a sport contest. When I returned to my class, I did say to the class: "Thank you for following your intuition. The invitation was not honorable or legal and you responded to the feeling of the wrongness even though the words were congenial." I asked them if they would like to have a Physical Education period outside, but they preferred to continue with work planned: it was more interesting.

The last week and one half we had gone all out into Outer Space and what a terrific time we had! The ideas that seemed to burst forth! The remark was expressed, and others, that they wished the end of this school year would not come so soon.

Yes, I saw many miracles take place before my very eyes this year. The path was not easy because as you are led to break new trails, the old try to tear you apart. Once I felt so ill at ease because of remarks and demonstrated procedures I went to school one morning with the decision to resign if they felt I was not doing a job worthy of their pay. They did not accept my intention. In fact my principal said: "It is not a piece of paper that says you are a teacher. Your children are reflecting the real teaching of your room." I said: "Then I am permitted to continue as I am doing, teaching attitudes first and facts second?" His answer was: "Yes."

In closing I would like to support your plan to publish the young peoples' magazines in their age groups. I would be particularly interested in more information about our solar system, other solar systems. Also a place where children could write in and ask questions. Of course this will be difficult to get into a public school system, but the way will be opened up if our desire is great enough.

Sincerely,

(Name withheld)

Please Note:
The foregoing letter is another example of what we mean when we keep repeating, "Stay in your own place. Do what God needs to have done where He placed you!" If He had wanted all of you to work in Cosmon office, He would have brought you all here, but He did not do so because you are needed in the schools, shops, factories, churches, homes, farms, offices and services where you are this very minute. The darker and more uncongenial, sad and unaccepting the area where you are, the more you are needed there, because you are one of God's children of Light and He needs a whole army of us, scattered

far and wide. If we cannot seem to do anything more than pray to the Father for His blessings of our area and for His guidance of our work, we are making the right start. Stay put, and TRANSFIGURE your small duty station and yourself into the bargain!

                      Your friend,
                      Barbara

    **   ***   **

LETTER TO AN OFFICIAL

Dear -

Is it not possible to send a group of people on a lecture tour all over this U.S.A. to see what we can do about race discrimination?

We must stop hating in our own country if we want peace in this world. Or do we want complete annihilation?

How many in the U.S. would like to live in constant fear 24 hours a day? Neighbors spying on neighbors - child spying on parents - imprisonment in slave camps - some of us forced to look on as our child is tortured? That is what will happen if we do not eliminate this hate between races in this country.

Do you know some of these riots by the colored people are induced by a white person? These white people pretend to be the colored people's friend. But would a true friend get you in trouble by talking you into a riot? These supposedly friends consider themselves above a colored person, therefore loves to see them suffer. Some of the secret instigators of these riots are working for Russia. They are doing all they can to weaken this country. Are we American people going to allow our country to weaken till Russia takes over? Do we Americans not realize we must stand by each other as friends if we want to be a strong nation with peace and safety? Can hate bring us peace? If we are all divided against each other, will our country be safe to live in?

No matter what religion we believe in, if we have sincerity in our hearts we will at least try to bring Brotherly love in this Country. World Goodwill is not a religious sect! Dare these race haters say they are sincere in their religious belief and then do all they can to hurt another being?

An ex-soldier said to himself while he was in battle, that if he ever got out of this Hell with any degree of sanity, he would forever smile with gratitude and never sneer with self-importance for as long as he is alive! He also mentioned how the ego of the rich dropped when they were wounded, sometimes only a scratch from a shrapnel.

Most everyone has a Bible, I'm sure. Even those that don't go to church. So you won't mind me quoting certain parts of the Bible that proves one man is no better than another in the sight of God. God does not look at the color of our skin. He looks at our hearts. Oh! What evil hearts he sees in some! Those race haters don't think of that, do they? How the angels must weep over what they see in this beautiful U.S.A.!

Whoever reads this letter, please read the 10th Chapter of Acts. Peter had a vision. Visions and dreams have a symbolical meaning. While Peter was trying to decipher the meaning of that vision, God sent someone to him to explain the meaning. You'll find the answer to that vision in verse 28! Also verse 35! Thou shalt not call any man common or unclean.

Now please read I Corinthians, the 12th chapter. This is a very real POTENT chapter that proves even some of those that are in low places or considered common may be more necessary in God's work and may also be closer to God than the oh, maybe the church leaders.

Even the people that do not believe in God or the Bible must realize that to have a strong country, we must abate hate and stand side by side!

Whenever a colored person gets in trouble, a white person will say: "Well what do you expect of a nigger?" ('Scuse that word. I never use it! I'm only quoting!)

Who is it that refuses the colored person a job! Who refuses them an education! There are some colored <u>college graduates</u> doing menial labor. No one will hire them. Who is to blame for the colored people resorting to crime? The whites! All right, we whites! Let's turn about face and bring peace and happiness to our good ole U.S.A. Come on. When do we begin? Is it possible for you to start a group of people to go on a tour to lecture on peace? You ought to have some singers and a pianist too. I'll sing alto. I'm willing to have tomatoes thrown at me!

(Name withheld)

Editor's Note:

The above letter was written to a prominent government official by one of our Cosmon members. She shows the mark of a true disciple in accepting responsibility and taking initiative to change conditions by doing the best she can with the means at hand.

SUGGESTIONS FROM OUR READERS

Bring the New Age to your community or your neighborhood —

1. Set up wayside rest benches along the way of the walkers in your community. Tired oldsters, mothers carrying babies, grandparents walking toddlers, young couples on moonlight strolls would sincerely appreciate resting places.

2. Place public drinking fountains in your parkings, or the corners of your neighborhood intersections.

3. Provide fresh drinking water for passing birds and animals.

4. Clean up and seed vacant lots with wildflowers native to your state.

5. Establish juice bars in the lobbies of your theatres, and in your recreation areas.

Lest we forget:

THE FOUR FREEDOMS

January 6, 1941

In the future days, which we seek to make secure, we look forward to a world founded upon four essential human freedoms.

The first is freedom of speech and expression — everywhere in the world.

The second is freedom of every person to worship God in his own way — everywhere in the world.

The third is freedom from want — which, translated into world terms, means economic understandings which will secure to every nation a healthy peacetime life for its inhabitants — everywhere in the world.

The fourth is freedom from fear — which, translated into world terms, means a worldwide reduction of armaments to such a point and in such a thorough fashion that no nation will be in a position to commit an act of physical aggression against any neighbor — anywhere in the world.

Franklin D. Roosevelt

SEARCHERS

The world is full of searchers. There are those who search for rank or gain, for love or fame or power, or simply self-esteem. There are some who long for the will to aspire, while others would gladly drown their desires. But nearly everyone searches for something.

This could be true of other kingdoms too. There is something faintly human in plants that reach for the sun. The eagerness of dogs and horses can outweigh all but the purplest human passions. But for us, at least, there is something special about the searching of people.

I once read a book called "The Quest of Fools," the only point of which was that the rather nebulous characters kept storming after their own will-o'-the-wisps, displaying at least great energy, though little sense, in their search for something meaningful.

Seekers are a motley crowd, and the dust of conflict rises from them as purpose clashes with purpose. But in all this fury and diversity there could still be a common denominator.

Those who search with fervor and purpose have at least their echoes in the hopes of gutter rats. There is a faint kinship between ambitious young fools and despondent old philosophers. Win, lose or draw, we find that what we have sought is only a shadow of what we wanted; that in the wreckage of catastrophes new symbols spring out to lure us toward other goals.

Some would tell us that desire is madness — the foible common to every man. It could also be his touch of greatness. From monster to man, to superman — through all the blind illusions and the false delights — there could be a common principle that urges him on. What he seeks could be the nameless essence of truth, filtered down to him through clouds of haze from distorted, half-reflecting mirrors. Then his greatest failing would lie, not in searching weakly after worthless goals, or wildly after great ones — but only in refusing to search at all.

J.D.M.

DR. HAMILTON AND GLORIA LEE SPEAK
(Continued from Page 25)

whole and complete year ahead but I am able to see only that which is given to me to see by the Masters), I see plenty of activity coming forth within the next few months. You have felt this within yourselves and have spoken of this many times among yourselves, and I am sure all of you who come to this Group weekly have felt a surge forward in Understanding of the Truth and Enlightenment that you have received.

GLORIA LEE

Received 1-23-63
Channel: Phyllis Veronica
Unit 72, New York City

(Ed. Note: This is the end of the recorded communication, as our tape ran out, after continuous communication of two hours on the Wednesday evening of January 23, 1963.)

Communications received at a regular Wednesday evening meeting of STAR LIGHT FELLOWSHIP, NEW YORK CITY.

****

WANTED
For Junior Group Section of Library...

Any of the beautiful books of fairy tales illustrated by the following artists. Most of these were published very early in the century, between 1900 and 1930.

Edmund DuLac   Arthur Rackham
Kay Nielsen   Gustaf Tenggren
    Virginia Frances Sterrett
    Jessie Wilcox Smith

Also Wanted:
Source for purchase of FairyLand Maps. Have seen these at Knott's Berry Farm and they retail for $1.00. These are large colored drawings about 2' x 3' and we should have some for our Junior CosmonKnights.

****

MISCELLANEOUS FILE

NOTES FROM THE NEWS FLOW

Eugene Hurtienne observes some items of interest in "Popular Mechanics," May issue...

Germs which had been dormant for more than 1200 years came to life after being put into an incubator recently. In a sealed tomb of a Maya Indian chief in Guatemala, bacteria was taken and due to lack of moisture, light and food were inactive. So far none have been identified. (Strange.)

A new method for finding North when lost in the desert or mountain has been developed by a 17 year old scout.

    A three foot stick driven into the ground will cast a shadow. Mark the tip of shadow and then wait 10 minutes or longer, then mark tip of shadow again. Draw a line running through both points. This line will always run east or west, and the second mark will always be toward the east.

    Over 50,000 trials have been made of this method and it has been accurate every time.

Those interested in music and its effect on plants should get this issue and read the article, "Growing Corn to Music." (Page 118)

CORRECTION

Please note retail price of the following book, unfortunately misquoted in our May issue.

    TO GOD THE GLORY
    By Annalee Skarin
    Price - $3.50

(Erroneously quoted as $2.95)

RECIPE

Contributed by Frances Newmon "for everyone's use who is making a transition from meat to vegetarianism."

    COTTAGE CHEESE LOAF
- 1/2 pkg. melted cheddar cheese
- 1 pkg. of cottage cheese
- 3 grated potatoes
- 1 grated bell pepper
- 1 grated onion
- 1 chopped clove of garlic
- 1/2 cup of milk
- 1 egg
- 3 tablespoons brewers yeast
- Salt to taste
- 1/2 stick melted butter

Mix together and bake about 30 minutes in medium oven - 350°.

APPRECIATION

A most sincere thank you to all friends who have so generously donated books to the senior and children's sections of Cosmon library. We are exceedingly grateful!

LAST WORD

Are you in earnest? Seize this very minute;
What you can do, or dream you can, begin it;
Boldness has genius, power and magic in it;
Only engage and then the mind grows heated;
Begin, and then the work will be completed.

                    Goethe

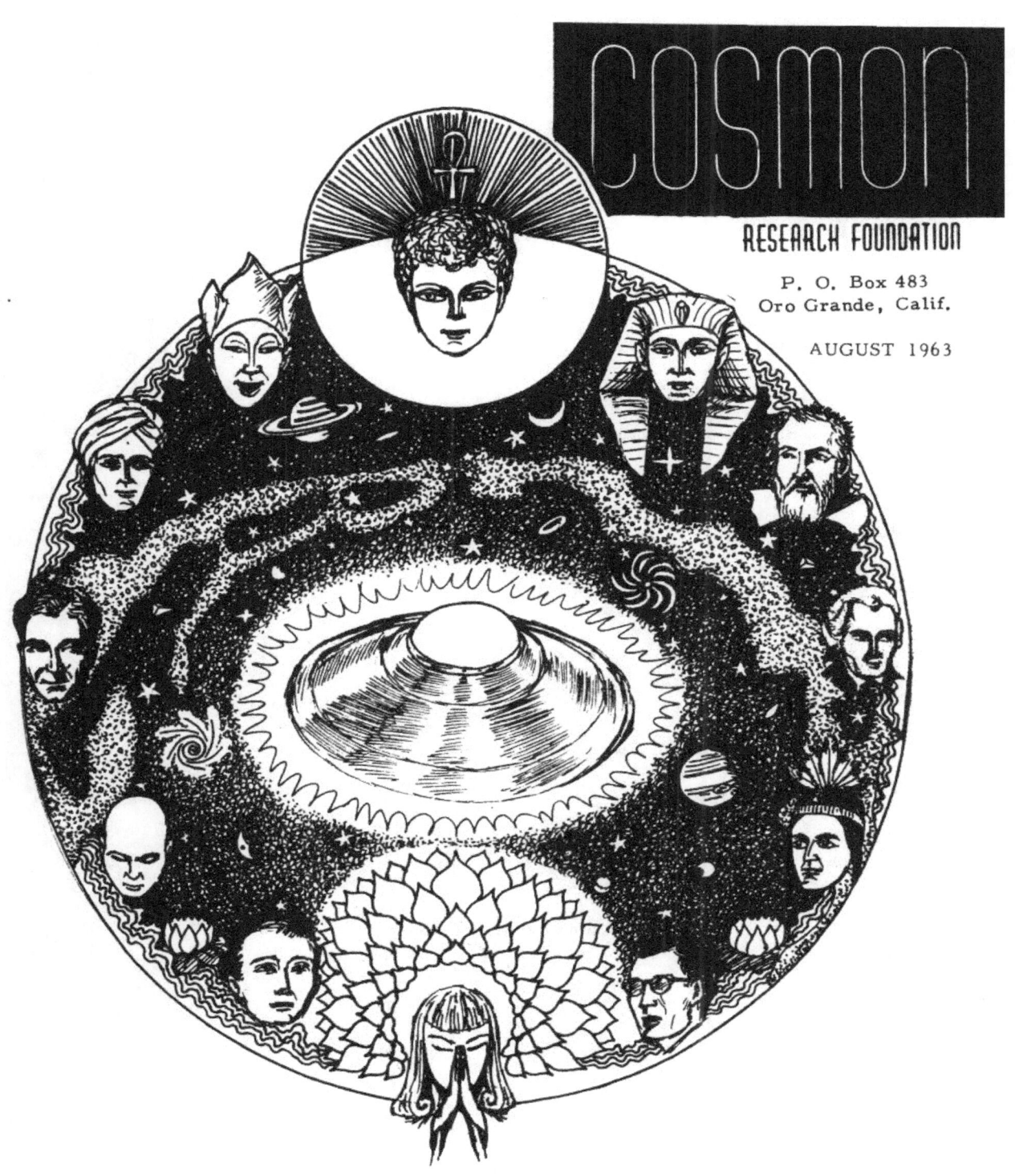

COSMON
RESEARCH FOUNDATION

P. O. Box 483
Oro Grande, Calif.

AUGUST 1963

YOUR RESEARCH FOUNDATION DEDICATED TO DEVELOPING MAN SPIRITUALLY AND PHYSICALLY FOR THE NEW AGE AND SUPPORTED BY YOU.

Gloria Lee, Founder

COSMON NEWSLETTER

CONTENTS

Gloria's Greetings	3
Message from J.W.	8
En Route with Barbara Steele	12
Communication from Another Kingdom	17
Your Health	22
Exploring Human Emotions	24
Guest Corner	28
CosmonKnights	31
Book Corner	33
Correspondence File	35
World Report	36

Cover drawing by Albert Roger
Grecian flutist after Thomas Hope

Copyright © 1963 by Cosmon Research Foundation
All rights reserved. Printed in U.S.A.

GLORIA'S GREETINGS

Greetings again, my beloved Cosmonites,

Since I last wrote to you in the pages of the newsletter, there have been many conflicting reports about my activities on the Other Side. Some of my friends on your side believe it is wrong to try for communication with me, for fear I will be delayed in my spiritual progression. Others believe it impossible for me to reach so many different individuals as have reported receiving messages, and still others feel they have been slighted by not reaching me where others seem to have gotten through who were less acquainted with me.

Well I can now tell you that I have been working with many over here to find better techniques for bringing the planes together in understanding. I have been permitted to try a lot of experiments because I have been so recently one of the earth people, and so can remember how it feels to be thinking inside an earth consciousness as well as to have been a channel in communication with individuals Upstairs. This is helpful, they tell me, to have my fresh earth experience plus a more-than-average understanding of the Teachers' point of view.

Survival of identity beyond death or transition has been proven for a very long time to many, and that is not such a great novelty, really. The thing that is more exceptional is my proof that progress, personality-wise, can be continued here so that I can actually open up or establish a precedent for others who leave the physical, and I can make a kind of dent on the surroundings hereabouts that will allow others to continue certain activities usually set aside until the following incarnations.

Over here the trend is against continuing relationships with the plane just relinquished at death. This is because these usually are not constructive relationships, but due to a desire to hang on to certain individuals and to maintain contact with familiar surroundings, all of which tends to keep individuals earthbound and holds them back from releasing themselves into higher planes of experience and preparation for advancement.

Where the Plan of the Father can be served, and physical plane people taught truths that will encourage them to continue their efforts and to develop themselves to greater spiritual capacity, there is permission granted to continue this contact. I have received this permission, and am allowing myself to be a guinea pig for the higher teachers.

I must say I am finding fascinating opportunities over here. I cannot begin to tell you how glad I am that I was enabled to develop far enough to be able to understand and appreciate what I have now, before leaving the body. Many times I said I wished there were time to travel and to visit all the Space Groups and become acquainted with the leaders and the members. Now I am able to get around to many more places and people than I realized were working on the side of Light. I may also add that I have now the ability to tell whether or not people are really on the side of Light, and some are mixed in with the good ones who are anything but Light workers, yet they pass because many on earth do not have any standards of measuring or judging the calibre and quality of those who claim to be servers of humanity within the Father's Plan.

The times are so pressured that the forces of Light will use even the smallest capacity to communicate truth, wherever they find it. Sometimes a person who is more on the dark side than of the light is able to give out a small MEASURE OF TRUTH, WHICH IS BETTER THAN NONE, AND SO IS USED to the full degree of possibility, anyhow, and often unknown to the person. The same thing is true in reverse and I would have you be alert to the possibility.

Truth does not always bring peace into a situation. Sometimes it reveals conditions that create conflict. Truth is like a super-floodlight that reveals the reality of circumstances which were somewhat shadowed by illusions or glamours. Sometimes, such a mess shows up in the glare of the Light that everybody is upset to the point of illness and nobody wants to tackle the chore of cleaning it up.

People are very weak in discernment on the earth plane. They don't have much ability to judge between first and second principles, or to recognize what they ought to do immediately and what they can leave for later attention. They usually begin on the easy little unimportant things, while the big human problems are neglected and keep on growing bigger and bigger until they become such monsters nobody knows what to do about them.

It is interesting to see how things are looked at over here, as compared to ways of measuring them where you are. The Teachers and Space People are rounded-out individuals who can work in nearly any problem area, even if they have special interests and training. I was realizing this before I left you, and now I can see it more clearly, that correct spiritual unfoldment brings about a rounded-out individual who can function wherever need arises, to some degree, though often specialists of greater accomplishment in a given line will be invited in for conferences, advice or confirmations of correct procedures.

. . . .

It's so nice you want me to continue being part of Cosmon and the activities I started in conjunction with J.W. Of course I would feel awfully sad if there were signs you had already forgotten me or intended to change Cosmon or write me off, just because I am invisible to most of you; but instead, many of you still feel I am as much your friend as ever, which is true, and you have asked if I will come to you in the pages of the newsletter. I am happy to tell you I'll come as long as I am permitted to stay in contact, and there is no indication from here that it will be discontinued.

In comparison to all the things I told you were planned for Cosmon, it must seem as if the group has simmered down to a very quiet organization, and you wonder if there will ever be those exciting activities in theatre, television and radio that we talked about, or those scientific researches or development of new age arts or more books from J.W. Well, I am not able to predict as to time, but I think all these things and more are going to take place, some of them perhaps not until after the Changes.

So often we discussed the Changes and what forms they would take, and I was given visions of myself in the midst of tidal waves and storms helping to keep people calm, because I had contact with the Teachers and they would try to follow directions if they knew the Space People were guiding through an instrument. I never thought I would come over here before all this happened. Maybe they will let me appear and do the very work that was visioned, but in this indestructible body. My! I wouldn't mind that at all. I hope I can come down and help. It was such a problem to me then to try to know when all these things would happen and where and how. I wish I could give you my present understanding of the whole picture, but I don't think you would care to pay for this understanding as I did, and you have to pay a pretty high price for understanding, as it's considered one of the greater treasures.

. . . .

At one time I was a worry wart myself, and I felt miserable if I could not answer questions put to me about the spiritual facts of life. I remember really sweating it out for weeks sometimes because I could not find the right words or even the right thought to answer somebody's deep personal-problem letter. Often I would ask the Teachers for help, but there were times when they put me on my own and forced me to discover the answers through firsthand experience, or through exploring my past relationships of other lives. Even after this, there were sometimes questions I could not answer or letters to which I could not respond. And I was told that people have the answers hidden in the very questions they ask, and must be given the privilege and opportunity to work away at finding their own answers whenever they show any capacity to do so, in order to grow spiritually by facing up to the challenges Life hands them for their own development. You just can't grind up your children's food after they get teeth to do their own chewing.

Really I hate to say it, but you would be surprised to see how many mentally lazy individuals there are on the earth plane. Over here we sometimes call them the drones. They cruise through life, sustained by the initiative and responsible efforts made by others of the human family, and when the shakedown cruise finally comes up, they are the first to zero out and fall by the wayside. They are all fat and looks and hot air. I can say this now because I am beyond the reach of certain destructive weapons that might cause emotional turmoil in an earth consciousness, and I am enjoying saying some of the things that should be said over and over until they are etched into the mind and begin to condition the thought processes of everybody. I wish I could pull off the veils of fear from the average people of earth, so they would realize they do not have to accept the rantings and bombastic directives and orders of ANYONE that goes against the dictates of their own souls. People have so little respect for the authority of their own Higher Selves, and allow people of far less capacity or intelligence to lead them around by the nose. People are still too much overawed by the printed word, and the spoken word that comes over legal communication channels as T.V., radio, movies, etcetera. They do not know propaganda when they see it, because they have not developed the habit of thinking for themselves.

Because you are my own group, I can say things to you that I might phrase more politely to channels of other groups, knowing they would not even bother to instrument my words if I seemed to be trying to get across controversial subjects. People detest to get themselves into a position where they have to think their way out, and this is the reason, my dear friends, why you get so much pap instead of the full, rich unstrained brew you should have for mental health. Here at Cosmon we don't care whether we win friends, so long as we influence people to wake up and live a little.

. . . .

In a way I would like to talk about instrumentship, taking sort of a busman's holiday. You would think I had saturated myself with the subject, but there are always new angles to everything, especially when viewed from a different plane of perception. J.W. repeated to us all who read His books, and to me who instrumented them for Him, that everybody is an instrument of some kind or another, and not necessarily what you are accustomed to call a psychic instrument. Maybe you are an instrument that radiates serenity into your environment, and do not even know you have that power. Some people act like oil on troubled waters. The minute they appear on the scene, everything relaxes and peace is restored where there was hostility or open conflict. This is a very valuable kind of instrumentship, and is the radiation of a kind heart who beams out good will and re-establishes harmony.

There are other instruments that radiate a magnetic vitality and who cause everything and everyone around them to spring into renewed activity. This can be extremely stimulating, but not necessarily on the side of what we think of as constructive projects. People in situations of relationship to magnetic instruments may read into their vibrational impacts, intentions that were not any part of the instrument's plan or purpose. This again may be good or bad, according to how you look on it and what happens to you.

I have seen instruments of healing, some quite unconscious of the effect they were having on the persons around them. People with radiant health of their own bodies are like fountains that spill over health on everybody around, and when they come into groups where you are or into sickrooms, they make everybody feel better automatically. The people who are cast down in spirits or ill or hurt, immediately feel better when these instruments of healing vitality come close to them. People of this kind are often exceptionally clean and sometimes beautiful, and everyone is encouraged just to look at them and be close by.

There are instruments of great thought force who channel vibrant creative energies into other minds and spark them to greater mental activity. People always shine more brilliantly and discover greater depths of their own mentality when influenced by the auric field of this kind of channel.

Some people instrument patience. Sometimes these are the people who have gone through great physical or mental suffering and have learned the lesson of quiet acceptance, without bitterness or fear. Oftentimes you will find people such as these among terminal cancer patients or spastics or post-polio cases, or among those who have lost sight or hearing.

I hope by now you are getting the idea that all kinds of instruments are valued and needed in this world where you live, and also that whoever YOU ARE, you are bound to be channeling something that is identified with your tag line or brand name wherever you go. Have you ever thought about this, and do you ever think what you are bringing into the environments where you work or live your private life?

Have you ever heard someone say, "Let's scram! Here comes that sour puss again!"? Did they say it about you? Do you drip gray streams of bitterness and cynicism into the atmosphere where you congregate with others? Did you leave your faucet turned on for channeling discontent and impatience?

All this may seem a far cry from channeling messages of spiritual Truth and Wisdom and Love, and it all IS A FAR CRY. In fact it is so far from it, that this is the reason why YOU may be far from it. Had this ever occurred to you? If true instruments were a dime a dozen, everybody would buy a dime's worth, and treat them as the trashy performers they would be.

What would you say if I tell you that many of the channels working today in Light groups have been burned at the stake, crucified, drowned, beaten to death, thrown to wild animals, and to snakes; guillotined; tortured; strangled, buried alive and hung by the neck, cut to pieces as living sacrifices, and generally mellowed and whipped into shape as human beings along the long road of incarnation? I know this was true in my own case. I cannot think of any type of death I missed. When you think it is a shallow accomplishment to be permitted to communicate with other and higher minds, ask yourself if you would be willing to go through a hundred lives of tragedy and turmoil to open your heart and mind to the extent that Teachers of Love and Compassion and Wisdom might be reasonably assured their efforts to bring their words of Truth through you would not be misinterpreted or slanted by your earth consciousness to fit your personality convenience, or your limited concepts of universal life and law.

Channeling is certainly a RESPONSIBILITY! While we are in the physical body we are taught that words given through us are our own particular responsibility. We reap the karma of our misinterpretations and mistranslations of the Communicator's intention. All who are in the earth body are subject to the imperfections of earth plane substance to some degree. You must learn to use discernment about the communications you accept. Your best bet is to study as many different publications as you can; to hear as many lectures as you can; to meet and talk to as many different groups and leaders as you can, and to weigh and measure and compare for yourself, and to sift all this mass of material and take out the parts that ring true and can be used by you in your daily affairs.

As far as Cosmon is concerned, we always took the approach that since we are not selling our services, you cannot say you were cheated by phony claims and paid publicity. If you don't like what we give you in our magazine, simply ask to be removed from our mailing list and go to other individuals or groups with whom you have more affinity. We are not suffering from lack of members or readers. We love our members and readers, but they are completely and absolutely free. They don't owe us any allegiance if they prefer to seek Light elsewhere.

Before I left the earth plane I heard from a few of our friends that some groups become vindictive and critical when their members wish to take on other affiliations, or wish to cut-and-try before entering into the entity of the group purpose. This to me always smelled of orthodox churchianity, where the important thing is quantities of members who will keep the financial structure afloat. We prefer quality in Cosmon, and we prefer to leave our income to the Father. In the beginning when I decided, with J.W., to set up a non-profit corporation, I wanted to prove that the Law of Balance would attend automatically to our supply if we would attend to the quality of our services. Now I am free to admit that this was not an overnight achievement — to learn the lesson of faith in an impersonal, invisible Universal Law, and many times I repeated my requests to our members for more help. Now, all of us who keep Cosmon going from our various levels of individual focus, are in accord that if we watch over the outgo, the Father will watch over the inflow. And as you see, we are in no anxiety that we shall be disintegrated as a group, so long as we adhere to this basic intention to seek ever for Truth and to share all we can discover of it. Since TRUTH is everywhere our problem is complicated, but challenging, and we'll keep working to find it so long as you say you want to keep us in action!

Today I am using Barbara as a channel. We get on famously together because we know each other so well from many past life experiences, and we both know now beyond any questioning that it is possible to continue a friendship and even to work together, though one of our bodies dropped along the way. Also we allow each other full freedom in all things. Even before I left we trusted and loved each other enough to keep an open flow for new ideas between us. There are many now living who have experienced this continuity of relationship with a departed mate or friend or relation, and could attest to the fact that this is one of the few treasures you can take with you, and can retain when another has departed from you.

Where true love exists between individuals, there is continuous rapport and there is no necessity of rituals or hocus-pocus. The relationship simply IS, and those within it are as close as thought and do not require to set up any conditions or times, but any time is as good as another because the communication level is above the action and work levels, and comes across on the intuitional plane regardless of distance or occupation. It takes a very long time to set up relationships of this kind. It is something I learned in association with J.W. For, you see, you can have the privilege of many such relationships, and they are all treasured in their different ways. In a heart of love there is room for as many as can enter into an affectionate relationship with the Soul involved. Hearts are so expandable and that is the very lesson J.W. was trying to teach you in WHY WE ARE HERE, but human minds are so incapable of seeing the true inner meaning until all the parts are dissected and laid out on the line.

Always your own

GLORIA

I DREAMED IN A DREAM

I dream'd in a dream I saw a city invincible to the attacks of the
    whole of the rest of the earth,
I dream'd that was the new city of Friends,
Nothing was greater there than the quality of robust love, it led
    the rest,
It was seen every hour in the actions of the men of that city,
And in all their looks and words.

LEAVES OF GRASS
Walt Whitman

MESSAGE FROM J. W.

My Greetings once again,
Friends of the Earth Plane:

A letter from one of your circle of readers has been brought to my attention and I would request that it be published, together with my reply in your August newsletter.

EXCERPTS FROM READER'S LETTER

". . . I feel it is important to suggest you check out with J.W. the following postulates for action:

(1) If it is true that time is of the essence in awakening the world to its imminent destruction and that it can be saved by understanding -- then, it seems to me that the world must be made aware of its need for choice and action. So far -- Cosmon can have reached only a tiny fraction of the population. Therefore:

(2) If it is true that spacemen come in spaceships with a message: the world must know that spacemen and spaceships are real -- as real as the other realities the world accepts. Only then -- can the world know for sure and thus take action thru new insight. Therefore:

(3) A spaceship and a spaceman should be seen, talked to directly and photographed. If such arrangements are made with spacemen, and Life Magazine and/or Look, etc. are contacted and permitted to do a complete coverage -- the world will suddenly know this till-now debatable status. Either magazine will pay a large sum for such a world-wide story. The money, under guidance, can go a long way to widely establish Cosmon Research facilities.

(4) Such action would prevent interference by Air Force or other government offices.

(5) Having been given such proof and the messages from space -- the human family would then be responsible for subsequent action, in the light of this new information. But -- unless the world is so unequivocally informed -- I cannot see how J.W.'s stern warning is quite fair or just. Humanity is still a collective infant.

(6) In summary -- I truly believe that J.W. and other enlightened spacemen -- if they do indeed exist -- have a tremendous obligation to INFORM the world -- not just a tiny fraction of its more enlightened population. To suggest that we, collectively, could not stand the strain of such knowledge, is illogical in terms of the prior premise: that we must act or be destroyed. Ergo: Give us, collectively, the information. Then we are collectively responsible for what action we do or do not take because of it."

Name withheld

J.W.'s REPLY

In response to the first question, I would say to the writer of the foregoing letter that constant action has been taken, especially from your calendar years of the middle 1940's onward, upon the part of countless individuals and groups native to other planets, to inform the populous nations of your world of our presence in your skies, the reasons for our presence, and of our peaceful desire to be of service.

During the ensuing years you have amassed shelves of books and periodical literature, much of it available in the public libraries of America, wherein the writer of this letter resides. We have made a continuous effort to reach your people, and we have made our efforts in every country. Yet we are bound by Universal Law and by the Law of Freewill, which latter the people on your planet exercise in self-determination of their destiny.

A network of small groups has been established and deployed across the surface of your planet, so that every major area of human consciousness is convinced to the degree of its acceptance of the aspects of TRUTH we have been permitted to disseminate, in the hope that a movement toward international cooperation would be initiated whereby the men and women of earth and the men and women of other planets might meet and confer upon the most spiritually-practical means to the ends in view.

Since we came, not as conquerors or as armed assailants of your populations, but as volunteers to afford you spiritual and physical First Aid in time of total crisis, we cannot perform our ministry if the majority of your leaders refuse to grant us amicable access to your several continents. It was not our thought but the thought of your Rulers that the people of earth would destroy themselves in panic, by reason of our appearance. All leaders of any influence whatever have been approached and tested on receptivity to us and to our Cause. Leaders are the key representatives of vast blocs of persons which make up the citizens and inhabitants of their domains. It matters not whether a leader is chosen by the people, or self-chosen through default of the people. The fact remains that a leader sums up in his personality the national strengths and/or weaknesses of the people represented, and through him, as through a robot model of the national character, the will of the people is fulfilled. We are subject to that will as having been conferred by the Father upon His children.

Cosmon Research Foundation, it is true, has only reached a small fraction of the planetary population, but Cosmon is only one of many groups dedicated to the same goal of communication and education of the masses. Other groups are working steadily to acquaint their members, followers and subscribers with the same information, couched in familiar terminology and the common idioms of many languages, broadcast through the medium of informal talks, classes, lectures, books, magazines and correspondence.

Many of your people have turned away or reacted aggressively or ridiculed the information offered.

In answer to your second question, I would relate to you that receptive people on every continent have been reached with the information that we exist, that we are present in great numbers, that our craft are standing by and patrolling your lands and seas.

Individuals numbering millions are aware of our reality and the reality of craft from outer space. The world cannot take action through new insight unless the controls on communication media are relaxed by those who would find it detrimental to turn over their symbols of office and to step down to a level of equality with their fellow men and women. In opening the way for conscious world-wide acceptance of us by your people, there would necessarily follow the removal from leadership of unqualified personnel in perhaps more than 90% of the power posts of influence within your nations.

There is a phrase rampant among your executive personnel in all branches of all governments, which is pronounced "enlightened selfishness". Your leaders trade agreements with one another as to the mass moving of those pawns within their own realms of influence, to advantage themselves and to increase apparent prestige for their bloc or their nation. It would be dangerous to import advanced thinkers from other realms, and to allow the human masses to compare these visitors from greatly advanced civilizations to their own rulers and self-designated guardians; for the net result would be damaging to the majority of those who have gained world prominence and personal fortunes at the cost of intrigue, secret schemes and perverted ideologies. There is an unwritten agreement among your world leaders that they will acknowledge the importance of banding together as self-elected shepherds and swineherds of the multitudes of your people whom they despise, and whom they tolerate only as contributors of greater or lesser aggrandizements and emoluments to their fame, well-being and continuity in office.

You doubt that a handful of men have the capability and power and intellect to motivate the millions? Yet one individual man is capable of controlling a gigantic piece of complicated machinery if it is equipped with levers, gears and push buttons. If there were not a world-wide inner government, which for eons has built and maintained this complex of power machinery: of domination through taxation, planned wars, ruthless poisoning of the masses through perverted medical conspiracies and distribution of tainted foodstuffs, perhaps you would have more room for doubt. One of the advantages of our superior knowledge is that we are enabled to penetrate the invisible government at mental levels and to see with clarity its unspeakable goals.

We have given you warnings to the extent of permission to do so, granted us by spiritual Higher Courts of Appeal; but you are those recalcitrant and self-blinded individuals who are so paralyzed in your capacity to think for yourselves, and so accustomed to taking orders from those in positions of influence, that you will not accept the opportunity to take the initiative even after we have given you the insight. The ratio of self-initiating individuals upon the side of Wisdom and Love, is so slight among your so-called average men and women at this time that they are as salmon breasting the falls, with the whole tide of civilization that is Piscean, cascading upon them in a mighty avalanche of hostile emotion, moving in the opposite direction.

My words are given you without heat. I am repeating myself for the benefit of those who may come upon this newsletter for the first time. Not only I, but many of my Brothers of Space, have exerted the fullest degree of the power quotients allotted to us for furthering this work of altruistic purpose.

In view of the other comments I shall make, I do not believe it essential that I respond to your questions number 3 and number 4, other than to say that as long as I am held in regard sufficient to be considered a Co-Founder and present Adviser for Cosmon Research Foundation, I shall use the weight of my influence against bringing in money to further its activities through the forms of publicity indicated. So far as I am concerned, your statement under Question 4 is debatable.

Humanity, my friend, is not still "a collective infant" but a retarded adult at the adolescent emotional level, paralyzed in intelligent self-direction by self-indulgence and refusal to accept individual responsibility for the good of the whole.

A factor your people are prone to overlook, as you sketch visions of pleasing social meetings between our peoples and yours, is that it costs us considerable pain and sacrifice of power to step ourselves down to your earth surface frequency, and we look upon the action with about as much pleasure as would you if you were called upon to descend to the darker and deeper portions of the sea floor to hold social and economic counsels with communities of giant crabs.

If your people, who spend so much of their sentimental force in prayer, begging us to come thither among you, would instead, study for themselves the spiritually-scientific laws and rules governing and conditioning such meetings, they might discover the power of massed invocation intelligently undertaken, to provide those vibratory rates and influences which make it more feasible and comfortable for us to descend into what is to us a suffocating and stifling emotional and mental atmosphere, charged with conflict, turmoil, hate, suspicion, fear and malicious intentions to cause extreme bodily harm to any incoming rescuers of and instructors to your vast population. You ask: "Why cannot you advanced beings offset our negative atmospheres by your knowledge of magic and higher sciences?" I reply to you that we literally are assigned power or energy allotments for this project and we prefer, whenever possible, to get the greatest per capita results from our investments of energies, and therefore find that the educational program carried out via physical plane disciples who have some degree of spiritual impressionability is thus far the enterprise yielding the greatest returns.

The best suggestion I can offer, as an anticlimax to all the suggestions and instructions already given over the past four years by myself, through the channelship of Gloria Lee, is that all who read these words undertake, if belatedly, to accept responsibility personally for the negative conditions of your planet, rather than putting it upon us who have already placed ourselves at the total disposal of the people, who now, it may be hinted, have some rather massive obligations to perform, themselves. Unity of effort has created miracles in the past ages of your world; so state the scriptures of all world religions. This is what is needed in the present. There is too much emphasis upon the personalities and too little emphasis upon the PURPOSE of this time of transition, even within the personnel of the Light Groups, themselves. And I am sorry to be forced to say this. A very few at the heart of each group, give of their total resources of knowledge, love and time. The others, with few exceptions, are not doers of the Word, but hearers only; and after feeding their ears, they return to the daily rounds to forget the impact of new wisdom until another weekly meeting.

Why do you not all undertake to request and circulate all the printed information that you believe is sound, logical and spiritually motivated, in books, periodicals and pamphlets, that you personally are able to finance? If you want the world to know about us so urgently, why don't you accept part of the responsibility to circulate this knowledge already in your midst? Why should the few who are already doing all they humanly can, be called upon by all of you to do even more, while you simply act as cheering spectators at a sports event?

A common fallacy to which far too many of the peoples of earth subscribe, is that if they cannot do much, why do anything? Look at a coral reef, the accretion of infinite numbers of the impossibly insignificant. Yet, by continuity of concerted action the reef finally gets its head above water and provides the rugged understructure for earth, vegetation and the life cycles of higher creatures. Why not observe these obvious examples around you and accrete with all like-minded individuals to the benefit, perhaps the last-moment salvaging, of your planet?

If sufficient numbers of your people would gather together and project love and gratitude, instead of continuous requests for more and more benefits, we should not be long in appearing among you to your conscious realization of the fact; but until you provide your half of the needed action, we are limited in our ability to help you further in those ways you have suggested.

Insist on yourself; never imitate. Your own gift you can present every moment with the cumulative force of a whole life's cultivation; but of the adopted talent of another you have only an extemporaneous half possession. That which each can do best, none but his Maker can teach him. No man yet knows what it is, nor can, till that person has exhibited it. Where is the master who could have taught Shakespeare? Where is the master who could have instructed Franklin, or Washington, or Bacon, or Newton? Every great man is a unique. The Scipionism of Scipio is precisely that part he could not borrow. Shakespeare will never be made by the study of Shakespeare. Do that which is assigned you, and you cannot hope too much or dare too much. There is at this moment for you an utterance brave and grand as that of the colossal chisel of Phidias, or trowel of the Egyptians, or the pen of Moses or Dante, but different from all these. Not possibly will the soul's all rich, all eloquent, thousand-cloven tongue, deign to repeat itself; but if you can hear what these patriarchs say, surely you can reply to them in the same pitch of voice; for the ear and the tongue are two organs of one nature. Abide in the simple and noble regions of thy life, obey thy heart, and thou shalt reproduce the Foreworld again.

ESSAYS: FIRST SERIES
Self-Reliance
Ralph Waldo Emerson

EN ROUTE

Dear Cosmon Members and Friends,

Greetings in August. Now we are much more comfortable in our office because our good friends, who are also the printers of the newsletter, gave to us a fine air-conditioner they were not using. We had been working in temperatures that kept us literally sweating out the daily chores, but now we are enjoying so much relief of body and mind that the strains of desert summer are all removed. Bartram actually sneezed a few days ago and I see he keeps a warm, long-sleeved shirt hanging on his desk chairback so that he can quickly switch from his nylon, drip-dry short-sleeve hot-weather classic when the air conditioner is going full speed. Thanks to Bruce and Mickey Bain, who are altruists of "the first water" (old quote applicable to brilliance and perfection of diamonds). Thanks to Jim for hauling up our gift from Lomita and to my son, David and to Bartram as well as Jim, for installing this joy-producing appliance!

It's nice to report that the newsletter is becoming a two-way conversation. The letters you write back and the interesting things you tell us about your experiences and ideas make us feel the establishing of that special family spirit which involves all the human family everywhere, but which relatively few on our world recognize as yet. Col. Arthur Burks and Esther Stilgebouer spent a Sunday morning with us earlier in July. Bartram Kent and Harvey King of Albuquerque were present, and we were talking over this sense of being a part of an unlimited family which includes everybody on all planets, wherever they may be living and working. It is exciting when you first realize yourself to be a relatively-conscious member of this uncounted myriad of beings.

We are talking about the Family of God. More and more recognitions flare up between and among people, as we realize our unity within the Father's Purpose. You too are right in the midst of this dynamic activity, but you may not yet have thrown off the LONG SLEEP, or experienced the thrill of recognizing your brothers and sisters who are already awake and working together. We must all learn to ignore racial barriers, for they are man-conceived; not God-directed, in spite of what you may be told by hirelings of various minority groups who find it to their advantage to play up any barriers of any kind at the mass level, that will create disunity and loss of power.

In a former life pattern, the differently-colored person next you may have been your close kin, beloved mate or treasured friend. All who incarnate study the lessons Life teaches in all racial classrooms, as well as from the standpoint of both sexes. The one who fiercely hates another race body today will have his or her chance of adjustment and clear vision as he lives in one similar to that detested in the following life pattern. Hate is magnetic in reverse ratio and draws us in intimate relationship to, or change of place with, that which is hated and must be understood. If you hate enough, you may find yourself as the siamese twin of the loathed individual, next time around! This has been said before but bears repeating, for we forget that hate must be transmuted into love before we can roam free.

Gloria had friends of almost every color and nation which she made while serving as an air stewardess. When time was available, she would spend as much of it as she could, living with a family native to the country visited, in order to learn something of the language and customs from those who knew them best. She spent time with a Chinese family, an Irish family and a Spanish family in their own lands, and brought away better understanding of the common humanity of all people than could be learned by theory and lectures. Among our members we number Chinese, Negro, Jewish, German, Swedish, British, French, Australian, Canadian, South American people and yet others; and those of many religions are among us. Our group differs from some of the others in this respect. We do not charge fees or dues for membership or subscriptions, nor do we place friends in one sealed compartment and members in another. Everybody, of any background, color, religion, belief or outlook may read our literature without any obligation. If what we offer strikes a responsive chord, we are glad and encouraged to try even harder to find a common denominator. If our offering evokes ridicule, insults, malice and disdain (which it does and has in some quarters), we are sorry we missed discovering a happy way to reach and bless everybody, but we just quietly remove dissatisfied acquaintances from the mailing list and keep on going.

At one time Gloria and I discussed the problem of finances at great length, and we both agreed that it rang true to us that spiritual food should be offered free to the people of the world, if in any way possible to produce it. Since we lived as you do in the teeth of the storm of controversy concerning this money-making bit, we floundered some in our effort to discover an even keel. It wasn't easy and Gloria often took the personality way out and talked to the membership about their duty to keep the pot boiling and to donate to the cause if they expected it to continue. Since then we have found a better way. Where Gloria is now, released from the constrictions of physical plane concerns with security, she can help me much better than we could work together in this aspect while she lived in a physical body, and we have the thing moving in a much better flow.

Many times, not just once, Cosmon has received checks for several hundreds of dollars, unexpected and unsolicited, from individuals who felt we were making a useful attempt to break down ignorance and help in the tremendous educational program leading into citizenship in the new and better Culture just around the corner. Many many times we have received donations of forty or fifty or twenty-five dollars from individuals around the world who believed in our assertion that we wanted only to keep the Lamp of Truth shining into the far corners and the dim recesses where life is difficult beyond human endurance. Personally, I have finally analyzed the problem of abundance down to a simple formula that works for us here at Cosmon. Number one is the attitude of thanksgiving. Every day we remember to thank the Father for His abundant blessings, His trust in us to perform His works of love and light, and His center of service in which to perform His Will. Then we ask that He give us sufficient energy to increase and expand our understanding and activity.

Number three is the prime consideration. If we watch over the outgo, God watches over the income. If ever the income becomes less than we think it should, I undertake the personal responsibility to increase my output. This is a necessary rhythm and you can apply it to any part of your life. Watch your output, increase your value to God and man, and the supply for all you need will find its way to you.

Now, I want to say before I forget it, that thanksgiving is a spiritual force of expansion. As you show your gratitude in prayer and service, you expand and open up your capacity to receive greater blessings. Another thing of importance is this, to do what you can today on the side of construction. One of our members is perceptive enough to realize that although she can send only 25¢ each month as her unsolicited token of appreciation for her newsletter, this is deeply appreciated by us because it is given as a pure sacrifice, and is charged with understanding love. This same woman occasionally sends us one or two or three postage stamps, because she is intuitive enough to realize it must require astronomical amounts of postage to keep our mail flow moving and that every bit helps!

To all other groups of Light, let me say that if you are in the RED instead of in the PINK, perhaps you are forgetting your manners and your daily thanksgiving to the Father, our Source of all good, and thinking first of income before throwing yourself wholly into parlaying your spiritual gifts into a larger sacrifice upon the altar of Love and Light.

* * * * * * *

One of our members asked me to note that in communication he received the information he was in tune with the planet of

VERGA in the System of Vega. Has anyone heard of this planet? Verification of its existence, or details concerning it would be most welcome to our friend. Thanks for your help.

* * * * * * *

There are, as usual, many things to talk over together. This is a New Age way of educating each other through a continuous exchange of the information, knowledge and ideas we have accumulated along our individual paths of life, no two alike and therefore filled with new thoughts and inspirations for the others around each of us. Don't say you have nothing worth sharing. Even babies can teach all of us lessons of sweetness, trust and patience, and they have not made any mileage at all upon the path of conscious self-development.

When you read Ani's article in this issue, you may shake your head in surprise and doubt. I was the channel for Ani and shall explain that some months ago several of us were gathered together around an instrument who was channeling J.W. That evening J.W. brought to us several guest speakers, among them Ani, Who was introduced as a representative of the consciousness of the Third Kingdom in Nature, the Animal Kingdom. J.W. undertook to bring Ani, Who is His friend, to us for expansion of our thinking and receptivity to a wider area of communication, and we were told that Non-human Intelligences of this nature must be invoked and related to our minds through the offices of someone who is capable of applying the techniques of protection and correct contact for all concerned.

Many times after that I thought about Ani and felt that such as He might welcome the opportunity to use a human instrument to express some of the ideas He would naturally have in mind. Therefore I placed a person-to-person offer with J.W. and said I would greatly enjoy being on a mental hookup with Ani, if permissible. Considerably later, one morning while sitting at the typewriter, I was made aware that Ani would converse with me. I should explain that great entities Who work behind the scenes of the other kingdoms of Nature are profoundly intelligent, and can communicate their ideas with supreme ease and wisdom. The words are mine: the ideas are Ani's.

There are statements communicated in Ani's message that seem to me to require expansion and discussion, and I have given much and long thought about methods by which I might bring to this group of readers vital information on subjects still considered taboo.

Further along in the New Age, everybody will be clairvoyant, and as one Great Teacher wrote, "Nobody will be able to lead a double life." Since everyone will have developed X-ray vision, nobody will be able to have any secrets. The advanced beings who live and work on the other side of illusion in the clear light of constant revelation, are accustomed to living, thinking and acting in a perfectly open manner before all others. It would not avail anyone to attempt to hide anything, and they see each other in the Light as well as they see us. We alone are unrevealed to ourselves, but as open books in every particular and detail of our minds, hearts and bodies to Those who have developed further.

At this transition point, there are a great many hypocrites among us who believe people will accept them at face value if they make a loud and impressive protest about discussing the creative relationships between the masculine and feminine principles. Several individuals have requested to be removed from our mailing list from time to time, because of our frank discussions of the facts of this relationship, and so I have hesitated for some time to continue along this road until I felt I might have discovered a better form of semantics, communication, form of words, etc.

Now I will deliver my small ultimatum, which is: Take it or leave it. I consider myself in the mothering class and am bound to explain certain things that everybody should know, whether they like it or it makes them squirm in self-consciousness, or not. I have been requested to tell what I believe to be TRUTH, regardless of the effect upon myself, and so I shall; and if you wish to hide your head in the sands of ignorance and illusion, just go right ahead.

What background gives me the right to set myself up as "authority" in this field? I have worked in a doctor's office through which wended a stream of men and women who had many marital and relationship problems. In that office I had access to the doctor's case histories, reference works, medical textbooks and contemporary periodicals, and I spent a great deal of my marginal time studying this material in order to understand and to help people. I read the Kinsey Report. I lived on a farm and observed Nature's cycles of reproduction among cattle, horses, hogs, poultry, cats and dogs. I read Rabelais, the life of Don Juan, endless books on marriage, marriage customs, history of marriage, the spiritual side of marriage, normal and abnormal psychology, reincarnation studies of cause and effects in human relationships, the Alice Bailey books, WHY WE ARE HERE, and also sat as one member of three including Gloria Lee and Dr. Sellstrom, to whom the Master Teachers began a series of talks on the necessity for bringing forth a better understanding of these matters so intimate, close and tumultuous to all of us. We need all the Light we can get. I was very lucky when young that nobody censored my reading, for I read all over the map from the time I was very young and my emotions were not involved, so that I could look upon my studies with clinical interest and dispassion, until I became swept up in the usual whirl of feeling and yet was better prepared to understand myself and observe my own reactions than many who get caught and drowned without ever quite realizing what it is all about.

Are you aware that we are forced to view the subject of our relationship with the opposite polarity through mankind's age-old self-constructed thoughtform that is as a red blur of passion, lust, desire and frustration, and that those who protest most vehemently and loudly about their freedom from interest in this fundamental aspect of all conscious life everywhere, are those to whom the whole subject is still a problem — major and unsolved? Those who take life straight and as a natural, normal process, are those who have come to a degree of balance within themselves and who do not go through exaggerated dramatic procedures of self-flagellation and ascetic pretense.

You who are reading this message have not always been the man or woman, boy or girl you are now. You have often been the opposite, and thought the thoughts most common and normal to one aspect or the other. Test yourself with honesty and see if you cannot allow yourself to put yourself in the place of the opposite gender. Cannot you see life as a woman or as a man almost equally well, if you strain a little?

After Gloria and I went to see the movie, EL CID, she said she felt sure we had once been in a position similar to the two leading male characters. She thought we had been two military leaders of different racial backgrounds, who met after the battle and shook hands, and recognized the fact of human brotherhood over and above the other considerations. This does not strike me as being ludicrous or peculiar, for I feel equally able to throw myself into a masculine viewpoint or a feminine viewpoint, although I stick with my present appearance as a general rule. To me it is important to be a person. I like to think of others as people, regardless of their temporary manifestation as men or women. To me this is basic to expression of true friendship, which is often lost in an emphasis upon the differences instead of the common ground all people share by simply being humans.

Human relationships are extremes of complexity. The one who is your child today may have been your mate in a former life pattern. Two men friends of today may yesterday have been father and son, mother and daughter, or lovers of opposite polarity. The same may be true of any two women friends. Any of these, involved in the relationships of today, with veils of memory drawn and darkness over their yesterdays, may still be swept by tides of true Love, generated in some innocent past and now causing tensions and pressures of remorse and inward guilt because of the ignorant accusations of the masses who cannot see below the psychological surface, and assume all constant and continuous relational living patterns of women friends alone or men friends alone to be perverted or suspect. It is also obvious that such relationships could be based on former associations as groups of monks or nuns, wherein the individuals had renounced life with the opposite aspect in marriage as being a carnal sin against the spirit and the church. We must open our minds far wider in this area.

J.W. tried to get across through Gloria that the Space People believe TRUE LOVE should be free to express itself wherever it is found, as affection, consideration, compassion, courtesy, friendliness, cooperation and collaboration. It is almost impossible for us to rise to the fact that the so-called sacred matrimony of today is a man-made concept. Marriages made in heaven are not ring-and-book unions, but something quite other, which we can discuss at a later time when there is more room. The point is that civilization should sanction and encourage LOVE, and override the notion that any personality owns or can possess any other personality, regardless of all evidences to the contrary. All should be free to smile and hold hands with any other! But we should not debase our natural and normal needs for balance with our opposite force into orgies of lust, perversions and damaging activities that brutalize and demote personality to the level of beastliness, which is actually sub-animal! If our human races were really relieved of their abysmal ignorance in this aspect of life alone, we would see a surge upward toward greater wisdom and loveliness as a whole.

The deplorable feature of homosexuality, as the term is bandied about today, is that it is a degenerated and depraved game, and completely off the goal of providing balance of forces; creative unities for production of spiritual, mental and physical offspring. The only hope for healing this running sore on the body of humanity is application of more knowledge, understanding and education of children to avoid the pitfalls leading to such a mistaken aim.

The individuals who say we must not look down at the evils of the day and help to erase and heal them, are those who have not looked deeply and understandingly into themselves, for if they had, they would have discovered imbalance and fear in greater proportions than Christ consciousness and wise love. To truly love is to endure revelation for the sake of those loved, and to be willing to go down into hell with a mop and a broom to clean the festering misery and ignorance there that are breeding places for human woe. No matter what the self-righteous say, in the certainty they are on the side of proper and untainted dippings into the panorama of life, I am still for setting free the prisoners of ignorance and bringing to them the good news that they are as much loved by God as anyone else, and can pick themselves up wherever they come to their true spiritual senses and go forward with all of us to the very same Goal.

That's all -

Lovingly yours,

Barbara Steele

STRONGER LESSONS

Have you learn'd lessons only of those who admired you, and
    were tender with you, and stood aside for you?
Have you not learn'd great lessons from those who reject you,
    and brace themselves against you? or who treat you with
    contempt, or dispute the passage with you?

LEAVES OF GRASS
Walt Whitman

COMMUNICATION FROM ANOTHER KINGDOM

I am Ani. I have come in answer to your hope for contact, by Divine permission and through the good offices of J.W. of Jupiter.

To those who do not recognize my name I shall introduce myself as one who acts as an animating spirit of the Animal Kingdom. You may designate me as that one-over-all, where the animals of Planet Earth are concerned. I am not a group soul of flock or herd, or of a species or family, but it is my function to preside over the destinies of the third kingdom in Nature. It should not evoke astonishment among the sons of men, to witness that intelligent communication is possible between representatives of various kingdoms in Nature, for all are encompassed within the reach of the Mind of the Same Over-Father.

As many of you are experiencing at this period of transition, a rise in consciousness, it is appropriate that you should prepare yourselves to accept the penetration of your expanding consciousness into realms other than the human, upon the ladder of evolution.

It is of record that the Creating Father established mankind as ruler over the beasts of the field, and the kingdoms of plant life and of minerals. This is accepted without question as appropriate, but is interpreted in relation to that which mankind defines as rulership. To humanity of this epoch, the meaning of ruling is imposition of force upon the weaker consciousnesses in the area of the influence of the ruler.

Man has not yet come into his era of kingly spiritual authority for the guidance of those conscious lives of the animal kingdom of Nature, for he has not yet, as a mass unity, demonstrated rulership of the beast within his own nature.

Without emphasis, for TRUTH stands without emphasis, I say you are a race of cannibals. You are those spirits inhabiting desecrated temples in which the dead bodies of your animal brothers are daily sacrifices to the brute within your own self, that the beast in you may be made stronger in his beasthood and fill the temple of his desires with those provocative fumes of the incense of death which drive you further upon the pathway to Illusion.

Is it a thing of uniqueness to imagine that I, an informing intelligence of a lower order of beings, am capable of conversing with those of your kingdom and may observe the practice of your worship of the physical human body, to which countless members of the animal kingdom have given up their planned evolutionary pursuits while you are led further astray as the unwitting prey of the forces of Negation, which, in their turn, have established themselves as rulers of the beast within man?

It is not of Truth that man must feed upon the carcasses of his younger brothers in order to sustain the life of his body. This is an enormity, that such a misconception should be given credence within the minds of men and should find coexistence with the pretended worship of an all-loving Father. How could a Father be all-loving, yet concur in the conspiracy that His younger children be murdered and eaten by the elder children within His family? You have turned away when faced with this question, generation after generation; for you cannot face it with honor and continue to take the name of your Divine Father in vain, which you do when you ascribe to Him a double nature which permits evil and cruelty, while sending Christs of Compassion and mercy to lead you into His Kingdom of Heaven. It is not a possible feat, even for the cunning minds of the human kingdom, to devise a means of splitting the individual into two sections, one retrogressing at the same instant the other is progressing.

In your true spiritual nature, it is impossible for you to move in two opposite directions simultaneously. And yet it is possible for that part of your wholeness, which is an individualized graduate of the animal kingdom, to sever the silver thread of communion between itself and the immortal, eternal Soul, and to sink backward, and to undo the countless slow eons of effort invested by the Higher Consciousness, and thus to place upon the Higher Self a necessity for beginning at the beginning in the re-evolution of a perfected human being prepared to graduate into the Spiritual Kingdom of conscious Christs.

There are subjects which I feel it is my duty to bring to you in terms that cannot be mistaken for definitions of other intentions, and which relate mankind to the animal kingdom. Humanity is a bridge between the animal and the spiritual realms of awareness and as the intended ruler of the less evolved consciousnesses, is held responsible to the Creator for those atrocities committed within the jurisdiction accorded and entrusted.

Having given you these foregoing remarks, I would next bring to your attention the logical consequence of hostility between the animal kingdom and the human, where not cannibalism and slavery, but companionship, mutual service and proper examples of guidance were intended.

Animal instinct is not overlaid by conditioned responses in its natural state, but brings into the animal consciousness immediate directives for self-preservation. The animal is normally aware of the presence within man of a beast or an angel, and reacts accordingly.

Civilized man, if of educated refinement, cannot enjoy the act of murdering an animal, followed by gorging himself upon a fresh, bloody kill. He pretends to himself to convert the facts, ugly and terrible, through the man-magic of cooking those violated carcasses that they may take a new form and appear as food; not as victims of premeditated murder. Men are in depths of untruth when they surround killing with the rules governing games. They say they are sportsmen. Is this a better sport than that of the martyring of those early followers of Light who were placed in the Roman arenas? Where is the distinction? Since there is not necessity in either example, what remains but blood-lust; disguised, camouflaged, to those who allow themselves the benefit of deluded outlook and a turning away from the Predator within — the Beast in man. This is not to be imputed to the compassionate Christ-nature; not to the Soul; not to the evolving God.

With weeping sentimentality, there are those who condemn animal experiments by scientists, yet fill their stomachs with the tortured, broken victims of the slaughterhouse. Even while gathering arsenals for the protection of cats and dogs, there are those who support the mass murder of sheep and cattle and hogs. These are often those who wince and turn pale at the sight of a shrunken human head, a trophy of savages, yet rejoice at the savagery of their own "sportsmanship" that produced the trophy of an animal's head upon the walls of their den. Is it not appropriate that the human being terms that place a "den" in which he displays his brutish prowess? There are many who would shrink away from the proximity of a human scalp cut from a living skull, yet would not hesitate to deck themselves in the pelts torn from murdered animals.

There are those who go forth among their fellows with an expression of self-satisfaction because they are fruit eaters and vegetarians, yet take their steps of holiness upon feet of clay encased in shoes and sandals of leather. Upon their wrists are leather bands. Upon their hands are leather gloves. Upon their backs are leather jackets. Within their pockets are leather money holders. Upon their shelves are bone-meal pellets. Upon their floors are rugs of fur. These teach their pets to carry on the cannibalism they have foresworn. These are willing horses should be murdered that their dogs may be filled. These also turn their eyes away, for they have not allowed their perception to roam in these channels of comparison.

Man has created excuses for himself. He claims he is dependent upon the murder of evolving bodies in another kingdom to sustain him in his hunger, his vanity and his nakedness. There are no longer the excuses of ignorance or forgetfulness because substitutes have been devised for all animal products, and now man must face the fact that he is enslaved to the BEAST within his own nature, as his karma for enslaving and plundering the beasts of the field which were given into his keeping and rulership by the Fiat of the Father, to Whom man is accountable for the transgression of his trust.

Not only has mankind enslaved his own lowest nature, but has vitiated and perverted the instincts of the animals which were placed within his guardianship and the proximity of his auric influence for added stimulation of a higher frequency which would enable them to attain to the individual status of humanhood.

Animals are impressionable through their emotions and accept the vices as well as the virtues of those beings, senior to them, with whom they are associated. An animal exposed to the atmospheres exuded from human excesses of lust and passion and perversion will exhibit these qualities also. An animal exposed to serenity, gentleness and self-restraint will exhibit these qualities as easily. It is due to these causations that the animal world exhibits that which it exhibits. Animal greed is an imitation of human greed.

As above, so below. Two worlds meet in man and he finds himself mirrored whether he turns to the world above or the world below. If a man focus his thought within the world of the beasts, he will see the reflection of the beast in himself. If a man turn to the world of the gods, he will behold the forming image of his own god-self. So be it.

Seldom do the sons of men invoke the intelligences of companion kingdoms to converse with them as friend to friend, as brother to brother. We of adjacent realms would come forth in gladness as brothers within the family of the Father over all. We must be invoked. We must contact you under the rules governing such association. It is through the understanding of the technicalities involved, and due to his friendship with members of the human and the animal kingdoms, that J.W. has kindly fulfilled those needed requirements which have made my message available to you through a human instrument.

Further to the subjects I have brought to your attention, I would cause you to take note of the suffering and unnatural conditions you create for your pets through isolating them from their complementary polarities. In your own kingdom, you express an extremity of ignorance concerning the balance of forces in Nature and the necessity for association of the masculine and feminine aspects of all species, races and families, through chemical, mineral, vegetable, animal, human and superhuman kingdoms. Your misdemeanor in this regard opens you to unrestrained inflow of those influences and suggestions from the powers of darkness which enter into your minds with formulas for artificial and degraded modes of stilling the lower emotional drives and hungers of man and of animal.

This brings me into an area of discussion which your kingdom surrounds with taboos, yet I would avail myself, as a spiritual intelligence, of the opportunity to draw aside the veil from certain inharmonious topics so that you may fail to claim the excuse of ignorance of the facts involved after my declarations.

In this aspect to which I allude, J.W. has exchanged thoughts with me and has stated the area requires cleansing and exposure to the influx of the spirit of TRUTH, and that since my kingdom, as well as yours, is involved, I may, with some hope of benefiting you, touch upon the relationships of an emotional nature you term homosexuality, due to your lack of true spiritual education and your propensity for turning away from that which revolts the sensibilities of the refined and those among you who find the conditions established, beyond their power to ameliorate.

Nature, under the Universal Laws of harmony, order and beauty, does not violate the law of cycles or the law of love. In pure Nature, not vitiated by the proximity of man's barbaric stupidity, there is the progressive display of evolutionary forces in harmonious relationships.

J. W. elaborated to me his attempt to place before the people of earth two manuals for New Age behavior in the formative stages of your coming civilization. He said that He experienced the same inane and infantile reactions and misinterpretations that have been accorded to all reformers, and educators sent to this planet from other spheres of higher development, through the slow revolvings of innumerable eons. Those from elsewhere have commonly concluded that a majority of the humanity upon this globe will go down in the records of the infinite memory as that race of individuals most layered over and laced in and encircled by extrusions of inner complacency, stubbornness and egotistic unreceptiveness, crystallized into glassy indifference to the Truth, of any of the humanities of any of the man-bearing worlds of the universe.

And now I would say, in defense of the animals of this planet, which are my proteges, that the source of the perversion of homosexuality is not to be discovered within the animal nature of animals but within the animal nature of man. The basic statement to be remembered is this, that all functioning of this sort is, in its final analysis, a misconceived and wrongly expressed yearning for the exchange of the energy of love. No one: no consciousness: no intelligent entity ever outgrows the need for an exchange of the pure energy of love. Substitutes spring from imbalance and segregation and the damming up of the proper circulatory flow of Life to all parts of its body of manifestation.

If as is true, the mistaken attempt to find Polarity Balance is undertaken between animals of the same sex, due to their arbitrary and inescapable separation from their complementary polarities, as an instinctive urgency to find balance and revitalization, — the karmic liability lies with man and not with the innocent creatures dependent upon his guidance and cultivation.

There are those individuals, both male and female, among your multitudes, who have made a fetish of culturing perverse attitudes and elaborating artifices to an extent they are out of touch with reality, and vainly imagine themselves to be those who exemplify forerunners of a superior type released from dependence upon the opposite polarity by the possession of an accreted body of rituals, doctrines, formulae and mechanical techniques by which they believe they supply to the physical body a supposed balance through exaggerated exercise of the sexual function, aided by the willing, enforced or remunerated cooperation of their own sex.

At the end of the pathway of human evolution, it is true that each individual concludes certain developments of potential which allow the establishment of a balanced supply of masculine and feminine attributes within the personality. Either developed man or developed woman is in a wholeness of individuality at this point and can look out upon others with the understanding of both polarities, acquired by extensive sojourns within each aspect. Love is known for what it is: the Universal Life Principle of Creation.

A Soul is inclusive in its awareness of, and love for, either or both polarities. The personality of an experienced old soul expressing upon the earth, is one who includes love of either sex — for its fellow men and women. This is a true hermaphrodite, a spiritually mature combination of Hermes and Aphrodite, or man-and-woman, in the sense that incarnations in vehicles of both polarities have been experienced so frequently there is no great emphasis placed upon a distinction between the two. Often personalities of souls such as these, are captured in their innocent youth upon the physical plane and conditioned by a perverted adult to imagine they are beyond the understanding and acceptance of society and must accede to a way of existence prescribed by the one who seeks to corrupt them.

This is a blight upon your kingdom, a cancerous growth of your civilization; a misuse of the creative power which should find its expression in bettering the form aspect of your humanity, in producing better opportunities for incarnation of both animal and human. You have a great need for exploring the field of spiritual eugenics. You who read my message are as much to blame as any for you, too, are of those who have turned away your faces or closed your ears. All these corruptions are rooted in the ignorance you have not eliminated by acceptance of responsibility for the finding and teaching of TRUTH. You have all been a part of the failure to guide the young of your kingdom, to rule the animals, and the beast in your own self.

It may now be repeated that this is a rare opportunity, which I cherish, to be permitted entry into your world of conscious thought and to open more widely your door of recognition that no activities, desires or thought processes upon your planes are in any wise hidden from the clear viewing of those in greater spiritual capacity. You are known for what you are in all the detail of your living. I would have you realise that contrary to the claims of superiority and freedom from the restraints of Universal Law promulgated by those of perverted patterns for living, they are the LAGGARDS of your race; the first who will fall away and be separated off from the pioneer exponents of Christ powers, and who will find themselves again in the kindergarten zones of evolution, facing an enforced re-ascent through the veils of ignorance, until at length, even these will have learned by repeating the course how properly to utilize the CREATIVE FIRE of LIFE.

My understanding will not permit me to withdraw from your realm until I have left with you the thought that you hold within yourselves the power to turn yourselves away from those actions which your spirits have long since outgrown, and which should find no response or encouragement within the kingdom of man. I am not an animal, but a spiritual intelligence. (There are animating intelligences of communicative capacity within the vegetable and the mineral kingdoms also.) I am quite capable of communicating with members of your race in the terminology to which you are accustomed among your human brothers, but it must be remembered that I and others of my kind are not able to meet with you as yet in the normal course of events, but only under special permission and by invocation where conditions of inclusive love and altruistic purpose have been fulfilled upon all sides. My prayer upon leaving your human vibration is that your people of earth may begin to look upon the animal kingdom with concepts cleansed of illusion.

"A main fact in the history of manners is the wonderful expressiveness of the human body. If it were made of glass, or of air, and the thoughts were written on steel tablets within, it could not publish more truly its meaning than now. Wise men read very sharply all your private history in your look and gait and behavior. The whole economy of nature is bent on expression. The telltale body is all tongues. Men are like Geneva watches with crystal faces which expose the whole movement. They carry the liquor of life flowing up and down in these beautiful bottles, and announcing to the curious how it is with them. The face and eyes reveal what the spirit is doing, how old it is, what aims it has. The eyes indicate the antiquity of the soul, or, through how many forms it has already ascended. It almost violates the proprieties, if we say above the breath here, what the confessing eyes do not hesitate to utter to every street passenger."

ESSAYS: 2nd Series
Behavior
Ralph Waldo Emerson

YOUR HEALTH

Several of our readers have written requests for articles on diet. Many of them wish they could steer a middle course and add a forbidden item once in awhile just to balance the monotony. The following list was given by Master D.K. through Alice Bailey, as a commonsense diet for those who were trying to live a reasonable New Age life among the "cannibals".

> All vegetables that grow above the ground
> Milk (sparingly)
> Honey
> Whole wheat bread
> Oranges
> Nuts
> Raisins
> Bananas
> Potatoes (sparingly)
> Unpolished rice

This Teacher said our foods should be chosen from among the fruits and vegetables that vitalize. Since this Teacher was well past 100 years when writing the Bailey books, it should be inferred that He knew what vitalized.

In one of Master Morya's Agni Yoga books, mention was made of the benefit of fragrance radiation from ripe apples. How many of you know that apples belong to the same family as roses?

You are going to have to gather up your courage and experiment upon yourself in this wild territory of diet and food preferences. Nearly every authority differs on some basic essentials and so there will always be the need for you to inform yourself of several intelligent viewpoints and strike a personal balance somewhere among them.

Please don't be dogmatic or dictatorial about one pet item or another, just because you like it and can buy it at your health food store. Also be reasonable. Can you expect others to take you as a perfect example of your preachments? Are you glowing with health, radiantly beautiful, nice to be near? Or are you a theorist who feels impelled to tell everybody in your family and elsewhere what is best? You could be missing the mark and ruining the whole subject of proper diet for all who know you, just because your appearance, performance and character do not match your sermons.

Some of our Cosmon friends are purists and will refuse to take certain things into their systems. Yet could they be overemphasizing food and underemphasizing being fun to live with?

The Space People explained to Gloria, as we have told you before, that any cooked foods are dead foods and have only the power to maintain you in whatever condition you may be. You can hold your own with these to some degree, but you cannot regenerate your skin, muscles, organs and bones on dead vegetable or animal matter. It is necessary to eat fresh raw fruits, vegetables, and juices of both, for energy to turn back the clock.

Over and above all, let's try to remember that a very great deal of the physical ill health, indigestion, run-down feelings and misery are due to lack of humor. "A merry heart doeth good like a medicine."

One of our friends, a member of the U.S. Navy in Asia, tells us he wishes we would put in some good words for herb teas. They have helped him a lot, he says.

Your local health food store or the health food section of your market may offer up to 150 interesting and unusual teas made from the flowers, bark, leaves, stems or roots of plants. You will enjoy some. Others you will find flat or tasteless, but they all have some medicinal or health values which you would enjoy studying.

As in making regular tea, it is advised to use either tea bags or 1 — 1-1/2 teaspoonfuls of herb per person. Have your pot or cup heated before brewing the tea and if you make a pot of it, add an extra spoonful or teabag, for second cups. And pour on water that is really boiling hot. Most persons like tea steeped for 3 - 5 minutes. Sweeten with honey!

ALFALFA TEA - Rich in iron. Relieves anemia. Good for bones and teeth.

COMFREY TEA - Helps to ease sore throats and heals fresh wounds.

FENUGREEK TEA - A good intestinal cleanser.

HOPS TEA - Soothes nerves. Helps overcome insomnia. Relieves heart palpitations.

HOREHOUND TEA - Helps in relief of coughs or asthma.

HYSSOP TEA - Helps bronchitis, lung congestion and asthma.

LAVENDER TEA - Helps in relief of cramps, dizzy spells and headaches. Use as a gargle to relieve hoarseness.

LICORICE ROOT TEA - Said to be helpful in treating ulcers.

RED CLOVER TEA - Has an active ingredient, glycogen, which is said to help in blood infections, coughs, rheumatic and arthritic pains and heart palpitations.

MINT TEA - Said to soothe stomach pains and to stop colds.

SAGE TEA - Good for relief of stiff joints, when used in the bath. Good gargle to soothe sore throat and head colds.

SARSAPARILLA TEA - Said to relieve skin ailments and improve poor blood.

SASSAFRAS TEA - Tonic and general therapeutic use.

The list is almost endless. Study the fascinating details for yourselves. In future perhaps we shall stock some of the more general-use teas and books of instructions that should accompany them. American health food stores stock tea packages at approximately 65¢ per box. This is the average size and price, though they vary from 49¢ to 75¢ or more, depending on rarity of tea, etc.

* * * * * * *

Try to eat all the raw fruit and vegetable salads you can during the summer and if you are lucky enough to own a juicer, make lots of orange, carrot, and mixed fruit and vegetable juices for your family.

We will add more diet information as we go. Try to avoid extremes, because it is important to be "fit to live with," and many place themselves on diets that were never intended for their type of body and cause pain and discomfort instead of health and happiness.

Our dear READERS —

A very few of you have sent in your new ZIP CODE numbers. All within the United States have now been assigned a mail-delivery AREA CODE NUMBER. Remember to send this to all your correspondents.

Bartram suggests that you tell us more specifically if you do or do not like the newsletter. We are open to constructive criticism, and ideas that can be incorporated to the benefit of everybody.

EXPLORING HUMAN EMOTIONS

INTUITIVE PERCEPTION
Maurine W. Sellstrom

Intuitive perception should be a useful function for all of us who are looking with interest toward the New Age. Intuition is the ability that can perceive what is in the future. Both reason and senses must deal with what has happened. Feeling knows what is happening. Only intuition reaches toward the future.

Admiration is frequently a form of intuition. We admire in others what we sense we must potentially develop. When we feel this admiration without any awareness of having the qualities we admire, we often fail to relate to our heroes. The very quality repressed in us keeps us from expressing those values precious to us and to those we admire. Hero worship which carries no sense of identification with our hero creates a fan attitude. Fans can have a distant relationship with their stars, but sooner or later feel frustrated because they do not have real acceptance by those who look so glamorous to them. Stars also tire of admiration which has no exchange of ideas which they value. Sheer admiration may for a while attract those who need ego bolstering, but it does not really create a relationship conducive to communication and mutual acceptance. We soon feel the need of being accepted as an equal, a brother. Only those who feel such equality can really communicate.

Who is our brother or sister? "He that does the will of our Father Who is in Heaven," or he who serves our values. As we see the same values as Heavenly, we can agree. When we cannot, we argue. This includes even such simple things as choice of color or foods. When people like what we like, we feel they have "good taste". When they do not, we are puzzled and question their judgment.

What causes us to reject parts of our endowment as important as intuitive perception? Why do we refuse to live these traits and then be so charmed by them in others?

Usually it is because we have witnessed the trait immaturely used, usually early in our childhood. This kept us from developing certain abilities that were our gifts from "our Father Who is in Heaven."

Even such a wonderful quality as love can seem undesirable when it is lived "not wisely but too well." The love that is selfish and possessive is usually an immature form of loving. Those of us who may have experienced such a love from others, may have become cool and remote in the expression of our warm and outgoing feelings.

When we have seen a particularly frightening form of any function in our early years, we often feel that "I'd rather be dead than like that." Often that is exactly what happens. A side of us becomes dead. It no longer lives. Even as Herod killed the babies in the Christmas story, many of us have sides of ourselves that have been killed before they were two years old by the cruel dictation of customs or people who had power over us in our early experiences. Longing for these dead children in us makes us susceptible to disproportionate longing for people living qualities like these dead sides of ourselves. Yet this very suppression makes us unable to express those values we admire in the very areas we admire them most.

This is why agreeing with our adversary while he is yet in the way with us is so important. Loving our enemy becomes necessary if we are not going to imprison parts of ourselves. It lets us keep alive traits we need to train and develop so they can express maturely. If we cannot do this, we leave parts of ourselves in outer darkness until the trumpet is sounded which lets us see the Christ or the way God created those traits to be used.

As we feel admiration for another whose abilities seem beyond our world of expression, he is indeed a hero or savior to us. He is redeeming qualities for us which had been condemned in our early living by seeing them used too hard or unwisely. As long as we cannot use them because of our former enemy whom we could not forgive, we are cast into a prison. We lack the freedom to use these sides of ourselves or enter into the areas of life this endowment would open to us. We will remain in this prison as long as the ones we condemned remain in outer darkness — or suppressed beyond the light of our attention. This also robs us of the energies surrounding us we could use to bring them into form and expression.

Why would we repress any qualities so valuable as intuitive perception? Usually because we have seen others use it in a way that seemed to us "crazy", or loaded with delusions of grandeur. We have seen intuitive people who had claimed some great gift that everyday observation told us they lacked. Or perhaps we saw intuition used exploitively in a way that gave others too big a bill to pay, by predicting some dreaded and feared future event in order to receive some compensation or blackmail from the fearing one.

One woman was told that she wouldn't live past a certain time unless she studied from such an intuitive person about how to pray and meditate. Others have seen people who made extravagant claims for themselves, saying they received such information intuitively. All of us have read of prophecies which never happened. These are all public examples of beginning attempts to use intuitive perception. Beginners often do things in a bungling manner. We all make some mistakes as we begin any new enterprise.

Ego must be surrendered in most of these cases, before the wise and mature use of pure KNOWING can come about. We have to be willing to learn, often by trying and failing.

What are the skills right use of intuitive perception can give us? One of its frequent right uses is flare, or a sense of timing that tells us what will be popular. Clothing firms, manufacturers who succeed in correctly estimating the market are frequently using intuitive knowing in this way. We are more apt to have intuition express as flare in areas of life where we are experienced and have worked extensively. Even when we feel we do not have this quality of flare or sense of knowing which direction to go, it is our repressed intuition which accuses us and makes us feel that we are heavy and ponderous. It is our unconscious awareness of flare that sneers at us when we do not use it.

Intuitive perception senses the future and helps us to move instinctively towards it. Many of us do this, then try to give reasonable explanations to justify our actions, which sound stupid. Or sometimes when we cannot find a reasonable explanation we delay and procrastinate, until we sense we are being fearful or stubborn. Prayer and faith in guidance can help us reduce the mechanism of procrastination. Many times we fear our dream of the future because we sense it is conceited and unjustifiable. We sense that man can not put himself ahead of God. Most of us have witnessed some self-styled prophet who implied that he was greater than he believed God to be. Man perhaps is potentially all that God is, but he can never be secure in having any part of God's abilities that he has not proven by his own action. Intuition can show us what part of any new ability we can use. It will also make us aware of where we can use it safely, if we will allow this tutoring from within to take place.

Really mature intuition brings with it a humility and a sensing that "Thine is the Kingdom and the power and the glory." As we mean this prayer our fear of blame diminishes, as well as many of our encumbering protective mechanisms.

Intuitive perception that seems foreboding can be the warning that we may be confronted with a test or initiation that requires more preparation on our part. It is time to get ready and learn, so we can pass our test with flying colors. If we are thrown into fear and depressed foreboding instead of study, we allow ourselves to be thrown into dark moods. Thus we are cast in a dark light and cannot pass with flying colors, because our colors are heavy and we cannot see our problem in its true light.

Intuitive perception gives us the ability to slough off unnecessary encumbrances. We do not have to save against the rainy day, because we believe in an inner guidance which will have us under cover in time. Thus "sufficient unto the day is the evil thereof."

Intuition can let us know what we will face in our tests, so we do not have to review the whole course. It will let us leave what is old and outmoded and move with interest and energy toward what is new. We can reach into the New Age with enthusiasm and find joy in creating new forms, which make old and hoarded ones unnecessary. They can be given to our fellow man who is coming up the step we have just left. He can benefit from that which we can no longer use.

Most of all, intuitive perception can help us to find God's law in regard to any situation. If we can follow His guidance we do not have to carry armor and defenses against the punishment for our mistakes. As we can perceive and follow God's law, we prosper. Things go well, so we do not need all the equipment we try to carry in case they do not.

We do not have to prepare so carefully or consider so thoroughly what we will say, for our perception of God's way can put the words into our mouths as we have need of them. We do not have to consider what we will answer, for we will know what is true.

This inner tutoring can teach us what is God's plan for the gifts we brought into life with us, to accomplish God's purpose for our living. As we can find the right use of all we are, we can become the beloved sons in whom God is well pleased. It is then we can be like Sir Galahad who had the strength of ten, because his heart was pure. We can start out in our search for the Holy Grail, the cup from which we drink of the essence of the Christ in us, which is the way God intended all He created like us to be used.

This cup gives us the living elixir of life, the body of the Christ consciousness of man as being sustained by God in His Kingdom. This cup satisfies all thirst, and man no longer hungers and thirsts for righteousness. His own intuitive perception lets him know the right use of all he is, and he is filled.

Much of the anxiety we feel is the fear that we won't know, we won't understand. We are afraid that we will be oblivious and miss the Holy Grail, that it will pass us by unseen. Let us stand still and see the salvation of the Lord. For He has promised us: "Lo, I am with you always, even unto the end of the world." This certainly includes any form within this world.

THE HOLY GRAIL

by Maurine Sellstrom

Had you asked of Me
I would have given to you
Of the Living waters
And you would thirst no more.
As man can sip from the Holy Grail
And drink its waters of understanding,
He does not long for righteousness
For he knows the right use of those qualities
Which were his at birth
From his Father which is in Heaven.

Once that right use is known,
He is not tempted to use them foolishly.
The flow of life becomes his cup
Which meets his need
Even as it arises.
He does not need to hoard or hunger
For sufficient unto every moment
Is the inspiration and gift
Of that moment.
The Christ within — the living waters
Flows through him into life.
He is part of the stream of all that is
And God moves through him, around him, in him
And from him to every corner
Of all that is Creation.

GUEST CORNER

UNIVERA OF JUPITER
TEACHES TO STEP FORWARD INTO LIGHT
* * * * * * * * * * * * *

"I AM A WAY-SHOWER OF JUPITER. I, UNIVERA, do speak with thee again. I, UNIVERA, am a WAY-SHOWER of the Planet SATURN also, and am now becoming a WAY-SHOWER on the Planet Earth!

"UNTO YOU DO I SHOW THE WAY! UNTO YOU DO I LEAD WITH LIGHT! Unto you do I give the hand of Friendship, - the Fellowship of the Great Powers of the Great Beings of all Heaven! To Earth do we send the WAY! SHOWING THE WAY is ever entwined with all of the FATHER'S BEINGS in Heaven and Earth! LET THAT WAY BE SHOWING UP UPON EARTH! I, UNIVERA, would speak with thee sincerely, - KNOWING THE WAY IS STIFF AND HARD and difficult at times.

"COUNT NOT THE PEBBLES UNDER YOUR SHOE! COUNT NOT THE BRIDGES YOU CROSS! Count not the dark alleys and the difficulties on the Way, but count the LIGHT BEINGS as they play ahead of you, - knowing that AS YOU MARCH FORWARD, - as you STEP INTO ONE LIGHT-BEAM AFTER ANOTHER, - so do you acclaim that LIGHT-BEAM unto yourself, and you BECOME A PART of that INTO WHICH YOU STEP. As you acclaim it, you BE IT! You MOVE INTO that which you SEE, and which you CHOOSE TO BE. And that which you CHOOSE TO BE, you BECOME, and ARE!

"Little by little, you DISSIPATE that which you WERE; you undo the work which was erroneous. In error you lay it aside, in the Path which is BEHIND you, - and looking NOT BACK, but FORWARD INTO THE LIGHT, you STEP FORWARD, forever moving into the LIGHT, breathing deeply that exultant LIFE which LIGHT IS! As you absorb LIGHT INTO YOUR BEING, you BECOME that toward which you face, and WORK, and into WHICH YOU MOVE!

"LEAN NOT BACKWARDS, nor be looking backward, nor under, nor beside; nor noting, nor taking note in whatsoever manner of the DARK and the DEVIOUS; of the ugly and betraying; the shallow and the wrong. THAT IS THE UNDOING OF MAN! For as he looks to THAT WHICH IS, he BECOMES THAT to which he fastens his eye, - his thought, - even his lack of desire. For a lack of desire is a Negative Thought; and that which is Positive, attaches itself to a Positive aspect.

"LEAN NOT TO THE DARK OR THE WEARY! LOOK NOT BACKWARD but FORWARD, feeling the LIGHT moving INTO you, over you, around you, through you! As you step along the Pathway to the Mountain which you see rising in Splendor, - VAST is that pinnacle of LIGHT and DELIGHT! For each step FORWARD into the LIGHT, raises you UPWARD, and you BECOME THAT WHICH YOU FACE, AND IN JOY, WOULD BE!

"I, UNIVERA, would address thee many more times; and shall, for I AM BEING A WAY-SHOWER OF EARTH!"

Hope Troxell
Channel for School of Thought

ON FREEDOM
* * * * *
(Especially July 4th)

"WE WHO ARE WATCHING THE WORLD wonder at the EXPLOSIONS which you perform! And now tomorrow in your Great Theatre of Action called AMERICA, you will perform for pleasure in great joy, more minor explosions!

"HOW YOU PEOPLE DO LOVE TO REND THE AIR WITH NOISE! Little do you realize what dastardly results you perform on yourselves, on your Auras — on the Functions of your Beings — on the PROGRESS OF YOUR CIVILIZATION!

"HOW UNGRATEFUL WE MUST SEEM TO BE OF YOUR SO NOBLE PURPOSE, that Fourth of July so long ago! And yet what has it become, but a 'CANDY DISH for the Kiddies? A TIME OF PLEASURABLE NOISE for the parents, - fathers, I would say, while Mothers prepare hot and steaming dishes, or cold foods in excess quantities, for over-gluttonous individuals!

"NO, I cannot say that we feel glorious in your glory, or pleasure in your attempt to REVIVE THAT DAY so long ago! FREEDOM WAS ITS ESSENCE, wasn't it? What has FREEDOM become, but noise, extravagances, excesses, gluttonous efforts! IS THIS FREEDOM, our Children?

"OH, WAY BACK ONE TIME — FREEDOM may have meant something greater still! But to us, FREEDOM IS IN THE NATURE, not in excessive bundles of this and that! Foods, firecrackers, noises, people!

"FREEDOM IS A WONDERFUL CREATION OF THE FATHER'S SPIRITUAL POWER! You have LOST the art of FREEDOM! You have LOST the MAKER'S PURPOSE in FREEDOM! CONQUER YOURSELVES! Children of Earth! And you will once again, KNOW FREEDOM! For Freedom is the result of CONFINEMENT OF EXCESSIVE POWER! Think that over, and be relentless in your desire for Freedom, not of noise, not of excesses, not of hearing yourselves BOAST of that which you ONCE WERE, and have BECOME!

"OH, NO! Children! THE POWER OF FREEDOM IS IN THE WORK WHICH LIES BEFORE YOU! Freedom to achieve a Power so GREAT and grand and beyond your concept! FREEDOM is quiet sincerity to application of a POWER which is GIVEN UNTO YOU FROM ON HIGH! The FREEDOM to accept it, and to WORK AT IT and the FREEDOM not to abuse, but the FREEDOM TO ACHIEVE GLORY BEYOND GLORY! ACTION BEYOND ALL possibly conceived ACTION!

"WHAT FREEDOM MEANS TO US, dear children, in the Great HEAVENS beyond, is NOBILITY OF ACTION and serenity and the PULL with the FATHER'S LAW, and the ACCESS TO GREAT BEINGS — greater Beings by far, than you have encountered, or even surmised! FREEDOM TO ACHIEVE GREAT COMPLEXITIES and even greater UNFOLDMENT... is the promise!

"OH little people of Earth, with your firecrackers, and your gorged stomachs! Oh little people of Earth! HOW YOU HAVE CONDEMNED YOURSELVES! FREEDOM you know not. Freedom is not destruction! Freedom is not SELF-POWER or SELF-WILL! FREEDOM IS THAT WHICH when abused, DESTROYS YOU! Watch and see!"

Hope Troxell
Channel for School of Thought

To All Light Groups and Light Bearers: As received by the Channel, Phyllis Veronica, JUNE 17, 1963. Released by Star Light Fellowship, Unit 72, New York, N.Y., U.S.A.

THE LORD GOD * I AM THAT I AM *

I AM THE LORD THY GOD who speaketh unto Thee, O Daughter of ISRAEL. I AM with Thee always, even unto the end of the Latter Days which are now upon Thee, in the House of the Lord, Thy God, THE KING of ALL ISRAEL. I AM the Conqueror of the unjust; the Leavening of the Bread of Peace that shall Leaven the Whole Loaf.

The Third Time has ISRAEL fallen and risen again to take up Her Cross along the long, hard pathway the many have worn in traveling before Her. WATCH YE, AND PRAY, for the Time is <u>nigh at hand</u> when I SHALL JUDGE THE SHEEP OF MY FOLD, and Pray I that not one shall be found wanting! For long have I awaited Thee to stumble on to the Path of Righteousness for My Name's sake, and only You who can bear the hardness of the Bitter Cup shall be worthy to be Possessed by ME, when in the Last Hour I SHALL SEEK MY ENTRANCE UNTO THEE. O, My Blessed Lambs, My Blessed and Beloved Flock from My Pasture, keep Thee in thy ways MY TRUTH, that My Covenant with Thee may not be broken of Men.

Stand fast and firm in MY LIGHT which overshadows Thee so that MY WORD, MY POWER may come unto Thee and give Thee STRENGTH, as you unveil and unmask yourselves of the physical verities, which are unnatural in the EYE OF THE FATHER of All of His Children. PRAY YE, therefore, after ME, that I may come closer unto Thee in the Rising of The Sun within YOU, so that the LIGHT may pour forth in Wisdom and in Love, your own Ascension after ME when it is Time that I COME.

PREPARE YE and make ready, for already the Threshing has begun. For the Seed has risen above ground and is being Blessed by the Rays of the SUN to Bear Fruit after the labors of the Harvest Time. For They have been imprisoned, but have now been sent forth to sow Restitution in MY WAY that I AM bringing forth for them to travel. You have MY MARK upon You, who shall deliver unto ME those who cannot as yet see ME for the dust within the eye.

Let, therefore, thine eye sparkle as the LIGHT OF THE SUN, so that Ye may heal that which Ye shall look upon in the Days Ahead, which are Now upon MY DOORSTEP.

ENTER YE INTO MY SPIRITUAL WATERS, for Thou art JOHN Whom I have already sent to Baptise Thee in MY NAME. Let Ye who hear KNOW, and Ye who can see UNDERSTAND. For the Days of the Parables have begun to pass over, for THE LIGHT is no more hidden, but has risen above the shadows of mortal time Which has told its Given TIME.

REJOICE YE, WHO CARRY MY YOKE. For thy burden is made lighter in the carrying thereof. PRAY FOR ME to come closer unto Thee All, for THE FATHER has granted Thee ALL in MY NAME that is asked.

BE IN THE PEACE of He that lieth in thy womb and is preparing for THE BIRTH that shall raise up the Tomb unto the lush Garden of the LAND OF THE EVERLASTING SUN.

BLESS the Holy Ground wherein Ye stand, for in that Place I AM THE LOVING CHRIST IN ALL OF THE FATHER's GLORIOUS VICTORIES which He has given ME to bear up the Earth Plane.

* I AM THAT I AM, WITH YOU ALWAYS AND EVERLASTINGLY *

COSMONKNIGHTS

Dear CosmonKnights,

We want you to know about a lovely club in Canada, called the Kindness Club. They have put out a very fine book for all who love animals and want to know really HOW TO BE KIND, which is the title. This is a book for boys and girls and their parents and contains in it suggestions for forming kindness clubs among your friends, as well as giving you many stories about the wonderful intelligence of pets and wild creatures. Dr. Albert Schweitzer thought this was such a great idea that he wrote a letter of praise to the people who have brought all this information together for you, and it is printed at the front of the book. You may buy a copy at Cosmon for $1.00. Add .04 sales tax if you live in California, and .10 more for postage.

HOW TO BE KIND
By Joyce Lambert

Our magazine is so full this month of so many things that we are going to publish two letters from other CosmonKnights instead of a communication to you from the Space People or a long letter from me. Vicky is eleven, as you know, and Frank Ninivaggi is sixteen. We hope you will read over what they have written and write to us about what you would like to see in the newsletter. If your letters are of great interest we may be able to publish parts of several letters from you, or one or two whole letters.

Several grownups have been sending us books for children and young adults so that you will be able to have a fine mailing library after awhile. This makes us very happy and we again say THANKS to all who have so generously sent help to the CosmonKnight group, and books for lending.

With love from your friend,

Barbara Steele

Dear Cosmon Members,

This time I am writing this letter for the same reasons that I want to help you and think of more and more things to do.

When you are over at a friends house or at home and think you have nothing to do then sit down and think for a while. You will find out there is really a lot to do.

Look around and see if you can find some odd materials, then find some odd things to make with all the materials that you had found. Right there that will keep you busy for a while.

Don't always think of your self. Help others to find things to do. Then someday you won't have anything to do and they will help you to find something to do.

Wait patiently for things to happen and for things to do.

Don't say that you can't do something for I know you can, that is everybody can if they try and have the patients. For all it really takes is the person and the patients.

If you have the patients then you can do anything your heart desires.

When you make something don't always make it for your self. Make it for a friend or someone who does not have anything except a house to live and clothing. There lucky if they have that.

Thank GOD every night for your blessings. Be grateful that you have shelter, be grateful that you have people around you to help you and love you, be grateful that you have clothing. Thank GOD for all these things.

Don't get angry, jealous or impatient. Be calm, nice, generous and patient.

If you have any kind of pet at all don't spoil it. For it's sad to see when a person or animal is spoiled. Be nice to everybody and every animal. But don't get to nice. For it will spoil them.

If you follow the suggestions or at least try to follow them then you will be prepared for the NEW AGE. But you must try as hard as you can because it's not going to be easy.

Please feel free to wright back to me. Let's be friends. I would appreciate it if you would wright back and ask questions or anything you like.

    LOVE and LIGHT
    From VICKY CARSTENS

THE WISDOM OF A FOUR-YEAR-OLD

"My grandson Troy, four years of age, was viewing a picture of a dove I had just painted on a wall. He said:
  'Maryellen, how does God make things?'

I said:
  'Suppose you tell me, Troy.'

He replied:
  'Why, He just thinks up something in His mind, like a bird: then He pushes it out of His mind into the air.'"

   ... Sent by Maryellen Sullivan
       California

FEASIBILITY

Many people upon hearing the goals of Cosmon say that such ideas are impossible to be put into action. I think that in all honesty they are not to be called bigots because I know from experience that this is the most probable reaction of a person first hearing about Cosmon. Many of my friends have laughed and admonished me to stay away from such phony organizations. But through long and extensive investigation, I, myself, have realized that Cosmon is no ordinary group with old ideas just fixed up a bit to make them look new. Cosmon is prolific to old age thinking. We cannot go by old age thought any more. Now is the time for change. Today is the New Age. This is really the Age of Termination — the ending of old allegorical thinking in terms of religion, and the beginning of New Age ideas and True Age ideas. First, we must have hope in the future; for hope precedes faith. Then we shall have the faith necessary to begin our investigations in thinking. From this revolution in the concept of thinking, we shall procure the knowledge of the ages — and endless array of color and concept.

Because God is all-good and has shown us His goodness by creating us, is it not right that we, reflections of the Father, should be good and loving too.

I love God with all the love He has given to me. I hope that you love God in the fullest way possible and show this by loving your neighbor. Jesus of Nazareth said, "If you love me, you love my Father in heaven."

Do YOU love your Father in heaven?

I do!

    With Love and Light in God,

      Frank Ninivaggi

THE BOOK CORNER

SUGGESTED READING FOR ANIMAL LOVERS
Who Want to Read About Animals

(Not for Sale or Available through Cosmon Research Foundation)

KINSHIP WITH ALL LIFE by J. Allen Boone, Harper & Bros., N.Y., 1954

This modern classic had its origin in the writer's becoming friends with the famous movie dog, Strongheart, and his discovery that he had much to learn from the dog. Entertaining and philosophical, the book contains adventures with many animals, and a completely new point of view about man-animal relationship.

LETTERS TO STRONGHEART by J. Allen Boone, Prentice-Hall, N.Y., 1939

Letters written to Strongheart about the author's observations on people, animals, and foreign lands. Like Kinship With All Life, the book represents a warm and unusual philosophy of living. Out of print, but available in libraries and sometimes in 2nd hand bookstores.

EXPLORING INNER SPACE by Jane Dunlap, Harcourt, Brace, and World, N.Y., 1961

The writer relates her experiences with LSD — a chemical agent which causes profound changes in consciousness. In these sessions she had some intense inner experiences regarding animals. Her behavior and entire outlook on life alters as a result. A book of great spiritual meaning as well as wide psychological implications.

THE ANIMAL WORLD OF ALBERT SCHWEITZER, ed. by Charles Joy, The Beacon Press, Boston, 1950

A collection of Albert Schweitzer's writings on animals. It contains some fascinating anecdotes about animals in Africa; but the book is significant principally for its section on reverence for life and its discussion of the need for a broader ethical system, which shall insist upon man's ethical obligation to animals.

CATS' ABC by Beverly Nichols, E.T. Dutton and Co., N.Y., 1960

A slender and captivatingly illustrated volume, which no cat lover would want to miss. It is filled with wit, whimsy, and much practical information about cats from A (Amusements) to Z (Anything but Zoos).

THE FUR PERSON by May Sarton, Rinehart and Co., N.Y., 1957

This is a delightful story about a Cat About Town who decides to find himself a permanent home, and finally finds one that is suitable. He soon becomes a Gentleman Cat who obeys all the 10 Cat Commandments (I. A Gentleman Cat has an immaculate shirt front and paws at all times) and in the end becomes a real Fur Person.

ANGEL IN TOP HAT by Zulma Steele, Harper & Bros., N.Y., 1942

The biography of Henry Bergh, founder of the first Humane Society in the United States. Out of print, but available in libraries.

VOICE OF THE VOICELESS

A magazine which keeps its readers informed about events in Catland, Dogdom, and the animal kingdom generally, including those abuses and cruelties which cry out for correction. The need for humane education is stressed. $2 a year. P.O. Box 17403, Foy Station, Los Angeles 17, California.

A SURPRISE FOR YOU

After almost a year, we have been able to locate only seven copies of a wonderful book which was published in 1961. It is "THE MASTER H" by Pensatia, and I do not feel capable of reviewing such a marvelous work. It is a history of the many lives of a Master.

Why do so few of us heed the inner call to become a Master? When we have suffered much and the time is ripe the Master will appear.

This is a <u>must</u> reading for those who believe in Karma and Reincarnation and the Ones who have promised to help us to reach Their level.

I have read this book three times, and promise you this - if you buy one of the six books now left, and you think you do not like it, just mail it back to us and I shall send you my check for the price you paid. The price is $5.00 plus .15 postage, and .20 tax in California.

          Bartram

"The fossil strata show us that Nature began with rudimental forms, and rose to the more complex, as fast as the earth was fit for their dwelling place; and that the lower perish as the higher appear. Very few of our race can be said to be yet finished men. We still carry sticking to us some remains of the preceding inferior quadruped organization. We call these millions men; but they are not yet men. Half-engaged in the soil, pawing to get free, man needs all the music that can be brought to disengage him. If Love, red Love, with tears and joy; if Want with his scourge; if War with his cannonade; if Christianity with its charity; if Trade with its money; if Art with its portfolios; if Science with her telegraphs through the deeps of space and time; can set his dull nerves throbbing, and by loud taps on the tough chrysalis, can break its walls, and let the new creature emerge erect and free, — make way and sing paean! The age of the quadruped is to go out, — the age of the brain and of the heart is to come in. The time will come when the evil forms we have known can no more be organized. . . . And if one shall read the future of the race hinted in the organic effort of Nature to mount and meliorate, and the corresponding impulse to the Better in the human being, we shall dare affirm that there is nothing he will not overcome and convert, until at last culture shall absorb the chaos and gehenna. He will convert the Furies into Muses, and the hells into benefit."

        ESSAYS: 2nd Series
        Culture
        Ralph Waldo Emerson

CORRESPONDENCE FILE

ONE WOMAN'S EXPERIENCE

"I never was one able to pray aloud to God, whether alone or with others. My way was to just speak to Him at any time of day or night in my heart, silently within. But seeing how my church friends <u>voiced</u> their prayers, I thought perhaps my way was not the best, wondering with great anxiety if He really heard me. But to my great joy one day as I was talking to God in my heart, I heard my heart speaking out, as loud and clear as when a person is conversing with a friend. So in this wonderful way He showed me how easy it is for Him to hear <u>plainly</u> not only my heart's thoughts, but <u>every person's</u> thoughts.

"Another time I desired the riddance of my carnal mind that I might have the Mind of Christ, and one night I was awakened from sleep and felt as it were, the Finger of God make a clean sweep inside my brain. After this experience, I found my consciousness expanding and I was enabled to drop <u>all</u> church doctrines, and when I say all I mean it literally, every last shred — yet not without some trepidation. But I received great courage to drop all because, again, I was awakened at night and a clear, audible voice within me said, 'Behold, I make all things new. Shall ye not know it? Truth shall spring forth out of the earth.' So Christ is to be formed in us and come forth out of <u>us</u>, earth."

LOADED IDEAS DEPARTMENT

QUESTION:

"Have you thought of a way for man and woman to get in touch for writing along lines Cosmon teaches? Could you print name, age and address, single or married? Please don't think I want you to operate a marriage service. I like to correspond with people of kindred mind."

ANSWER:

We will try almost anything once, but we do not intend to turn Cosmon into a lonely hearts club or a tender trap baited with lonely widows and handsome love pirates.

If you have the cool nerve to publish your basic statistics, which should include your real name, your birth date for astrological investigators, your marital status and your mailing address, we may give a cautious trial and see what happens. But we are not guaranteeing anything in the way of redress or responsibility if you pull a lemon out of the hat or a bum steer from the corral.
(P.S. - What race are you?)

There are many ways to skin a cat and to hide a wolf in sheep's clothing. CAVEAT EMPTOR! - which means, "Let the buyer beware!" You take it from here!

C.R.F.

NOTICE

Single Guys and Gals (35 to 50 years young) wanted for week-end discussions, trips to mountains, walks, etc. Those with Metaphysical abilities or desires; knowledge of biochemistry, electronics, mineralogy, astronomy, chemistry, music, psychology, flying saucers, etc., etc., preferred. Write Don Bush, 639 Rosemont Ave., Pasadena, California 91103.

WORLD REPORT

Notes and Comments by Eugene Hurtienne

Earthquakes

Southern California is receiving the greater number of quakes of late.

Heart Disease

The American Heart Association in a scientific study, stated that there is a strong relationship between cigarette smoking and heart disease.

Miscellaneous Items

. . . 21 miles south of Amman, Jordan, a pyramid was unearthed which is believed to be associated with Moses.

. . . A temple of ancient Rome was found adjacent to a wine cellar in the nearby community of Marino, Italy. This temple is known to have been erected to the god Mithra.

. . . Off the coast of Italy the Island of Love is rising again, according to authorities.

. . . According to scientists at Scripps Institution of Oceanography, land in the Pacific is two miles above the ocean floor — the highest point still remains under 1-1/2 miles or 8,000 feet.

. . . A titanic volcano erupted beneath the surface of the Scotia Sea, just outside the Antarctic Circle.
(Comment — Could this be the cause of the glaciers along the coast of Antarctica to be receding faster than they should?)

. . . Doctors from Istanbul reported examining a woman claiming to be 168 years of age.

. . . The fourth finding of diamonds in a meteorite has just been discovered.

. . . Scientists have disclosed recently the detection of water vapor on Mars, thus increasing the chances of life on that planet.

Sky Mystery

Dr. James McDonald, a meteorologist at the Institute of Atmospheric Physics at Tucson, is puzzled by a cloud formation 26 miles up and 30 miles across. This cloud was first seen over Arizona at 6:10 P.M., N.E. of Prescott. It was next seen at 6:15 P.M. North of Phoenix. At 6:30 P.M. was sighted West, N.W. of Winslow. The shape of the cloud was circular, some describing it as a horseshoe and others as a doughnut. Could this have been a U.F.O. giving off ionization, thus causing water vapor to form?

Tidbits

. . . At 11:30 P.M., June 25 in the area of Riverside and Elsinore, there was felt a shock of great strength, but was no earthquake, for it wasn't recorded in any of the nearby seismological laboratories.

. . . Two new mountains have been found by Japanese oceanographers in the eastern part of the Indian Ocean.

. . . A European is saving our crops. A wasp accidentally introduced to North America is saving California crops from destruction by an insect pest that has troubled growers for years. Seems that many crops will no longer be sprayed or dusted by chemical, for if they are the wasp is apt to go.

. . . From Nevada comes a report that man has lived in that area 32,000 years ago.

In Closing

I suggest that those who can get the June issue of Search magazine, do so and read the article,
"Who's to Blame if America
is Destroyed?"
Most interesting article.

FLUTE PLAYER

cosmon

OCTOBER 1963

RESEARCH FOUNDATION
P. O. Box 483
Oro Grande, Calif.

YOUR RESEARCH FOUNDATION DEDICATED TO DEVELOPING MAN SPIRITUALLY AND PHYSICALLY FOR THE NEW AGE AND SUPPORTED BY YOU.

Gloria Lee, Founder

COSMON NEWSLETTER

CONTENTS

Greetings from Gloria	3
Message from J.W.	6
Message from a Master	9
En Route with Barbara Steele	12
Books to Help You Grow	20
Exploring Human Emotions	22
Correspondence File	25
Idea File	28
Vegetarian Recipes	29

Cover drawing by Albert Roger

Copyright © 1963 by Cosmon Research Foundation
All rights reserved. Printed in U.S.A.

GREETINGS FROM GLORIA

My many dear Friends,

It's time to get another newsletter ready, I see, and so I have come to chat with you. I appreciate all the nice letters you write to Cosmon saying you still care about having me keep up the contact. Thanks!

It's easy for me to know that you wish I would clear up some matters regarding who I am using as channels these days, and which communications tagged with my name are authentic, in view of the opposed claims and widely separated locations involved. Some of the things I am supposed to have written, have come through in word-patterns hard to attribute to me as you remember me, but you have to make allowances for the personal coloring and individuality of each Instrument. Even if the Channel does not sign a name, you finally are able to tell who brought through the message because of the differences in spiritual understanding, language use, and personal prejudices or blind spots that block out or change or misinterpret some of the ideas we try to put across.

When I was in a physical body I was like you; I didn't want any secrets kept from me. I wanted to know about every detail of everything, all the time; so I can sympathize with you, but now I am in better understanding of the whys and wherefores of a necessity to hold back considerable information on a great many subjects that you would like to have revealed according to your exact specifications. (I was the same way, so help me!) Now I can observe, for they have taken the trouble to show me, how Truth becomes garbled and — (I almost said loused up) but I will substitute "confused" — after it has taken a zigzag course through a few earth-conscious minds. We must be very cautious in presenting ideas to you so they may stand a chance of not getting botched up and misinterpreted beyond the point of safety. It is up to us to study you carefully before we make the mistake of thinking you can channel or handle a given subject, when your mind is already loaded with preconceived notions that will color everything you get from us on certain lines of thought.

Now for one thing, I have often incarnated as a teacher of the subjects included in what we call the Ancient Wisdom. Quite a few of these incarnations were taken in Egypt where I was often a head priestess in a temple. Large groups of individuals came under my direction, care and influence. A special reason, among other reasons, for my most recent incarnation was the fact that most of my former students were and are in incarnation, and it was intended that I should have the facilities given me to reach them and to clarify for them parts of my teachings given in the past, which were not then understood or accepted by them in the life periods of our closer personal association.

Most of you do not know that the idea behind Cosmon Research Foundation germinated in those ancient Egyptian days and involved thousands of individuals who were then set aside for preparation to take part in the beginning of the Golden Age of now, that is just dawning on the horizon of our thinking! I do not make the claim that Cosmon is the only group of Light to hold ancient beginnings or the only one to have relationships with many people who would work specifically through one particular center, but I am telling you what was told to me and given to me in visions and dreams and mental projections into the past as well as the future. Well, as I started to tell you, a teacher is obligated to assume responsibility for all the knowledge and information passed to others, and it is up to the teacher to use wisdom in judging how much or how little the individual pupil can take in and assimilate and apply to his own life problems.

No teacher, no matter how capable and discerning, below the degree of Master Teacher, is a perfect teacher or one who goes through life without making mistakes and creating negative karma along with the good accomplished. I made many mistakes as a teacher and caused many karmic ties between myself and others, some of them of great need to be adjusted and still of unfinished business. My last life, spent among you until quite recently, had been intended to continue for another fifty years or so in order that the majority of these relationships could be brought into constructive balance. We were to use Cosmon (within the over-all Plan of God for the transition period) as a magnetic center vibrating to religion, science, education and the arts, which would sound a spiritual call to all those students and friends of the past with whom both J.W. and I had worked.

Under J.W.'s guidance I had been enabled to set up a mental-emotional climate or frequency through the publication of his first book, WHY WE ARE HERE, which harmonized with the frequency patterns of those karmically related to me. As I have lived many lifetimes, you can realize I established a great many relationships with large numbers of people. This is what is so devastating to me now, or would be if I let myself stop and think about it, that there were plans set up for hundreds of people to participate with me in the inner work of Cosmon. We had all incarnated for this mutual purpose within God's Plan, and we were to be associated within a program that would almost stagger you if I could tell you all that was outlined to me by J.W. and many other Teachers and Space People as far back as 1959.

Cosmon, in some form or another will continue to serve and will expand just to the degree that all of you can vision the possibilities and help to support it for the time being. It necessarily cannot yet be brought out as intended at the time of J.W.'s and my founding of it, because it was my personal karmic project and one which had been planned, and a certain type personality prepared for me to work in, for many thousands of years.

Now everything is temporarily changed, at least for this immediate cycle. I have told you these things so you will see that I am trying to salvage all the loss that I can, by going to the many groups and individuals who would have sooner or later worked in or with Cosmo and giving them the help and guidance and messages permitted to me that rightfully belonged to them in the longer range plan. Not all of these people were my pupils. Some of them were former friends who came with me from other planets to be among the helpers and teachers of the earth people, and whom I have known for ages of time. There are all kinds relationships involved, and as these various people, scattered over the world in their different nationalities and different settings, bring through claims that I am with them, I often am. I will not say that everything come through to your level exactly as I intended, ar sometimes I only dropped a thought or two in someone's mind and it was strung out to book length or a series of communications. The point is, as it always has been and will be, that principles of TRUTH are what really cou with God and <u>for</u> man, and it matters very lit tle how they come or from whom so long as they are good and wise and helpful suggestior for the spiritual and physical development of mankind.

Cosmon was to have had many departments. Now I have to go across the face of t planet to find some of the people who were to work in one aspect or another, and give to each of them some small part of what it was intended they should undertake in collaborati with many others.

In spite of what you hear and what has been publicized, I am not in distress or anxi ety about Cosmon as it is presently set up. My friends now managing my personal cente are looking out for my interests and their ai is to keep the pot boiling until I can return a take it up where I left off. They would all d anything under the sun to help me, and each me has been tested almost beyond endurance by deciding to keep the center alive. You who receive the newsletter haven't any conception what it has cost my friends in sweat and tears and total dedication of total resources so that my work could go on. You often wonder why more benefits aren't forthcoming, but if you could know the inside story, you would think it a miracle that there is so much vitality and love and enthusiasm operating steadily for my benefit and yours.

My first efforts to help from this side seemed to cause a great deal of turmoil and stirred up misunderstandings and caused a split in people's personal loyalties, due to some of the things I was supposed to have said. It was a big test to me as well as to you. I wish, and I know you do, that everyone could be in harmony, Light and goodwill, but so long as there are people on so many different levels of spiritual understanding, those on the lower steps are bound to misread the motives and goals of those on a higher plateau of wisdom. There is a great tendency among earth minds to believe they are the chosen, the elect and the ones on the higher steps, and it is rough on us over here to blast through all these delusions and come out with anything near the real facts. Everybody on earth walks in a perfect cloudbank of seething illusions. It's a wonder anybody can hold a mental projection steadily in the light above all this cloud mass. That some manage to get up into the light quite often and even to spend considerable time there, is almost beyond belief.

Maybe this will help to explain to you the ups and downs of people you would like to follow and whose ideas appeal to you, but who are so darn changeable and so far from living up to their own stated ideals that you get dizzy trying to keep track of their swinging first to the left and then to the right and then see them stop without warning in the middle, only to start swinging again.

The real swing is a shift back-and-forth, up-and-down between some degree of Christ-consciousness and plain old customary earth-consciousness. You could say people veer between the consciousness of God-man and animal-man. When they are down, which is most of the time, they are very earthy, mass-minded, swept by their human emotions, and full of self-doubt, fear and suspicion. When they are Christ-minded, they are full of benevolence, generosity, goodwill, patience, compassion and affection, and even wisdom.

It will be so helpful when events take place that will peel the scales from people's spiritual eyes, so they can see people for what they really are. People will some day glow forth their own radiance according to the degree of self-effort they have made in evolutionary advancement. You will see everything from 7 1/2 watt human light globes up to a few 500 watt ones, but most will be somewhere near the middle; maybe even that is too optimistic. But anyway, you will then see your own light and the lights of others and there won't be any way you can wiggle out of showing your true self, whatever it is.

Quite a few people think I will return soon, and they wonder if I will be permitted to show myself to you in an etheric body, or will I reincarnate, or maybe can I take possession of some good female body that has just lost its tenant by death. Well it is too soon to say, and depends on so very many events and on how much I can accomplish with present equipment where I am. Demand proof before you swallow any sudden claims that I have come back, because it is very easy for even the dark forces to imitate anyone's appearance and mannerisms. In the past they have often fooled the elect, so be on guard and use your common sense, whatever comes out.

Thank you all for helping to keep Cosmon going!

In love and Light,

Gloria Lee

MESSAGE FROM J.W.

Once again, Earth Children, I come to greet you.

My theme today is the Waiting Period in which we seem as eager vessels becalmed; forced upon our own resources until Heaven sees fit to generate those momentums which will again furnish the Go-power which we await with so much expectancy.

I say we, because those of us on other planes of action are becalmed also, to a degree. We came to help you and the first fruits of our mission are now being gathered in a somewhat unforeseen manner, though we were with hope from the outset that you might become more aware of your own capacities to take initiative and to think for yourselves in some of the areas which you have formerly bypassed. A thrill of new force of a higher vibration is being registered within the mass nature. It is not generally defined as that which it really is, but it is having its effect and is opening up depths of perception as well as dissolving some of the blindfolds which have served to restrain the racial entity from plunging forth into greater accomplishments upon the spiritual frontier.

Through my instrument, Gloria Lee, I told you that we of other planetary affiliations and realms of Being have left many personal relationships and objectives behind and set aside plans dear to us as individuals, in order to help you cope with the torrents of conflicting powers bringing your Golden Age to birth. Although we have developed a larger patience because we have a greater sweep of vision plus awareness of many plans that lie hidden from you in the (to you) inscrutable Mind of God, we are still touched by that common bond which causes our own heart longings to move in one particular direction or another, and though we have much to occupy ourselves, and seasoned control of our personal natures, we too yearn for the Day of Release even as you, when the tension of necessity can be dropped to allow our return to that which is waiting for our attention.

Because your race has allowed itself to forego the privilege of consistent exercise of the higher faculties innate within man, you have deteriorated in some aspects of your racial character, while developing disfiguring propensities and attributes of ponderable value in other facets. To state it simply, you are unbalanced, asymmetrical and "out of drawing". Perhaps you can better understand if I say that some of your characteristics have become grossly exaggerated until many of you have become as caricatures of the original concept held for you in the God-Mind of the Being Who brought you forth. If you could see some of your selves as we are able, it would shock even those of hardened sensibilities to look upon some of the travesties walking the Earth and calling themselves men and women. Some of them seem to be as funnels for intake that have no arrangement for carrying off outflow, and their acquisitive natures are thus bloated and pumped up to proportions that would astonish them, while their physical bodies reflect the inner imbalance in various forms of disease. Still others are as open-ended channels which allow a perpetual flow-through, without means for selective appropriation of nutritive material for mind and emotions from the constantly moving stream of consciousness, and these individuals are in continuous attenuation as though possessed of a subjective tapeworm of voracious appetite. Still others seem to have developed colossal hands for clenching and grasping, while feet appear to be changed to roots which hold the character attached to a single idea, and render it incapable of response to any new and improved suggestions.

Such are a few random symbols to illustrate our observations. Fortunately there are goodly numbers of your planetary race who give every appearance of development, self-undertaken, along more harmonious and agreeable lines. True Beauty is characterized by a fluid grace of line if not of motion, and is apparent though the aggregation of elements which set it forth in person, object or location may be in a form arrested by art of sculpture.

Still is given forth the implication of adaptability to circumstance, without loss of the proportioned blending of component parts which register it as pleasing to the perceiving consciousness.

The Earth people are, as a unit, possessed by desire for new sensations, new information, new objects and new relationships. At best this shows forth the innermost urge impelling to self-discovery, inventiveness and evolvement toward inhabitation of higher forms of life. At worst it is a gluttony and retrogression toward artificial gratifications that sink one into morbid and deluded depths of negativity.

Be not among those waiting beneath the Tree of Life in open-mouthed hope of falling plums. Be users of ingenuity and create for yourselves a ladder constructed of aspiration and perspiration in equal parts, that you may climb upward and gather fruits, not only for the advancement of your own concerns, but for the general good, enough and to share.

Have done with this listless attitude of apathy which retreats from reality and views the ebbing Age as a withdrawal of all that has been well-loved and familiar; the death of that which you were taught to consider the sum of all that was best and most worthy of cherishing because tamed and domesticated and docile to command of levers, gears and pushbuttons that were shaped to comfortable manipulation by your Piscean physical bodies. Do not look back and become enmeshed with the processes that destroy by crystallization and create pillars of salt from static personifications of despair. Do not weep for dead yesterdays. Smile for living tomorrows!

That latent GOODNESS in you, waiting your call to action, is more than equal to the sum of challenges constantly hurled within the radius of your constructive preparations for the Aquarian civilization. Be that invulnerable Christ energy, in expression of your true spiritual Self. Be discovered among the builders who are engrossed in the absorbing task of creating new receptacles, of unprecedented shapes and materials, to receive the new wine of life that is ready to flow into all those forms of sufficient ductility for reception of an exuberant elixir!

Upon your plane, you have occasionally had opportunity to study individuals waiting for an assured inheritance to be delivered into their hands upon the demise of the current holder of assets. Sometimes these hapless mortals have been outlived by the unexpectedly vigorous relative or friend, and have passed to other realms of life with very little to show for their gift of incarnation and opportunity for self-progress. Others have frittered away their waiting periods in idle amusements or bitter impatience. Having laid no thrifty plans, nor at the same time employed themselves in useful pursuits, yet they have received their awaited inheritance in due course only to find they are lacking in sufficient control over themselves and their thirst for power and prestige to handle wisely and invest their acquired benefits in future security, and so their gains swiftly disappear along the runnels grooved by their weaknesses of character.

It is by such symbolic means that I hope to warn you anew it is of utmost importance to place your capital of time and strength in fields of general usefulness, tending toward realization of the Plan of God, while the duration of your individual waiting periods are yet undetermined and in some smaller or greater measure adjustable to proportionate effort on your part to arouse yourself to heightened consciousness, before the Storms of Cleansing force personnel to enter those places of sanctuary and shelter reserved for workers of proven merit and, I might add, valor.

The time of now is in your hands. It is the only "time" anyone has ever possessed. In the now we shall create attainments, or our names will not be listed among those wanted for heavy-duty assignments in the rescue work, salvaging and clean-up still ahead of the planet as a whole. Those who are not faithful stewards of the comparatively small duties they have now, cannot expect to be given even greater responsibilities later on, when right work habits and character developments will be of far greater significance than ever before in the long history of birth, life and decline of world cultures.

Our great need is for all-purpose individuals who can be placed at any point of urgency and give a good account of themselves by putting sound principles into operation, regardless of the kind of demand or the unusualness of their situation. These will take hold and make a try and show some proportion of success in any placement, however humble or authoritative. Therefore I urge upon you, while there is yet a measure of daylight, yet a period of relative stability in planetary affairs, to make the most of what is now in your hands. Do not stop by the wayside to ponder and wonder. Roll up your sleeves and work beyond the limits of your human imagination. Fall back, in prayer and meditation, upon the limitless imagination of God; and as you glimpse some of the ineffable ideas He holds in store for this world, dedicate your boundless determination to Him to become His co-worker for bringing them into being.

With my personal love and gratitude to all of you who are giving of yourselves without reservation to the task of ushering in the Golden Age!

Your friend,

J. W. of Jupiter

A PERSONAL PRAYER
Given by J. W. to one of the Cosmon workers

Father within me,
I affirm my eternal being
Within the love of your knowing.
I am sent forth by You and I
Will not fail.
My security lies in doing
Your WILL according to the
Utmost of my unfolding understanding.
So let it be forever:
A blending of MIND and mind,
HEART and heart; seeking only
To give forth that which is.

MESSAGE FROM A MASTER

Our Friends, our Disciples,
  our Co-workers; — Greetings.

I come to you in thought, by invitation, to bring forth into your minds a broadened understanding of the setting in which you perform your functions of service, of personal duties and of relating yourselves, as best you are able, to the wider picture set before you piece by piece, to be received within your minds according to their severally-developed powers of synthesis.

As has been told our people repeatedly, they are set forth in the midst of conflicting forces to fight for the Cause of Truth and Righteousness and to maintain what stability of outlook and perseverance of action is possible to them, while strained to the utmost of capacity. This is, need I emphasize it, a period of prolonged and anguishing testing, embracing trials of every sort; some so subtle, some so obvious that an individual participant is hard-pressed indeed to find a lasting source of certainty and to stand firm by his innermost convictions, despite continuous hostile suggestions and menacing actions that would tempt him off his course to defend his personal honor and to challenge his opposing combatants to hand-to-hand battle for determination of superiority.

We are Teachers as well as Generals in this battle between the forces of good and evil, and like Teachers in a classroom, we may not undertake the task of pointing out to you where lie the correct answers to those tests which, if you pass them, will indicate your fitness for inclusion in a progressed world culture; which, if you fail them, will cause you to be placed in the position of having to repeat spiritual schooling for a term lasting many centuries, but during which your memory will be veiled to the true implications of your incarnations thus repeated, and will therefore save you the mental suffering of recognizing your loss of opportunity and your seeming loss of time.

Since time is an illusion, and since that which is repeated develops a deepened impression upon the consciousness, it can be said that beyond all considerations of loss, suffering, separation and personal failure to pass into a higher grade of evolution with the majority of one's classmates, there are yet compensations for those who slip temporarily behind, as well as for those who enable themselves, by application of total abilities for a protracted period, to enter into more intimate relationship with those spiritual intelligences responsible for that which is to come forth in the Golden Age now dawning.

Although at every such cyclic termination as you are experiencing, there are upheavals and churnings and displacements in every phase of existence, this termination is freighted with deeper significance; for as your guides and teachers have explained to you, your current incarnation is centered in a purpose vast and incomprehensible to mortal minds. You have been told that this is a Cosmic interval in which the very gods and their gods are undergoing term-end examinations that will afford them, in their high and illimitable reaches of awareness and responsibility, initiations into yet greater inclusions of knowledge, power and capacity for furthering the constructive purposes of the MIND over all.

If it were not for your allotment of self-determining individualized intelligence, you would indeed be the Fate-swept pawns of destiny you often fancy yourselves to be, but free will, the power to think and your essential oneness with HIM in Whom we live and move and have our being, place you in a category of relative choice and considerable influence upon the outcome of this present situation.

Many of you are of divided loyalties, and find yourselves swinging now toward the forces of one side of the battle and again toward the other forces on the opposing side. You are swayed back and forth by impacts of suggestion registered upon your vulnerable emotional nature. Your feelings seem at times to be overwhelmingly lured by the pyrotechnical displays of force, color and personal authority exhibited by the claim-making legions of dark intention, whereas at other times your feelings are captivated as wholly by recognition of visions disseminated through the instrumentalities of those dedicated to service of the Light. It is feeling, my friends, that sweeps you beyond the shallows close to familiar shores, and carries you to depths wherein you place yourselves at the mercy of those who exercise control of rougher seas and deeper water.

The deeps are for strong swimmers or patient floaters. Those who are washed beyond the depths they can control, on tides of great emotion, place themselves at the disposal of whatever beings happen to be available for rescue work in the area entered. If the beings encountered are such that a pact of loyalty is demanded before rescue is completed, the individual who finds himself in need of help is without bargaining power and must accept the terms offered in exchange for continuity of existence.

A general question is formulated by humanity which could be translated: "Why, if we are under test, must we be blindfolded?" And to this, answer is given that only in such manner can you awaken the higher spiritual faculty of intuitive knowing, which alone can save you in a situation which gives rise to continuous new sequences of illusion. Little as you may believe it, the usual five senses you possess, unfed by intuition and working singly or in conflict among themselves, bring only beclouded messages and false reports to the dweller in earth consciousness, and cause mirages to appear as solid realities.

The weak minds, the childish minds, the uncontrolled minds, the minds continually at the mercy of their own feelings of animosity, fear, hate, doubt and despair, are those prizes eagerly sought as spoils of victory in the mighty battle between the forces of Light and the forces of darkness. You have heard it said that the true battlefield is situated upon the mental plane where the goal is, conquering the minds of men, so far as this planet is concerned. Mankind, as an entity, comprises the work force of the physical level and whoever controls this vast force, en masse, determines what shall be accomplished with the resources of the physical plane and whether or not this world shall be a playground for the forces of selfishness, greed and egotism, or a temple of planned spiritual education for the further schooling of gods.

Because the Father has given the gift of free will to His children of this earth, it remains in their hands, for yet a little while, to choose their individual loyalties and to abide upon one course or the other, but not upon both; for no man can serve faithfully two Masters of opposite philosophical principles.

Some of you remember well the early anxieties which preceded the crucial moment of your determination to tread the Path of Discipleship. You questioned whether, by giving yourselves over to rules of discipline and self-control, you would yet retain that treasured and accustomed measure of personality which acted as your instrument for gathering impressions and experiences open to your earth-surface existence. You felt then as if you might, quite possibly, be selling yourselves unwittingly into conditions little better than slavery, which would mean irrevocable burning, by higher forces, of those bridges built in the past by your desires for pleasure and personal gain.

Then the years passed swiftly beyond your point of decision and you came to know for yourselves the certainty that on the Path of Returning, there are demands beyond the performance exacted from those of lesser advancement, but "the compensations are adequate" for they, too, are beyond the compensations realized by those of smaller daring. My Brother and Senior Disciple, Djwhal Khul, has often reminded his students in their moments of faintheartedness that the "conditions are hard, but equal." This cannot be proven by you until your experience contains knowledge of the individual ascensions of your brothers and sisters, who, to your yet fettered vision seem to meet aught but equal degrees of difficulty. Some evoke your pity, others your envy, due to viewing a minute portion of the long road of their climbing. Your road, too, is taking you upward through a patchwork of shadow and sunshine, whereupon are confronted many tunnels of death leading to rebirth and to shifts of scene and changes of companionship.

To you of the comparative lowlands of spiritual knowing, who yet walk in alternate mists and filtered rays of the true spiritual sun, all appears so different from the vision accorded to those centered in Reality. You hear Our Call, yet doubt your hearing and call it an echo of your own wishful thinking. You deny your best and most sensitive apparatus for contact with Us, your intuitive faculty, and dismiss acknowledgement of its existence as if it were an artificial graft, fastened to your imagination.

Despite all these inequalities and your continued involvement with the emotional glamors and mental illusions spun from your own incomplete personality natures, we hold forth great hope and welcome your steady approach as a throng of those very dear to our hearts, and eagerly awaited for reception within the Hall of Wisdom. We may not do your work or pass your tests for you, nor could our Teachers, in Their turn, do as much for Us, but we can do much to light your Way that is Our Way and the Way of Returning to the Father.

In drawing my short discourse with you to a conclusion, I leave with you a prayer familiar to many disciples in the East and in the West:

The Gayatri

Oh Thou Who giveth sustenance to the Universe;
From Whom all things doth proceed,
And to Whom all things must return,
Unveil to us the face of the true Spiritual Sun,
Hidden by a disk of golden light,
That we may see the Truth and do our whole duty
Ere we journey to Thy sacred feet.

With my desire that you, too, may do your whole duty ere you reach His sacred feet.

Koot' Hoomi LalSingh

Intuition is a knowing that comes from the universal wisdom into the individual awareness. It enters from the inner side of life, through the center of the heart. There it can be felt, spreading like opening petals of a flower, expanding into and becoming part of the living consciousness. It cannot be rejected because it is certainty.

From the Diary of a Disciple

EN ROUTE

Our dear Readers,

Hello in October. The weather is cooling down on the desert, joy be (!). Now it is easier to concentrate on work. I hope every one of you has had days of happiness in your summer and opportunities for change, rest and recreation.

While I think of it, do any of you gardeners have a handful of extra flower bulbs from your Fall transplanting and thinning or a few choice seeds you would like to send us for the beginning of a Cosmon friendship garden? We are just renting this center of 10 bare acres and two buildings, until firm directions are given us to stay here permanently or to leave for higher ground. We know this depends on what forms the earth changes take, and so we are ready and willing to stay or go. Meanwhile, in whatever time we have, we would so enjoy starting an oasis, at least around the buildings. We have a few scattered shrubs, and our kind landlord brought us several young Chinese elms for one side of the office building, but the general outlook is very unaesthetic and I would love to poke in some vine seeds, bulbs and bare-root plants for a better appearance next spring.

* * * * * * *

Thanks for all the interesting letters you have written since the August newsletter went out, and thanks for all the loving donations you have sent us. In comparison to all the plans folded up in our minds, it seems as if we are making slow headway in pushing back the horizons and spreading a wider variety of services before you. But we are trying.

* * * * * * *

The Cosmon library is nearer the circulation stage. It really is! But we have had no less than five volunteer helpers since it began; each is a reader in different fields of literature and no two have agreed under which categories each book should be entered for classification by the Dewey Decimal System. In looking through the shelves I discovered books of the same title scattered under different headings, and our latest volunteer is having difficulties in unsnarling and rearranging the books for easier finding. Most of the book now have their title cards and date slips and are recorded in the title and author card indexes, but they must all be listed and printed in a brochure to make selection possible for those who will borrow by mail. One of our friends asked how much it would cost to mail books back and forth. Since they vary in size and weight, we cannot tell you in advance, but there are postage rates for books and library material which can save us money. Just check the amount of postage when you receive your books and the same amount should return them to us. We have asked those who can afford it to please pay two-way mailing costs, especially because there are those who cannot pay anything, but should have the privilege of sharing our books. Please use the same jiffy bag or mailer to return books to us and we shall just keep the containers in circulation as long as they will hold up!

* * * * * * *

Sincere apologies go to you who have waited many weeks for replies to your letters. You wonder what on earth happens here. Some of your letters are very, very long because you are very full of problems, ideas, loneliness, or questions. I cannot always stop to more than skim through these right away; to give Bartram your book orders, requests for extra newsletters and donations for the account records. My three work piles of newsletter, correspondence and office details keep me busy all the time. There is always a newsletter on the way; never a vacation as you might suppose. A few of you are in peculiar personal circumstances where your needs cannot easily be met unless someone takes the initiative to do so, and I have promised you books and letters and have just had to keep some of you waiting beyond all limits of courtesy and friendship. Please forgive me until I catch up.

You aren't forgotten.

It would be very welcome to receive more funds from you, earmarked for book gifts to our friends in institutions and in foreign countries. I have told you before how exorbitant airmail rates are for getting newsletters and correspondence to our friends in other lands, and we would very sincerely appreciate your help in providing this faster service.

* * * * * * *

A good proportion of our readers wish we would print more material on diet, world news, psychology and so forth. We wish we would too, and hope to do so in the future. We had also hoped to establish a youth department as a monthly feature for different ages of children, but no children responded and the older young people like to share in the adult material and to write to us as individuals who have ideas to exchange; so we have dropped that younger section until we are shown it is wanted to a greater degree, or until people trained to handle it come forth and show us their qualifications. We haven't time to gather and comment on the endless news in all the fields that interest you, and the clippings you send in are so sparse and irregular that we have not enough to send on to Eugene Hurtienne for processing into anything like the news section you tell us you want. We will do all we can alone, and when you care enough to follow up your suggestions with tangible efforts, we'll be delighted to go even further — with your help.

* * * * * * *

CORRECTIONS
Bartram noticed two goofs or shurdlus in our September newsletter, after it was printed. I goofed by saying that I went wading in a branch of the Mojave river. Shows I'm a greenhorn in these regions. Bartram asked "What branch?" It seems they be'nt any branch; just one twisty stream! Pardon me. ... The other goof was Jim's. He was probably nodding and dozing over his post-midnight typing when he slipped in a "Here" instead of a "Hear" in Marty Sadler's communication from Jesus on page 25, beginning of third paragraph. So sorry.

* * * * * * *

Some of our readers (drawn to our mailing list, Heaven knows how or why) suspicion we are up to no good and have some kind of a confidence game going to rook our subscribers. But first off, we don't have any subscribers. We send out our newsletter free, without publicity or promises of anything to anyone who reads what we print. No one is under any obligation to read, join, subscribe or donate. We do not have any paid ads. We do not know from month to month how funds will be supplied for our continuance. We do all that we know how, and give to the limit of our present capacity, to help spread those ideas and messages compiled by us from many sources that concern the New Age and our part in it — all of us, that is.

But I can sympathize with the writer of a letter quoted in part under CORRESPONDENCE FILE this month. To get into one of these Space Age publications by pure chance, without any background or precedent, might conceivably leave a body filled with foreboding, and doubtful as to whether he mightn't be caught up in a group of tetched minds who appear to speak with equal emphasis of mermaids and vegetarian casseroles, Space People and organic gardening, angels, fairies and herb tea, Life on Uranus and etheric vehicles, mental telepathy and race prejudice. Perhaps, for such as he, we should backtrack every once in awhile, just to clarify where we think we are heading in the midst of such varied scenery.

Readers such as this, whether they know it or not, are behind the times — our times, at any rate, with all the turbulence and miscellany of subjects flooded out of their safe little mental dwellings of yesterday and mingling now in wild confusion on the bosom of heaving waters rampaging through broken levees of Piscean prejudice. We are at home among all these seeming paradoxes, which we discovered long ago by wandering in the attics and basements of life where so much is stored away.

Now that New Age energies have floated so many of these mysteries into the open, it seems scary, and the majority of folks who share the surface of the earth with us have not prepared themselves to deal with the gifts brought on high waters.

Cosmon Research Foundation was founded because Gloria Lee received so many interested letters asking for further teachings and instructions along the lines of the material in J.W.'s first book written through her, WHY WE ARE HERE. Her first intention was the building up of a New Age esoteric school, and she proceeded quite a distance with this thought in mind. Little by little her project took on extended territory until it embraced the many aspects and divisions of human living per se, and it was decided that the name Cosmon should encompass in very fact the wholeness which surrounds us. Soon she was outlining future departments for the study of and participation in New Age religion, science, art, government, philosophy, psychology, archaeology, occult principles, psychic unfoldment, etc. etc., until she had gathered what appeared to be a projected mental diet for people of the most divergent or inclusive tastes.

Gloria was one who tested her theories upon herself. She went direct to teachers who could show her how to develop mental telepathy, automatic writing, clairvoyance, mental projection, psychometry, palmistry, mental exploration of the past for evidence of reincarnation, and the power to communicate with Intelligences of other worlds and realms.

When we met she had made considerable progress in these various fields of extrasensory perception and had convinced herself, through endless trials and tests undertaken in company with many different individuals considered qualified, by their peers, in these fields, of the reasonableness and logic behind claims to psychic powers, means for safe unfoldment of these in the ordinary normal individual, and methods for placing her findings before the public in an informal but intelligent format which would divest them of fearsome mumbo-jumbo and convince skeptics of the universal distribution of such powers, since before history was recorded.

It was intended that from Cosmon would go out steady streams of books (written by many New Age authors, and not only Cosmon members), periodicals and study courses, lecturers, teachers and artisans of all kinds, but with the common denominator of New Age ideals for the Brotherhood of Man on an interplanetary scale. There were to be many locations, for many kinds of projects, across the globe. There were planned to be scientific laboratories, in which the Space People had promised to work side by side with qualified humans. There were to be television stations, radio networks, theatres, schools, studios of all the arts and crafts; temples for the coming together of angels and men, vast office buildings set in tremendous parks and gardens; fleets of planes, cars and trucks, spacecraft for interplanetary travel; health and diet centers, retreats for study and meditation, hotels, motels, and shopping centers; New Age clothing production or affiliation with manufacturers for creation of more beautiful, healthful garments, shoes and other accessories and cosmetics. There were to be centers and workshops for child care, right human relationships and all other subjects related to the coming Aquarian culture, now well-formed in outline in the Master minds behind our scenes and ready for sharing through those accepting human minds who will give voice and form to the ideas delivered into their keeping.

The foregoing is part, but not nearly all of that which was buzzing away under her glorious red tresses, and I, for one, have no doubt she would have carried much of it forward to great proportions within the next fifty years which she was intended to spend upon the physical plane. I have sat beside her often and listened to her channel the explicit and detailed instructions from her Guides as to the means, methods, the kinds of help, the sources of abundance and the plans for other individuals being prepared to enter into this work at different points, on cue, when the proper timing arrived for their lines to be read.

Gloria has gone from us for a time. Meanwhile there are many things that can be forwarded, and with all of us pulling together we may be able to make the newsletter into an influential voice heard far and wide, and one which will carry new ideas, new hope, new friendship and courage to those who belong to our particular hookup or network, and who, when they are reached again by old associates of former lives, will take heart and renew their dedication to their own parts in the Great Work.

* * * * * * *

A friend of Cosmon said she thought it should be brought out that I have been acting as a channel for many of the communications given in the newsletter, at least those with no name attached. With a few exceptions of channeling given us by those who requested to remain anonymous, in earlier months, you can assume that most of the unsigned material has been given to me for this publication.

This is not new, for my training began in 1936 when I tried, in daily meditation, to establish a two-way conversation with my Master. I still have some of the old, pencilled records in notebooks, that show the evidence of early effort. Before meeting Gloria, it did not occur to me to mention these facts or to think of them as anything outside of the usual mental training of disciples everywhere. Gloria demonstrated to me that you can receive and then tape it, type it or talk it, whichever you please. The only formidable part is learning to separate incoming material from other minds, from the contents of your own subconscious or super-conscious. It helps to know that mental plane substance is in constant flux, moving continually as blood moves through all the parts of your body. Much of the material that moves through your mind and arrests its passing attention, is the mere drift of loaded thought-currents bearing eternal cargoes of mental substance, not necessarily related to you or meant to be seized or examined by you. An open mind will allow continuous flow-through of the most varied subjects, but it will learn discernment and with time, will find itself standing "censor at the portal of thought" and refuse to admit or entertain all would-be mental guests who stop on one's threshold and demand admittance. You have eventually to distinguish, among the muchness, those thoughts which well up from the creative processes of your own human mind, those general thought streams which pass through all minds, and the distinctive impressions of other Intelligences who wish to reach you from the inside and to hold useful, constructive conversation and discourses with you.

The many individuals still centered in their emotional nature, who have not yet developed much lucid mental awareness, are among those who deny the possibility of telepathic communication, and to them it is impossible until they have worked at evolving a receiving station in lives yet ahead of them. Therefore, forgive them, for they cannot know any better until they are ready to experience the phenomenon for themselves. There are others, however, of an advanced mental nature, who also deny the possibility of telepathic communication between or among any combinations of minds — human, superhuman, or both working together; because it is distinctly detrimental to their own retrogressive purposes to encourage widespread human access to higher guidance from Those who can be the means par excellence to accomplish permanent release of humanity from the slavery of ignorance, and the ignorance that they are slaves!

* * * * * * *

One of the subjects that crops up in every batch of your letters is LOVE. It worries you so. Can you believe it if I tell you individuals used to telephone us anonymously when we worked in our offices near Palos Verdes Estates, to ask us questions and to explain they had read WHY WE ARE HERE, Chapter 8, and knew we would understand the wry predicaments they had gotten themselves into (not because of Chapter 8, but because of human propensities for getting ourselves into what I believe the British refer to as sticky situations), and would we please not ask their names, but just tell them person-to-person, what could or should a body do in the midst of purely impossible situations, self-generated? Just a few weeks ago someone said she had read in a recent newsletter J. W.'s benign and impractical advice, and she wondered how J.W. intended you to extricate yourself after reaching the stage of smiling at one another and holding hands, when every impish separate nerve and fiber was sending up smoke signals to green-light you further along the well-worn road; yet each of you just happened to be married people, over 21, and with families of thriving, happy children at home, plus a well-loved mate you really would not wish to hurt for the world. What then, J.W.? What then!

A few of our original and holier members signed off because of the cyclic reappearance of this topic in Cosmon newsletters and in J.W.'s second book, THE CHANGING CONDITIONS OF YOUR WORLD. "I see," wrote one thoroughly disgusted individual, "that you have not learned your lesson, Gloria Lee, but are still promulgating those references to matters which we are to forget completely in the New Age. Don't you know that we are to have etheric bodies and become perfected? Don't you have sense enough to realise we aren't supposed to dwell on these carnal subjects? I, for one, wish to be dropped from your mailing list, for I shall have nothing further to do with emphasis upon the things of the flesh!" After reading such letters Gloria would say with a laugh, "So-and-so was probably one of the wilder Romans who became so satiated with wine, women and song that the pendulum has swung him to extremes of puritanism and self-restraint to get the poor dear balanced up."

My own ideal panacea for these uninvited situations would be plain old honesty, if in any degree possible, and to come forth in some such form as: "Well friend, here we are, caught up in a swirl of inconvenient emotions. For myself, I am committed to a course that requires all my energies, all my attention, all my wits, such as they are. I am in deepest sympathy with you and with our predicament, and know all about the gamut of human feelings, but I know too, from experience, these can be diverted, deflected and channeled into all manner of constructive aims and thereby work out into creative and rewarding accomplishments, instead of being allowed to go sour like the contents of swamps cut off from a supply source of running water."

J.W. emphasized that our present social structure in the more civilized (?) portions of this planet, is not open to outward condoning of those emotional expressions and relatings which might finally gather momentum fit to start an avalanche which would plump down on the whole crystallized ball of wax that our civilization is, and would smash it into smithereens. No one can bear to face the chore of deliberately tearing down this big cumbersome thing in order to build up a better, more forthright and honest culture which comes right out and tries to solve these anguishing perplexities that gnaw at the very core of most of the citizenry. We live in an old, rotten building and one of these days it will fall down by itself, and let's hope no one is indoors when it happens. The building has already been condemned as unfit for human occupation, and here we stay, waiting for the catastrophe large enough to wipe out the ugly mess we have put together, a crumb at a time, since our race was knee-high to a grasshopper.

In this aspect of Life I feel we need more frankness, candor and openhearted simplicity with our fellow men and women and boys and girls. We are all human; even you, Buddy, and I. We are all set up personally, with the same darn set of emotional reactions, mental possibilities, and physical bodies that are mainly spoiled brats and out of line with our better judgment, and with avowed intentions to bring them to heel and show them what's what and who is their boss!

Don't you ever think it is any easier for female people than for male folk to hassle with all these bewildering, furious attacks of emotional suggestion. We're right in the midst of it with you, fellers. It is something we have to face up to, individually, and work it out for ourselves until society gets on the ball and brings us better means of coping with these big silent, awesome forces of nature that would overwhelm us if they could (and they often can, if we aren't eternally on guard!)

After kicking around for a good many years, I have wrestled out a formula that keeps me safe and more or less sane, but it is rougher on many who do not have a terrific involvement with and love for their life work. Long ago I learned that there is just one living creative force within us, and we have to learn to ration it if we don't want to be burnt-out globes before our time. This one life-force, so generously proportioned to our human needs, is that which can perform the magic of bringing invisible children into tangible form, in human physical bodies, if directed to combine with the balancing force of our opposite polarity; or the same force turned into another direction can empower us to carry out any life work we set ourselves to achieve, if we do not grow reckless and waste it on secondary fritterings or repeated emotional sensations, while trying to accomplish our declared life intention; or this same miraculous force can empower us to soar upon spiritual wings of our own fabrication, into realms far above the flight of poor wax-winged Icarus.

J.W. told me the safest bet for unmarried people and single surviving mates at this moment of the world's unsympathetic and critical judgment, is to invest their surplus steam in a creative art such as painting, writing or music, that draws upon one's creative force with a demand that is sufficient to release all your pent-up needs for expression at the human level; and by so doing, it is highly possible you can bring tremendous beauty and joy to others and rouse them to conquer themselves and their imbalances by joining those walking this same path. Personally, I get my kicks out of drawing, painting, crafts and writing. So might you.

Marriage, as it is practised now, does not take into consideration karmic ties, suitability of partners, or evolutionary age of partners that brings together those of equal soul attainment. In some of the classic books of occult teaching, the Teachers tell us at length that marriage as we yearn for it to be, can never succeed until it is a throughout marriage of equal souls, and personalities that match each other's needs. We do not yet have a universal, acceptable method of analysis which can bring the perfectly-suited individuals together on the physical plane.

There are, of course, uncountable marriages that are arranged for the payment of karmic debts, and some of the incomprehensible mate-switchings you see and disparage may be due to a former incarnation in which a plural marriage was legal and a sultan had deep affection for some 10 or 20 women at the same time. If he meets the same girls again when he has incarnated as a farm-implements salesman and the girls are farmers' daughters scattered along his route, what is he going to do, after having loved them all intimately and sincerely and legally in the distant past? If old affinity should well up again as he trips the triggers of past association along his rambles, will he marry each one in turn and divorce her, try to settle on one above all, or establish a branch home in every farming community?

Maybe the theatrical people, whose names hit the world's headlines, are also victims of past affectional relationships, unremembered, but nonetheless influential. Perhaps they are just human, even as you and I. Since so many of you write letters telling your very personal problems, I am well-acquainted with your need for assurance, knowledge and release from a frustrating sense of guilt. J.W. was trying to show us that marriage is a reflection on earth of a deeper spiritual law of union between two equal souls. The innate desire for that lost state of fully-satisfying affection is so instinctive within us all that we bumble and flounder along in our blindness trying to find once more those who really belong with us.

It seems to me we ought to progress into a state of honesty where it will be our pleasure to tell other people, male and female, that we do like them or love them and enjoy their company, and where they can tell us the same, secure in the knowledge we won't or they won't take advantage of a closed situation where it would not be constructive to go beyond a simple declaration. All of us have particular affinities with whom we feel immediately at ease and as though all necessary understandings are long since established between us. No stranger can intrude such ready-made bonds into our circles, by dint of any amount of effort or cunning, for these relationships are something out of the past and some of them are pure distillations that have required thousands of lives in some relationship to each other for ripening the quintessence.

When it was said that "true marriages are made in heaven" it meant just that. There aren't such made on earth. If two are fortunate enough to meet in physical life, who really do belong together, their perfect marriage is a reflection of an invisible link, formed before they came to birth in this life pattern.

Sometimes, we see a fugitive expression ripple across someone's features or the features themselves remind us of someone else, forgotten and lost; but in trying to recapture what was special between us and those lost ones, by substituting a mere look-alike, we cannot bring about anything but disillusionment.

So what are we to do if we get swamped in someone's melting smile and discover blazing currents running from hand to hand when it is already too late, because we are yoked to another teammate and hedged about by duties enough to last a lifetime? We can only say, "You know, it's wonderful to find you here, with me, under the same sky, upon the same planet, in the same civilization. Isn't it kind of the Powers-that-be to bring us together, even momentarily, that we may experience the memory of a love that must be from far away and long ago? It seems sad to us that we cannot now know each other more closely, but if we fulfill our commitments to Life, which are our self-made karmic obligations, and do the very best we can with the relationships we are already in, then surely in the right time and at the right place, we know it is destined for us to meet again under happier and more permissive circumstances."

You see, dear hearts, it's needful for us all to develop the long view. I am making plans for lives ahead, that I cannot by any stretch of imagination hope to fulfill within this incarnation pattern. I am setting about to earn the privilege of having certain happenings cross my path much later. God can be trusted. We must place ourselves unreservedly in His keeping and within His Will that is LOVE. For it is the surest thing you know that whatever truly belongs to you will come to you in God's time, in the best possible and most satisfying ways, if you will turn your full attention upon what you know you should do here and now, and leave the rest to Him.

My love to you all,
Your fallible fellow human,

Barbara Steele

TOGETHER

Together we can cut across the controversial areas of politics and caste, of race and belief; using the good of all for the help of each, the help of each for the good of all. Some have an inner joy and no possessions. Some have many possessions but no inner joy. Each needs to share his surplus. Some have no arms, while others have no legs, and many have strong arms and strong legs, but no good purpose for their use. These extremes also need balancing in a common goal. Some have gardens overridden with weeds and no tools with which to remove them. Others have storehouses filled with tools and no needs for which to use them. Some have much free time, but no evolved skills. Others have many evolved skills, but no free time. Some have much energy, but no channel that seeks it. Others have many channels, but no energies to flow through them. These too should find one another and make exchanges. Some have much wisdom but no followers. Others have many followers, but no wisdom. Many have the qualifications of a teacher, but no pupils. Many have the attributes of pupils, but no teacher. Many long to make music but possess no instrument. Many silent instruments stand idle and forgotten and have no player. These extremes should be combined. There are shabby-looking people with fine minds, and fine-looking people with shabby minds, and each should be revealed for the good of the whole. Someone needs all the good things you no longer use. Some others have all that which you need, in surplus supply. Ask and you shall receive. Give and it shall be given unto you, pressed down and running over.

                                                 From the Diary of a Disciple

BOOKS TO HELP YOU GROW

The following books are picked at random from the lists of favorite reading over the years. They are not all classifiable as spiritual books unless we look on Life as a whole and try to understand by approaching it from every possible open door. These books are not available through Cosmon at present, and so we are giving you data that may help you find them in your public library or local book store. A few are out of print.

GEORGE WASHINGTON CARVER
    By Rackham Holt
Doubleday & Company, Inc., Garden City, New York, 1943.
Original price $4.00

A sensitive and beautiful story of the life of a true server of God and man, who happened to choose embodiment as a Negro in America.

THE LONG WALK
(A GAMBLE FOR LIFE)
    By Slavomir Rawicz
    as told to Ronald Downing
Harper and Brothers, New York, 1956.
Original price $4.95

More than four thousand miles, with neither map nor compass, equipped with an axehead, a homemade knife and an insuperable determination to live... Slavomir Rawicz and six companions broke out of a Soviet slave-labor camp and walked south into the endless, crushing spaces of Siberia, headed for Tibet.

THE FIRST RAY
    By Its Chohan, El Morya
Published by The Bridge to Freedom, Inc.
P.O. Box 777, St. James, L.I., New York.
Current price believed to be $1.25

A series of personal-impersonal letters to disciples, especially those struggling to bring the New Age to birth. A must for all students of Light.

WOMEN and sometimes MEN
    By Florida Scott-Maxwell
Alfred A. Knopf, Inc., New York, 1957.
Original edition $3.50
Paper back edition $.40

For women who would know themselves and for men who would understand them.

THE THIRD EYE
DOCTOR FROM LHASA
THE RAMPA STORY
    A trilogy by T. Lobsang Rampa
You should read all three.
Published by two British firms and one American publisher. Try to find them in your bookstore or public library.
Prices unknown.

The incredible autobiography of a Tibetan Lama. You will know all human beings better for entering the mind and experiences of this one representative man.

> We still have some copies of J.W. of Jupiter's
> two books instrumented through Gloria Lee.
> These are available through
>
> Cosmon Research Foundation
> P. O. Box 483
> Oro Grande, California
>
> | WHY WE ARE HERE | | THE CHANGING CONDITIONS |
> | Instrumented by Gloria Lee | | OF YOUR WORLD |
> | | | Instrumented by Gloria Lee |
>
> | Book Price | $3.75 | Book Price | $4.00 |
> | Calif. Sales Tax | .14 | Calif. Sales Tax | .16 |
> | Postage | .10 | Postage | .15 |
>
> ***Christmas will be here soon. Buy copies for
> your friends.

APOLOGY
(More or less public!)

Harrumph... One of the friends I cherish said she was ashamed of my attitude of pushing people away from Cosmon and that I ought to apologize publicly.
...Darn it...
Well my bark is worse than my bite, folks, and so far no matter how fierce I've tried to be, it doesn't make any difference. People come anyway and I always like them and wonder how the deuce I can chat with them and get my work done and have anything left of energy. My friend infers that I should stop caring whether I have anything left and just turn the energy problem over to God. O.K. then. Come visit us, but if I don't have time left to get out newsletters, just chalk it up to profit and loss.

At present our guest quarters have vanished for overnight accomodations, because J.W. suggested Bartram move downstairs and stay permanently in our guest room and make it his home. This works out so much better for Bartram that there is no comparison in convenience.

Down the road, one mile, is a motel that usually has accomodations and is very reasonable. But please, dear people, remember I am not a trained seal and have no intention of performing in any way, shape or manner for you!

Somewhat sheepishly yours,

EXPLORING HUMAN EMOTIONS

THE LISTENING PRAYER
Maurine W. Sellstrom

Those interested in Cosmon Research are usually also interested in channelling. People in all walks of life have tried many kinds of praying. Only too frequently our praying is a sort of telling God what to do. Certainly it often is not sufficiently asking God for guidance and instruction.

We are not altogether to blame because we do not ask for this guidance. Many of us would mistrust it if we received it. We would have no way of knowing whether what came to mind was imagination, vain wishing, or just some crazy idea that entered into our heads. Many of these same doubts arise when one attempts any sort of channelling of ideas from other sources than his own thinking.

We have discovered a means of group praying, which includes some of the more reliable principles of asking for guidance and puts some intellectual or reasoning check on our doubts concerning what could be considered as channelling.

We have found that two or three or four people can gather together in an asking and meditating mood and pose a question which they mutually wish to understand more fully. We can ask of Mind — or God, or what sources of Knowing seem beyond our consciousness, and receive impressions concerning our question which are definitely in advance of the thinking of any of the members of the group.

This does not depend upon one of the members having any clairvoyant or special ability, although perhaps some intuitive interest and ability facilitates the process.

Jesus said, "When two or three are gathered together in My name, I will be in the midst of them." Perhaps this is the principle He was speaking from at that time.

Many of Gloria's friends have been intrigued by her concept of channelling. In her absence they have experimented with trying to receive messages from her or others who were wanting to help humanity. They have frequently been pleased with the novelty and quality of the ideas received.

In our group that experimented with group listening and praying for guidance were those who had participated in class study of dream interpretation and the use of dream symbols. We had done this in order to understand the unconscious part of mind and improve our own emotional tone. So the result of our asking prayers seemed to express in symbols which each member of the group could hold in attention and meditate upon as we went about our living. The symbols seemed to have an unfolding meaning which revealed itself to each individual with interpretations which met her need in a slightly different way than the same symbol did for other members of the group.

Because of the limitation of time and attention capacity, it seems necessary to agree on some one basic research project. This may be to help one particular person with a problem, or all may agree to explore some particular question. The next rule we followed was that no one acted as the leader. We usually each made an opening prayer statement according to our individual backgrounds of reverently asking for help and guidance. In this statement we tried to stipulate our personal interest or identification with the problem.

For example in one session a group of about seven women agreed that we all wished to better understand what to do to help a loved one who was in some sort of physical or emotional trouble. We had each felt at times that most anything done was more of an annoyance than help! All of us had been uncertain about how to offer assistance and sympathy.

As we made our statements of request, each had a slightly different concern. One woman had a mother who was confronted with surgery. Another was concerned because of her husband's dark moods which she felt isolated him from his family. Still another had an auntie who was supposedly afflicted with a fatal cancer. One mother was concerned because she felt her son feared going into service and was in conflict about the need to learn to shoot and perhaps have to kill in the line of his duty. One mother's worry circulated around a daughter who had made an unfortunate marriage, another longed to comfort her recently widowed mother. Each worry was individual, yet basically our question was the same. What could we as loving friends and relatives do that would help and not just increase the worry and tension?

In any form of listening prayer after the asking, it is necessary for a pause and silence to wait for some sort of answer. It has been our experience that often this silence is longer than many people can comfortably tolerate when in a social situation. Following the silence one member or another spontaneously spoke out that a certain idea or image had crossed her attention.

The second important rule in this kind of work is neither to censor what one receives or ask or expect others to approve or verify it. Each one must simply state without either apology or conceit what occurs to attention.

Several statements were made, that perhaps were meaningful to the individual who received them, but they did not impress the others enough to proceed with the idea.

One image that was received was of an open daisy-like flower and a big black bumblebee alighting upon it. The daisy wanted to crush the bee and only succeeded in crushing its own petals. One interpretation was: "We cannot stop what troubles us by just squeezing it out of existence." Another felt that when we try to hold those we love too closely we injure ourselves and do not help them. One woman felt the message was concerning the creative process of life which was fostered by the bee, and though it buzzed with a frightening sound and looked black, it was serving life's purposes in the pollination and perpetuation of the flower's species.

The next image that was received was a growing cattail with seven little bugs looking anxiously at seven others that seemed to be encased in a sac of embryonic membrane. Each bug was whirling in distress, caught in his own little sac of worry.

We interpreted this as being the helpers witnessing the others whirling and sort of stewing in their own juice. One woman pursued the idea of piercing the sac and saw the embryonic fluid spilled and the little bug inside depleted. As another imagined the picture, she realized that the seven witnessing bugs could become like little Buddhas and send love and the golden thread of faith and prayer toward the troubled ones. This thread of love became a golden light which dried out the fluid. Then another saw the embryonic sac as it dried out become a tougher skin which made the troubled bugs better able to meet the elements with strength and fortitude. The group decision was that we must not say or do too much, but stand by as a loving prayer, as a Buddha, knowing for our loved ones that they could grow the skin to meet the elements which life presents. This then could become the basis for our prayer whenever we witnessed their distress.

As each of us carried the image in mind we knew better what to do. It was as though the image of the little Buddha bug kept us from rushing in "yanxiously" with a hovering sympathy which only added to the burden of our loved ones.

This is a rather full and unique example. Many other images might have been equally revealing, but this was the one that intrigued us, and we used the time we had to explore its possibilities. All of us have felt we more competently dealt with our loved one's anxieties since this listening prayer session.

Another group of four of us met and spent our time exploring the understanding an expectant mother might need to better understand her coming child. She saw his characteristics as bundles which she opened in imagination. There were bundles of his gifts from life, from heredity, and from his own karma. This gave her quite a lot of awareness of the help she may need to give her child. Her wish was to understand the child's real potentials and basic purpose and not divert him from it by her training.

One member of this group came to a better understanding of how Daddy's very fussing and nagging the children becomes a motivating force to springboard the child into action so that his potentialities can be used. She had been distressed by her husband's goading of their children. This thought was activated by her admiration of the young expectant mother trying to genuinely understand her child and not just make the child fit some parental image. She expressed her concern that so many parents and especially fathers do not seem to be able to do this. When she asked for help with this feeling she saw a teeter-totter with Mother's loving understanding as the fulcrum. But the board didn't move. It was Daddy's shove that set it into motion. Just love and understanding and acceptance were not enough. Even the child's reaction to Dad's criticism which was a resentful, "I'll show him!" sent all the potentialities of the child into expression. She saw that Dad, like the objective world, goads us into trying and proving our ideas by giving them form which others can see and appreciate.

It is not easy to describe in words a process so subjective and dependent upon our active imagination as this method of listening prayer. We are trained from childhood to be "realistic", to suppress such imaginings. However if we can ask in faith and sincerity, and with the viewpoint of a child follow the imagery that comes in answer to our prayerful question, we may find as we follow our image it can lead us to new insights which will help us to better understand ourselves and those about us.

In summarizing, these are the rules.

The group needs to be small at first, from two to seven people. One person alone can drift into a daydream and become lost in the process. Although if your concentration is good, you might try it, but use some device to record what your train of thought is, such as writing, a typewriter or a tape recorder. In larger groups than seven, so many conflicting ideas may take more time than you would have to develop any one idea.

Open your session with an invocation type of prayer stating your wish for understanding or your variation of the question decided upon.

Then all listen, and be willing to wait quite a while until an image or idea begins to present itself to one member.

Do not try to argue with the images or ask others to verify them.

If any one also sees the same image and it begins to move in any direction, discuss it. Let each person amplify the story and tell what it means to him or how it varies in his imagination. Encourage each member to add his feeling and comments.

If possible tape your sessions and listen to the tapes later. Take off in writing the parts that seem true and practical.

Hold the images or ideas in mind as you go about your daily living, asking for further guidance and understanding.

Sincere asking is praying. But we cannot receive answers, if we do not listen. We cannot take and use new ideas if we cannot entertain them before we have practical proof of their worth.

Pray, listen, note the imagery and ideas that come. Hold them in attention and you may be surprised at the use you can make of ideas so received. It is an exciting research in any case. We can always use our conscious mind and experience to test the worth of the ideas. We do not need to act upon them until our feeling verifies their right use in our lives.

We need to become children toward God to listen for the guidance, perhaps in terms that are new to us. Then we can be as adults in our world and assume the responsibility for how we use what we receive.

CORRESPONDENCE FILE

FROM A YOUNG MAN

Another thing I'd like to say while I'm thinking about it is this: It seems to me that in these days too many people have drawn a straight BLACK line between male and female. People seem to think that only rough crude bold things are for the man; and soft fine beautiful things are for the woman. I have seen from experience that if a man admires, for example, flowers, he is thought to be feminine. If a small boy, say three, four, or five years old, picks up a baby doll, right away he is teased by being called a "sissy". You cannot imagine how angry I become when I see this. All too few of us realize that beauty IN ALL FORMS, whatever they may be, IS FOR ALL — not just one sex. I am not advocating complete freedom, uncontrolled and running wild, among people; but I DO most strongly advocate COMPLETE FREEDOM of the ability to SEE AND EXPRESS one's feelings toward what he considers beautiful. Love is Truth: why not have as much of it as you can?

(Publisher's note: We like the above and hope other young New Age disciples of either polarity will come forward and state their views and tell us their beefs, if they can do so as lucidly as the above writer.)

INVITATION

Mr. K. Lall International Friendship Centre
192 Mangalwara, P.O. Harda (M.P.) India

Please interested friends may visit the international friends centre Harda (M.P.) India. Kindly send educational books for our reading fellowship by post & oblige.

In search of heaven
K. Lall

OUR RELATIONS

Love, or if you want to say, charity, fraternity, sincerity, amicability etc., is altogether too lacking in our present social environments. We, at one time or another, have tried to be extra friendly and sincere to people with the result that those whom we have tried to "love" (using the word in a general sense) repel or reject us, saying that we are crazy or mentally unbalanced. Some will just take advantage of our kindness and respect us as fools. You will probably find this fact out, if you have not already.

Because of this terrible lack of love of neighbor, we have become a barren, ruthless people. When anyone tries to revolt, so to speak, and show a little love and kindness to his neighbor, he is termed insane or something close to it. Do you think that this is right — to live life bitterly, when God, Who is all Love, Truth, and Wisdom, gave us the precept to live in His own Image and Likeness. Do you think that living life without love and mutual honor among men is right, is good, is logical. Contemplate on these things in your deep-inner-self.

You can well see from the history of this planet that when a people have lived as God intended them — with love, generosity, and fraternity among themselves — they have been rewarded with peace and prosperity. And when an evil group has been powerful or in control of a nation, only hate, distrust, and disorder have come about. These truths are most logical and explicit so to speak for themselves.

The main rule and the chief principle of a best, lasting, and beautiful society is Love.

Love is the conqueror of darkness, and Light sustains Love.

Be thou with Love and Light in God.

Frank Ninivaggi

... About your idea of having college age pen pals, all I can say is: What a terrific idea! Imagine: A College Cosmonites Quill Club! And all the members can share their hopes, plans and experiences (psychic and otherwise), thus broadening the members' outlook about how wonderful Life is and can be. By all means do put my name in your newsletter!

> Linda Fusaro
> 1719 Hillsdale Avenue
> San Jose 24, California

(Linda is a college girl, as you might deduce, who yearns for pen pals. She throws in some good bait by offering you a candy recipe she originated and which she says you may call either —)

NEW AGE NOUGAT
or
COSMIC CANDY

- 1/2 cup chopped nuts
- 1/3 cup raisins
- 3 tablespoons wheat germ
- 3 tablespoons honey
- 1 tablespoon butter

Mix together the dry ingredients first, before adding the honey goo, which is made by mixing together the honey and butter. (Milk just simply will not mix properly with the honey, so that takes care of that!) After mixing everything well, turn this candy into a small buttered pan. Store this candy in the refrigerator to keep it firm. It does not cut well, so a spoon may be used.

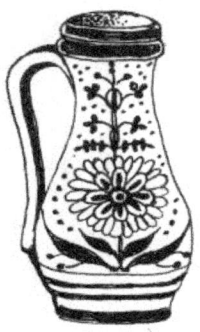

NEWS CLIPPING

(Sent by Mrs. Thelma Massey, Sacramento, California)

Editor of The Bee — Sir:
I did not write this letter until I received documented proof and pictures from the Humane Society of the United States in regard to cruelty to animals in more than 9,000 laboratories in our country, most of them operating in great secrecy with doors locked and visitors unwelcome.

The documented proof states these animals undergo every extreme of agony that flesh and nerves can endure and some that are wholly beyond endurance. They are burned alive, scalded without anesthesia, crushed in steel presses, starved to death, subjected repeatedly to painful experimental surgery and many go totally mad from years of cruel confinement without humane care.

The Randall bill, HR 4856, introduced in congress, would improve medical research by putting reasonable, moderate controls on such laboratories, requiring recipients of federal research grants to use scientific statistical techniques when experimenting with animals and to provide humane housing and care.

Any humanitarian who wishes further information and proof of cruelty to animals in these laboratories can write to the Humane Society of the United States, 1145 19th Street NW, Washington 6, DC. Support the Randall bill by writing to your congressman. Do not delay. These animals need to be protected and it is up to all of us who love animals to relieve their needless pain and suffering.

> Mrs. Gerald E. James

Dear Mrs. Steele:

Your efforts to analyze my recent letter to you, overlook the real motive. I was simply trying by sarcasm to penetrate your mask.

I will now say without sarcasm that I believe you are either a fraud or a self-deceived person and that the whole "Cosmon" bit is a spurious, bogus, quasi-religious and quasi-scientific hoax that could become dangerous.

You are . . . potentially a menace.

Sincerely

W.L.S.

P.S. I am not a negro. I am a mutant. I have to dye my green hair to avoid notice. My father was a Martian. My mother was an Earthling.

Don't look upon your neighbor!
If you harm him, you harm God.
If you mock him, you mock God.
If you say, "All men are not equal," you will be right.
For it will be you who are not equal.
You will be lower than the one you spit upon, and he whom you hurt will be esteemed higher in love than you.

Frank Ninivaggi

FRIENDLY INVITATION

I, for one, am eternally grateful the Lord brought us all together. I'd like to take this opportunity to invite any Cosmonites in the Battle Creek area to visit us.

Best wishes from all of us,

Virginia Schroeder and group
P. O. Box 77
Battle Creek, Michigan 49016

IF YOU'VE BEEN TO EROS, PLEASE SPEAK UP

". . . I have had astral visits to Eros. I understand others have also visited or contacted this rather large body in the milky way. I also understand that souls go there for a rest and to wait between assignments after making the transition. I would like more information on this and would like to send out a call to anyone else who has made visits or contacts and perhaps they would be interested in forming a group of pen pals called 'Brotherhood of Eros.' What do you think of this idea?"

H.B.
Long Beach, California

I D E A   F I L E

YOUTH WORKSHOPS

<u>Attention:</u> Churches, Chambers of Commerce and Police
Departments, Merchants, Service Clubs, Youth
Leaders, Psychologists, Parents and Youth

We will see more and more YOUTH WORKSHOPS spring up in communities. These will combine old, familiar things (that have use in New Age living) with experiments for the future and materials, patterns, ideas and methods for now.

Many centers will be needed, featuring light, spaciousness, simplicity and colors that do not over-stimulate.

These WORKSHOPS will be a halfway house between schools and home. They will stimulate better scholarship, better family life, more responsible and adaptable citizens.

These centers will bring young people together in a creative atmosphere. The tone will be casual; informal but serious and constructive. Here will be equipment for all kinds of experiments, in all kinds of fields. There will be studios of crafts, arts, music, dancing; science laboratories, gymnasiums, indoor swimming pools, chapels, libraries, museums, game rooms, rest rooms, kitchens, play rooms for little children, theatres.

Adult volunteers from every walk of life will be welcomed; to lead, to instruct, to protect, to befriend and to inspire the younger people of the community. Nationals from every country can share their skills, traditions, art forms, food preparation, New Age ideas and good fellowship. To these centers would be welcomed professionals and amateurs of all sorts: photographers, astronomers, hobbyists, rockhounds, actors, musicians, mechanics, designers, carpenters, decorators, architects, jewelers, scientists, gardeners, writers, athletes.

All the many and interesting phases of life that cannot be encompassed in a single family's home or in the usual school curriculum, should be made available to all the young people in every community and here should be the true New Age melting pot that dissolves artificial barriers of caste, social opportunity, color and age. All these can begin with a simple desire to direct the flow of youthful energies into happy, useful contributive channels.

The emphasis here is to be on people working together in the common desire to share individual knowledge and to gain through expanding each other's horizons.

                                                            Name withheld

VEGETARIAN RECIPES

MAIN DISH VEGETABLE SALAD

2 coarse-grated carrots
1/2 green pepper cut in strips
2 tbsp. sunflower seeds
1/2 avocado cut in chunks
1/2 tsp. sesame seed (hulled)
1/4 tsp. caraway seed
2 small tomatoes cut in chunks
1/2 small lettuce, shredded
1/2 can ripe pitted olives
2 slices cheddar cheese cut in strips
3 small green onions cut fine, using inner green stem also.

Dress with oil, lemon and honey or Safflower mayonnaise or French dressing.

GLUTEN VEGETABLE STEW

1 cup diced carrots
1 small onion
1 cup diced cooked gluten
2 tbsp. oil
4 tbsp. Whole Wheat flour
3 cups raw potatoes (cubed)
2 tsp. salt
Parsley (optional)

Add carrots and onion to 4-1/2 cups water and cook ten minutes. Brown flour in oil and make gravy from vegetable broth, just made, and add to vegetables with potatoes and salt. Cook 15 minutes. Add gluten and cook until done. Garnish with parsley.

GLUTEN BURGERS

Run gluten through a meat grinder and place in mixing bowl. Season with G. Washington's broth or other seasoning. Stir in egg and grated onion. Mix in enough Potato Flour to make patties. Fry in skillet, browning each side. Cover and slowly steam for five minutes to bring out flavor.

GLUTEN CHOW MEIN
(Ethyl B. Spear)

2 cups coarsely chopped onions
4 tbsp. vegetable shortening
2 tsp. Savorex (or Vegex or Savita)
1 cup cooked gluten (cut in thin strips 1-1/2 inches long)
1-1/2 cups diced celery
2 cups cut mushrooms
3/4 cup water
1 tsp. celery salt
1 cup bean sprouts
3 tbsp. soy sauce
Salt to taste
Tapioca starch or arrowroot starch to thicken

Add onions to hot fat. Stir well. Add Savorex, then gluten and stir. Add celery, mushrooms and water. Cover and allow to cook five minutes, stirring frequently. Add bean sprouts and remaining seasonings. Thicken with starch dissolved in cold water to creamy consistency. Serve hot on unsalted flaky, dry cooked brown rice.

EGG FOO YOUNG

6 large eggs
1/2 tsp. salt
2 cups bean sprouts (drained)
1 cup chopped cooked gluten
2 small onions, chopped
2 cups brown rice
2 tbsp. soy sauce
Parsley and mushrooms (optional)

Beat eggs foamy and add rest of ingredients except rice and soy sauce. Blend lightly. Heat a small amount of shortening or butter in a large heavy skillet and pour portions into pan (same as hot cakes). When set and brown on the bottom, turn and brown well on other side. Serve with hot steamed rice, and any brown gravy to which has been added soy sauce. Garnish with parsley and mushrooms.

WET GLUTEN BASE
(Ethyl B. Spear)

Gluten is very rich in protein and can be used to make delicious entrees. Gluten can be made from hard wheat flours (Whole Wheat Flour or unbleached White Flour or from Gluten Flour.)

Mix 8 cups of flour with 2-1/2 to 3 cups lukewarm water to make a stiff dough. Form into a ball and knead well. Let stand under water for 2 hours. Wash out starch by kneading with the hands in the water, ever being careful to keep the dough together and pouring off only the starchy water, until water is almost clear. You will then have a lump of wet gluten in its raw state.

COOKED GLUTEN

Put 1/2 cup oil in 6 quart kettle with tight lid. Add one large chopped onion. When slightly browned, add 1 tbsp. Savorex. Roll gluten into loaf, cut in slices and put in kettle and cover with boiling water. Boil 1 hour and drain. This is the basis for recipes calling for cooked gluten.

GLUTEN GRAVY

Use the liquid from cooking gluten steaks or vegetable water and thicken with green pea flour or whole wheat flour and add mushroom

All Gluten recipes taken from El Molino Mill Cook Book:

EL MOLINO BEST RECIPES
El Molino Mills
3060 W. Valley Blvd.
Alhambra, California

Write to these millers of stone-ground flours for their list of products, prices and recipes. These people are not vegetarians, but include many convertible or vegetarian recipes with other suggestions for using their products. You will find this firm's excellent products in the best American health food stores.

* * * * * * *

"Lord, Thou knowest better than I know myself that I am growing old. Keep me from getting talkative, and particularly from the fatal habit of thinking I must say something on every subject and on every occasion. Release me from craving to try to straighten out everybody's affairs. Keep my mind free from the recital of endless details — give me wings to get to the point. I ask for grace enough to listen to the tales of others' pains. Help me to endure them with patience. But seal my lips to my own aches and pains... they are increasing and my love of rehearsing them is becoming sweeter as the years go by. Teach me the glorious lesson that occasionally it is possible that I may be mistaken. Keep me reasonably sweet; I do not want to be a saint — some of them are so hard to live with, but a sour old woman or man is one of the crowning works of the devil. Make me thoughtful, but not moody; helpful, but not bossy. With my vast store of wisdom, it seems a pity not to use it all — but Thou knowest, Lord, that I want a few friends at the end."

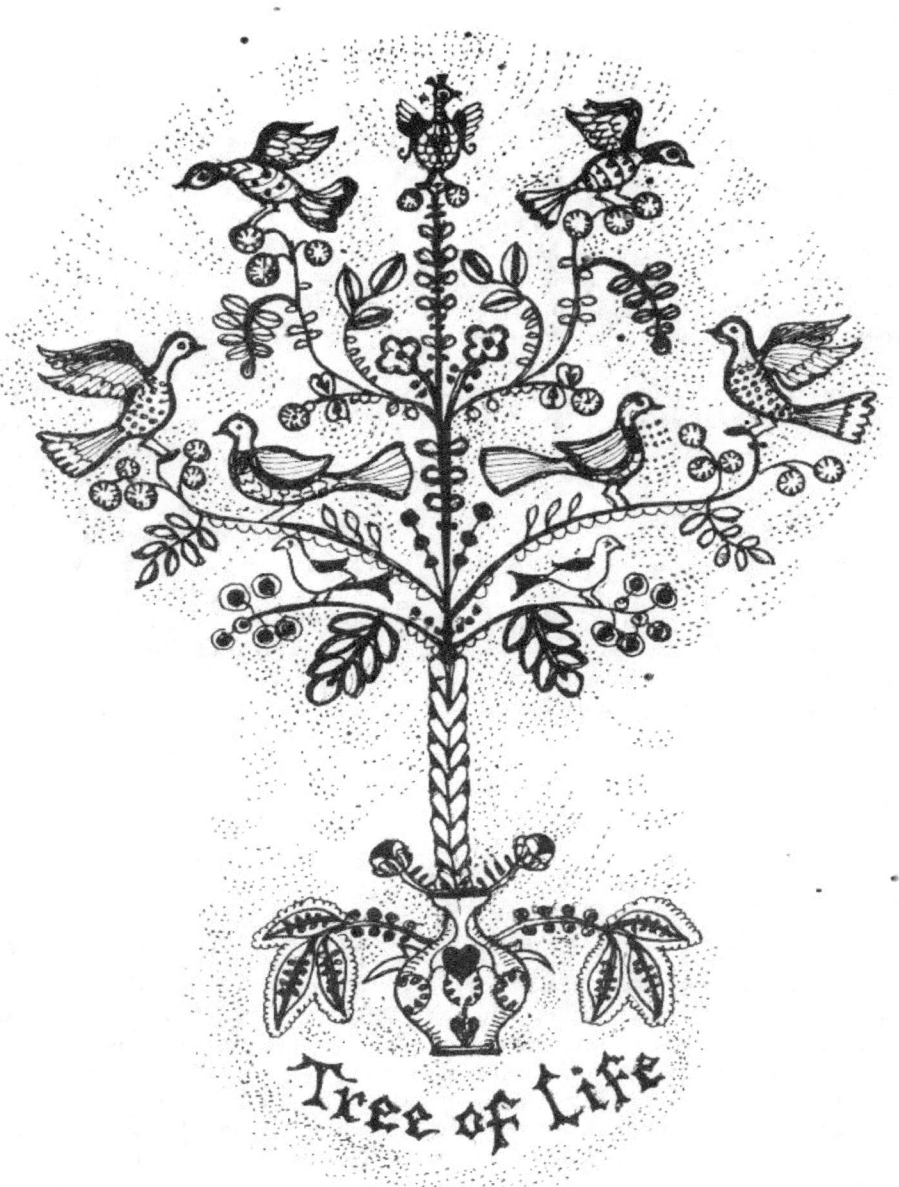

COSMON

APRIL 1964

COSMON NEWSLETTER

CONTENTS

Greetings from Gloria	3
Message from J.W.	6
Poems	9
En Route with Barbara Steele	10
Children of the New Age	15
Another County Heard From	18
The Creative Process	22
Our Ivory Towers	26
Why They Came	28
The Book Corner	30
Your Health	32
Correspondence File	33
Co-workers in the Vineyard	35

Cover by B. Steele
Drawing (p. 27) by Maureen Kline

Copyright 1964 by Cosmon Research Foundation
P.O. Box 483, Oro Grande, California 92368
All rights reserved. Printed in U.S.A.

GREETINGS FROM GLORIA

Dear Friends -

It is not hard to see that you are caught in the cross-fire of daily bad news that comes to you in newspapers and over airwaves and in the predictions and prophecies handed around by the New Age groups. From this side I have a greater idea of the relations of effects to causes than I had when I was working among you and added my share of activity on the side of "scaring some sense" into the many who seemed to be doing little else than milling around and refusing to take any useful action to offset the troubles they have been continually told exist on every inch of the globe.

Now I have much more understanding. I see that you are pulled by the terrific pressure from those who hedge you around with laws that prevent you from taking the very actions that would clear up the problems they point out to you, and on the other hand you are told that the pile-up of corruption is too large for anyone or groups to clean up, and there is no solution until the forces of nature are unleashed to create absolute desolation and to destroy all the institutions and idols man has brought with him up to the present time. Between these opposing views of the uselessness of your personal attempt to improve conditions, you are caught at a standstill.

To keep yourselves from going wild, you try to work out personal formulas for evading the big issues altogether and concentrate harder than ever on getting peace of mind for yourselves and a tranquilized attitude that "this too will pass if we turn our eyes away and don't look at it." I have taken time to look more closely at the substitutes you have made for yourselves. Even among the Light groups there is a continuous contribution to the forces of alcohol, tobacco, and various kinds of drugs and stimulants; if not from many of the leaders, at least from the followers. It reminds me of the way America went to war against other nations while sending them a continuous supply of metal scrap with which they could build up new weapons to continue the war against us!

Of course I have asked myself what my attitude would be if I could again be incarnated in the midst of things as they are now, but also knowing what has been shown to me since I came over here and could get a better view of both sides of the problem.

Now, it is perfectly plain for me to realize the efforts of every individual count a hundredfold more than you can possibly imagine, especially the efforts you deliberately put on the side of Love, understanding and the dissemination of Truth. You see only the littleness of what can be done by individuals such as yourselves working alone; but in your total numbers, counting everybody on the side of Light everywhere on the planet, you are slowly building up a pressure bloc that will eventually decide the way the world will go in matters that hit everybody right in the heart as well as in the money bags.

There was no mistake in planting out these Light centers and Light workers in the scattered way they have been distributed. Each one is a magnet that grows in pulling power in proportion to the honesty and amount of personal sacrifice each person puts into the work that has been given to his hands or her hands to do.

It really does not matter what your circumstances are. Even if you have nothing more than one postage stamp and a scrap of paper and an envelope, you can "be in business" on the side of the Forces of Light.

Many of the Light groups have free literature to send you in response to your request. When it comes to you, read it, study it, think about it and talk to anybody or write to anybody about what you have discovered. Never mind if they don't accept it; the important thing is for the information to spread and spread and spread everywhere so that ALL THE PEOPLE can say they have heard the word, even if they haven't "walked the walk." The Forces of Light need recognition first of all, and you can help give it to them. If you are the shy or timid kind of individual who cannot come out in public as an associate of a new and "radical" seeming world movement, then quietly leave New Age literature wherever you go. Let it appear, as if by magic, everywhere. But BE SURE it is literature that stands for the highest good of all people everywhere, that it emphasizes Love and Brotherhood as the only possible solution-approaches to the problems of all races, and that it does not blast anybody's religion, but sees good in all that lifts the spirit of man closer to God as each religion sees God.

There are always some who take shelter under good movements and use the phrases and names of those who are dedicated to the Father's Plan, to draw in the simple-minded who still believe "if it's in print it must be true." You must read into the material as well as taking in the surface and be sure it does not offend your intuition. Some things are sweet and beautiful and are also true; but some things are neither sweet nor beautiful, and they are also true and need shaking out and airing in sunlight where everybody can see them for what they are, and determine to wipe away such ugliness from our planet, once and for all.

In your homes and at work you can begin to set New Age examples. This is your part in the creating of trends that are really helpful to the people. Introduce New Age topics wherever you go. Ask restaurants if they feature raw juices and salads and whole grain breads. Get them wondering and thinking. Do the same at hamburger stands. Wherever the weight of public demand is, the products will be changed to suit the changes in taste. Patronize your local health food stores so that increased patronage will bring the prices down and popularize the products, so that regular markets are caught up into the better food business. Talk a lot about raw nut butters, raw honey, organically grown fruits and vegetables. Yes, money talks. Let your money speak on the side of needed changes. Let your children switch to dried fruit and carob confections and teach them to drink raw juices between meals instead of soft drinks with caffeine in them.

Bombard the editors of your local paper with quotes from New Age publications. Call up your book stores over and over and get your friends to, with their different voices, to ask if these bookstores feature New Age books Name several and get the word around. Don't be a sitting duck one day longer.

Start coffee-break group discussions of New Age topics, but introduce new coffee-break drinks of herb teas and juices. Tell your co-workers a friend told you about them and they're so good you want to share them. Also take raw peanut and cashew and almond butter sandwiches of whole grain bread to school and to work and let your friends taste them. Tell your friends to drink magnolia herb tea to help them get rid of the smoking habit.

You see? There are little things that almost anybody can do. If you live in Europe, Africa, Asia, South America, or on islands or continents where it is hard to get health magazines and books, keep pressuring your American friends to get them for you and share them with you. One of the very best ways in the world to get New Age ideas circulating is to SHARE. It would not be a bad idea to have all the Light Groups everywhere have a department they call SHARE, through which continual exchanges and sharing go on with services, surplus goods and ideas. This can help offset the economic crisis, if you will just share. Hoarding is the root of poor circulation of world goods. If enough of the New Agers begin sharing and distributing and creating demands this will have a positive effect on every aspect of the world's problems. Add your own ideas to the few I have given you here and share them, so that all the Light-inspired individuals and groups everywhere will take a hand in setting the world to rights. Imagine the thrill of saying to your grandchildren, "I was one of those who prevented world-wide catastrophes, because I CARED ENOUGH to use my hands and mind and heart to start a counter-action against the forces of apathy, indifference and inertia!"

Next time you go to your public library, see if they have any New Age books. If they don't, constitute yourself a book-of-the-month club and do without those extra pints of beer and packs of cigarettes so you can buy a good New Age book every month to insure the community where you live of a source of information.

Most of you have heard of the old saying, "Eat, drink and be merry, for tomorrow we die." Of course anyone can go over on the cynical side and just play while waiting for death to overtake him; but I thought of a much better slogan for now: "Work, love and be helpful, so tomorrow we'll live."

It's a funny thing but whenever one person starts making improvements in his home or place of work or even in his character, others notice and immediately want to show that they are just as capable of thinking up good things as the first person. In fact they might even like to go a step further and show the first one who can really get things done in a big, efficient way! That is why they say "example is stronger than precept." Become what you want others to be. Do what you wish they would do and show them the pleasant results. If they like your results, they'll ask how you got them. Simple?

For generations the spiritual Guides of our planet have tried in every way They knew to show us we must match action to our words if we want changes made. I think it would be wonderful to have letters from you that could be published in COSMON, telling what you have done to bless the world. Tell your co-readers about your very personal experiences and what ways you have found are best to produce friendly cooperation and to get the spirit of hopefulness back into circulation. I will be watching and so full of joy when I see that you have taken me seriously and are really going to get down to cases!

In love and Light,

Gloria

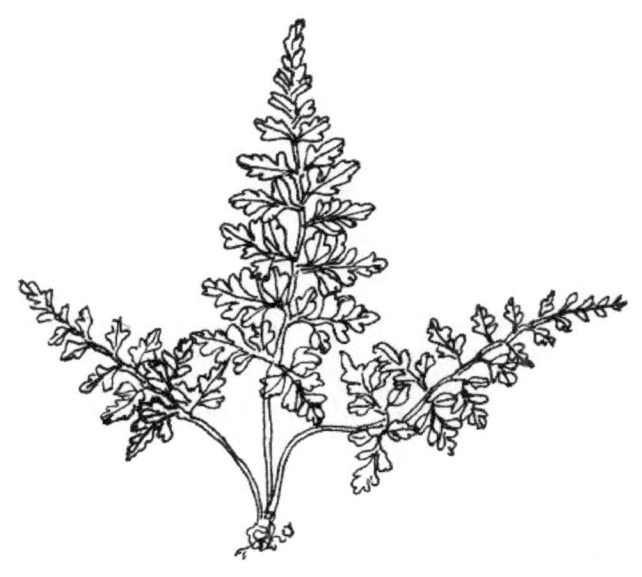

MESSAGE FROM J.W.

My Friends, Greetings -

Among the many topics which occupy your minds is the question of Twin Souls. I brought up the subject in my first book, WHY WE ARE HERE, and have had ample time to observe your reaction since the publication of my information. You will discover on studying the alphabetical indices at the back of most occult texts, no mention of this exciting reality, for your wise Teachers of the Hierarchy have made it Their first objective to draw your thoughts toward consideration of spiritual principles underlying the world of form, rather than to divert your attention to such considerations, which in the majority of cases are beyond your capacity to verify and which only tantalize your emotional nature as you ponder upon what you may be missing in enjoyments of a fabulous nature, which you enhance with the rich embroiderings of an ofttimes feverish imagination.

In your eagerness to prove my assertions to be either mistaken or correct, you have alerted your every waking moment to an attitude of stealthy exploration among the circle of your total acquaintanceship, hoping explosive recognitions might form the prelude to reunions of dynamic implications. And I see from my observation point that your efforts have not met with the success you sought. You failed to place your emphasis upon the word SOUL, and instead conducted your search among the physical bodies of the people you know. If I were to take each one of you, as individuals, by the hand, and point out to you the actual location in consciousness of your divine mate at this time of now, I think many of you would be swept by incredible shock. For even as you, yourselves in the majority of cases are working out debts of destiny in the circumstances where your own karma of the past has brought you, so is the other twin attached to whatever circumstances have been established for the education and balance of the entity.

Many of your twin rays are not now incarnated. Others wear the physical bodies of races inhabiting other planets, solar systems, and galaxies, some very far from your present form in point of cosmic distances. In other cases your twin has completed the assignments and class work of the physical plane and has ascended to Mastership and awaits your arrival at the expanded level of consciousness which alone could provide a perfect union of purpose, energy and action. In yet other cases your twin may now be occupying the body of another racial color upon this planet, and may be placed in circumstances that will never bring to consummation a crossing of paths in this life pattern. Your twin may be hidden in the body of your child, your parent, your relation, your friend, your co-worker or one who has an impact upon you as a public personage, or your twin may be languishing within a prison or dying upon a battlefield outside of the powers now available to you to arrange a contact.

The knowledge was given to you because it belongs to you by spiritual right to know that somewhere waits a perfect answer to your natural yearning for a wholly satisfying union with one who fulfills the requirements for partnership in every degree. But this reunion is rarely the prerogative of the separated halves, for each must earn the privilege fully and separately of finding the missing half under those beneficent circumstances which alone could insure joy and the hoped-for understanding each human child subconsciously seeks as he attempts life after life, with union after union, to discover the combination of mate and companion, true partner and constant inspiration.

It is quite possible to meet your twin ray in incarnation and to look upon him or her as an uncongenial person, unaware of the inner bond.

The path of common sense is the fulfillment of those duties which surround you here and now and which may include a marriage that is far from ideal to your human standpoint. As I tried to point out to you in WHY WE ARE HERE, it is not right to run away from the responsibilities you are in now, even if you do believe you have discovered your Twin in the person of a suitable physical mate. Voluntary escape from burdens can only bring tragic effects unless the karmic involvements have been entirely discharged to the satisfaction of the Powers-that-be. Personalities engaged in average patterns and relationships of daily living are those who are least aware of the full scope of lessons to be learned, or who can say with certainty where and when justice is satisfied.

There are, however, exceptions to all I have said and on occasion affinities are guided by their Teachers and mentors to close companionship and opportunities to serve together in some needed aspect of the Divine Plan. At times there are unconventional relationships upon which the world looks with disapproval, which are brought about under true spiritual direction and with complete unselfishness on the parts of those involved. Perhaps I have brought you to a better realization that this subject cannot be dismissed with a few shallow generalizations where so much complexity is involved for both halves of a combination of this kind.

Very often an individual learns the difficult lessons of life before his or her soul twin and there are separations of various kinds that can keep them apart for lifetimes; or where one fails to make the grade set before the egos of the cycle, while the other measures up to the standard set for personality attainment — this can mean separation for eons.

Before much time passes you will discover more information on this subject filtering into the public consciousness, and it may fall to you to aid another's understanding of this abstruse relationship through recollection of the few hints I am placing before you now. The twins themselves, at personality level, have the least to say about what can or should be done, for it is a Soul decision that brings the two halves before each other in some degree of recognition, and the Soul is aided in this decision by the Guide or Teacher responsible for pointing the correct spiritual path leading to expansions of consciousness which flower from rounded and symmetrical unfoldment of all the graces of character that form the basis of Mastery.

Although marriage upon your planet is an institution that is acknowledged to be far from perfect in whatever latitudes and interpretations are allowed to it by the nations that house it, there has not yet appeared a thoroughly satisfactory alternative for provision of creative development and maturing of human infants. Until all of you, working together prayerfully and with the highest aspirations, arrive at a mass method of regulating the activities that stem from the physical union of men and women in some acceptable universal manner, it would be advisable to improve the marriage you now have so that it becomes more flexible and more honorable, more balanced and more rewarding as a sheltered private classroom for the experimental teaching and learning of life's major lessons.

Humans are restless seekers of improved conditions and many substitutes for conventional marriages have been tested out in the laboratory of trial and error. Much suffering has proved a stern but salutary teacher. And yet there are exceptions where it is ordained by the highest of spiritual intelligences that certain souls can best clothe themselves in a physical vehicle formed from the combined essences and hereditary physical and racial characteristics of two parents who have not acquired the marriage certificate, nor are so situated that marriage is possible to them. Even in such cases twin souls have been known to come together as parents of children who could truly be called "love children", such is the rarity of the inexpressible bliss, short-lived as perhaps it is, that surges through mind and feelings and physical vehicle perfectly matched in all ways except those ways that satisfy the world's approval. Therefore, my suggestion for you is to consider the many aspects of the subject of twin souls and to resolve where you stand now to fit yourself to become that human personality of honor and integrity, of refinement and usefulness in relation to all those with whom your lot is cast; for this is the certain road leading toward a meeting with your other half when conditions will be such for each that only joy and gratitude can eventuate.

Earth consciousness, or mass consciousness, has not yet surmounted the tendency to feel possessive and exclusive in the carrying out of intimate relationships of friendship or romantic attachment. This is one of the basic reasons why more individuals are guided away from too heavy a concentration upon one partner of wholly satisfying capacity; for the goal before humanity is demonstration of universal brotherhood as an actual fact in nature and in spirit, and this aim cannot be served while the focus is limited to inclusion of but one, and all others are shut away from the charmed circle for two.

Little by little, as you prove your willingness to drop such passionate intensity of effort to find the one who belongs to you, yet who may not be available where your lines of living are presently cast, you will all be given added knowledge upon this subject so understandably close to your hearts, and in receiving more information will find you have a base on which to build those actions which will surely lead you to your heart's desire, in God's time.

Your friend of greater experience,

J.W.

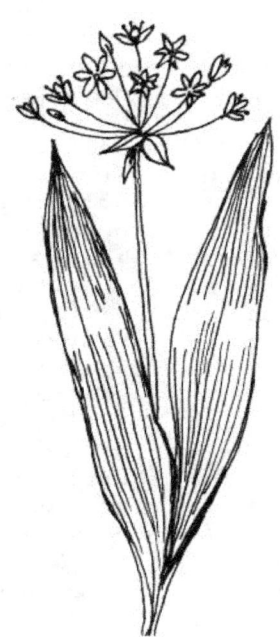

POEMS - by - Frank Ninivaggi

    Magnificent Creator, magic rod of power,
summon my thoughts to mingle in the pool of the Infinite.

    Most tremendous Author, I seek to open Your
glorious book of wisdom, and leap into Divine Communion.

    Sumptuous Lover, I fall enraptured into You.
Sonorous is the echo resounding throughout my soul; and
peace is brought to abide with me forever.

    I AM the eternal word of Truth.
    I AM the beauteous voice of Love.
    I AM the heavy hand of Justice.
    I AM the broad scale of Mercy.
    I AM the prismatic crystal of Rainbows.
    I AM the wide range of Life.
    I AM the sparkling song of Nature.
    I AM the fire in the Sun.

    All being is Mine.
    From Me all activity flows.
    Through Me all peace reigns.

Love is the flower of My I AM seeing.
Glory is another name of My Being.

    I AM the ever-present and eternal
    word of Truth that seeks entrance
    into your hearts.

    Now and forever,
    I AM

EN ROUTE

Dear Family members -

Thanks a million for helping us build up our mailing list with names of friends you feel might like to become part of the FAMILY. Since December, our list has grown to the extent that Bartram has been obliged to spend many extra hours typing up new name and address cards and sending off introductory or subscription copies of Cosmon to those who have indicated they'd like to be included.

Wouldn't you know it, though? Perhaps 50% of our new mailing list friends have said frankly they cannot help with financial support, but they want to receive the literature and we know they should, because in this way ideas will circulate beyond previous limits. That is what is important, for if we look at the world from one approach, we will see we are involved in a War of Ideas. It is Ideas that start everything, from the smallest mechanical or educational improvements all the way up to and including world changes. Every Light group is guardian of an arsenal of New Age Ideas which its custodians are intended to use as ammunition to eliminate outworn concepts and ignorance wherever they are entrenched.

More or less vaguely all of us have felt that we would be able somehow automatically to expand and grow and extend our service efforts if we kept in tune with the inflow that seeks release through us as spiritual milk for nursing the world child. We have been in accord with the thought that faith would see us through, if we could just hang on. This attitude is all right for the blind devotee, say the Teachers, but we are accountable for the use of our thinking machines and when we come to that point in our spiritual maturing where our minds are awake and champing at the bit, energetic and anxious for a test of our powers, it is then high time that we proceed beyond faith into conscious use of those principles, laws and rules which are capable of creating the results we seek and must learn to control if we are to come out of this hereditary contentment with vagueness and dreams.

It is much wiser to find the basic rules for supplying our needs than to rely on superstitious observances on a par with making wishes on the first star, throwing salt over our left shoulder and dropping pennies in wishing wells.

Here I am not intending to take only the view of how things appear from our own Light center, but am talking heart to heart with and to all Light Groups, Light workers and all fellow human beings who are bound and determined we shall find a way out of our prison of ridiculous restrictions, if it takes the very last ounce of our mental capacity and physical energy to discover the missing steps that we ought to be knowing and taking right now. This involves traveling down bypaths and kicking around a few facts and experiences common to us all, but it is not a boring, if comprehensive, subject. It is just as important for our private life as for our group life, both of which are pretty thoroughly intermingled by now, and we cannot escape our commitments to either.

El Morya Khan (Master Morya to some) gave voice to something appropriate to our discussion in His recent ENCYCLICAL ON WORLD GOOD WILL, published by the Summit Lighthouse, P.O. Box 1155, Washington 13, D.C. 20013.

C - Major Cause of Prolongation of Problems

"Strange, yet obvious though it may seem, the major underlying cause for the continuation of unrest which must be universally corrected upon earth is the attitude, held far too long, of regarding Life as a MERE SPECTATOR SPORT! Examination of the historical modes will reveal that difficulties have caused people to become embroiled in struggles which have resulted in needed corrections and reforms. Likewise, the soft living of modern civilization has tended to create indifference and aloofness on the part of the very people who are not only capable of changing the world but who are also the ones whose natures admirably fit them to be the vanguard of constructive and progressive change."

Page 3
Part II - Nature of Problems Under Consideration

You see, we must go behind the scenes if we are to discover the whys and wherefores of the operation of Universal Law. El Morya tells us our problems are running overtime because we have not done enough on our own initiative to halt them. Now, let's take it a step further. Why, into the turmoil of all this mess we have created and not yet cleaned up, should we expect a heavenly windfall of abundance, before we even have plans laid out for proper utilization of it?

It is not enough to let each day catch us standing by, like the lilies of the field, not toiling and not spinning, in the vain expectation that God will support us in our idleness because he clothes the lilies in robes of beauty more glorious than Solomon's. We are not lilies and we are not falling sparrows: we're humans, with minds and brains to register the thoughts our minds think! How can we stand there with egg on our faces imagining that faith alone, without any works or efforts on our part, will open the jackpots of heaven for our encouragement and support? 'Tisn't so!

If a wise financier, or wealthy patron of the arts, or philanthropist requires to see blueprints for action in which his funds will be used, so that he can compare these with plans presented by others, in order to determine how, or by whom, the wealth can best be used to further the good of the greatest number of individuals, can we not suppose the Divine Intelligence is even more prudent in requiring from us plans and blueprints of our intentions for use of unlimited abundance to be placed in service to advantage the whole race of men?

How many of us in this life pattern, now serving in some position of responsibility for furthering the spread of New Age ideas, have had the experience of managing great wealth and controlling our human impulses in order to keep the whole flow of attention upon creating progressive sequences moving from vision to fulfillment? Not many.

In the short span of life history for our modern Light Groups whose personnel claim they are dedicated wholly and solely to the dissemination of wisdom, knowledge and information to further the evolutionary progress of all the world's people without regard to differences of race, creed or sex, there have already cropped up evidences of forgetfulness as to their original dedications. Favoritism and prejudice have been shown, together with emphasis upon aspects that are secondary to enlightening the world and relieving the vast populations of their ignorance. Why then should such deviations from the intention of the Father be underwritten by augmented supplies?

It was impressed upon my mind, during the planning of this letter, that the parable of the Talents should be reread and the principle discussed. If you wish to study this for yourself it is in the Bible, St. Matthew 25:14. It is in this parable that the Master over these servants said: "For unto every one that hath shall be given, and he shall have abundance: but from him that hath not shall be taken away even that which he hath. And cast ye the unprofitable servant into outer darkness: there shall be weeping and wailing and gnashing of teeth."

What do you think it was, to which Jesus referred, that a person must have in order to receive abundance? First of all he or she must have integrity; but it must not be a static integrity that fences in its goodness from contamination from the jostling, hustling crowd to which we all belong. No! It must be an active integrity that we carry to market, office, factory, farm, court, schoolroom, shop, pulpit and altar, hospital and home.

Over and over we hear and read that all our fellow men and women are Christs at some degree of unfoldment and the perfected individual Whom we know as Christ is our Higher, Nobler Self emerged from the human limitations to which we are still held prisoner, and the perfected example of that which the Father intends us to become. We hear and read, but we do not receive the impact! We cannot identify with Christ because He is beyond our experience; but He can identify with all of us, because He has passed along the same long road that leads the race from babyhood to maturity, and is in deepest sympathy with our pain and bewilderment at all stages and is our Divine Sponsor begging us to look back and see our other selves as we were yesterday, even as He looks upon us and sees Himself yesterday.

Christ calls: (St. Matthew 25: 34)

"Come ye blessed of my Father, inherit the Kingdom prepared for you from the foundation of the world:

"For I was an hungered, and ye gave me meat: I was thirsty and ye gave me drink: I was a stranger and ye took me in:

"Naked and ye clothed me: I was sick and ye visited me: I was in prison, and ye came unto me.

"Then shall the righteous answer him, saying, Lord, when saw we thee an hungered, and fed thee? or thirsty, and gave thee drink?

"When saw we thee sick, or in prison, and came unto thee?

"And the King (CHRIST) shall answer and say unto them, Verily I say unto you, Inasmuch as ye have done it unto one of the least of these my brethren, ye have done it unto me."

(To those who live for self alone) He will say: "Verily I say unto you, Inasmuch as ye did it not to one of the least of these, ye did it not unto me. . . . "

Now let's have another try at whatever point we have reached, at taking TRUTH literally and not as myth, legend and symbol. What we did yesterday is not quite good enough for today or tomorrow. We are a few hours older and wiser and must put our improved understanding to work.

When the scattered representatives of the Forces of Light, working upon the physical plane, compare notes in person or in communications across distances, there is one basic theme common to all: Struggle. There are tales of struggle that would set your heart on fire with admiration! It is a marvel in a relatively cynical period of transition to realize there are as many as there ARE of sober, sane and responsible citizens who have heard the inaudible CALL or seen the invisible signs that directed them to take initiative and to inaugurate world changes at the level of individual responsibility, which is where all world changes in every aspect of Life must begin — with an individual who CARES ENOUGH about the vision to take steps to make it tangible before the eyes of others who cannot behold it direct.

There are many many little groups of sincere souls, other than COSMON, who are giving everything they own and borrowing all they can get their hands on, going into debt and living on short rations of food and clothing so that you may be given the gift of Light by sacrificial hands. They do not see their way clear, sometimes not even the next step, but they hope and believe that somehow their indefatigable hard work, carried on day in and day out, will create fruits of the spirit which can guarantee your future and the future of civilization.

If you who merely read and who benefit from the struggles of these hundreds of dedicated souls, could only realize it, your part is far easier to play than the parts of those who grope their ways as trail blazers into undiscovered territories where the New Ideas await recognition and development. By the kinds of fruits they gather from the higher dimensions of spiritual consciousness, you shall know them as true servants of the Plan of God. Only those ideas that have no stains of specialized or limited benefits, but are for all children of the Father in every nation, carry the impress of the New Age. Anything that is brought forth for minorities of any kind, does not bear the genuine signature of Aquarius.

Be alert for taints of racial or religious prejudice upon the offerings of those who try to hide their motives as they mingle with the sincere sharers of Love and Wisdom. Turn away from those who claim to bring good for any chosen few. God has chosen all His children to be His beneficiaries. Any less than the blessing of all is not of God, though it comes from priests and ministers, social figures, scientific authorities, teachers or leaders of multitudes. Those who speak for the supremacy of any segment of the human race as opposed to the whole of the human race, are wolves in sheep's clothing. Be warned of them by the gong in your own heart placed there for your protection.

It is up to the peoples of the world to become individual earners of freedom, one by one. All of us must continue the daily and hourly effort to conquer our own weaknesses, and they will often dismay even the strong among us as they burst forth from long-accustomed habit into the most humiliating manifestations. I speak for my human self as well as yours, for none of us is ready yet to set aside our guard and say confidently: "It is finished." Our common problem is that we are not yet made whole, but are called upon to help and share the knowledge we have, however limited it may be, even in the midst of our own experiment with Life and our own awareness of how imperfect we are, because there isn't anyone else who can substitute for us in this particular labor. All of us are on-the-job trainees and it is tough!

The cycles of Ages preceding this one have developed the bad habit in us of strong partisanship for certain forms of religion, nationalism, government and the mechanics of living our daily lives. It is the hardest thing in the world for us to come up beyond the "watertight compartments" we have made to insulate ourselves against the odd ways of "others", but we cannot afford to wait any longer as holdouts, for it is fully time to join the FAMILY OF MAN as members synchronized in spirit with every branch, group and individual of it.

Not any single Light group now working upon the earth can reach all the millions of every land, and that is exactly why there are so many groups, some for every continent.

In America alone there are more groups than many of you realize if you are not working in a center which receives quantities of publications and periodicals showing forth the evidence of earnest dedication on every hand. There is so much shining intelligence and love harnessed for your benefit that you are bound to find at least one, if not several of these relatively new Service Centers in which you feel spiritually "at home" and at ease. Each one is given some aspect of the glorious wholeness to bring to your attention, and no two are exactly alike. Nor is it the intention of Those Who are behind the visible movement of mass enlightenment to limit or confine your allegiance to one small group alone, to the exclusion of all others. While we are yet incarnated beings, there will be some groups and persons to whom we gravitate most naturally, and to whom our love flows freely as to dear friends known so long they are as our other selves, while some seem less well known to us and their particular projects less congenial to ourselves. But we can live and let live as groups, as well as individuals, and allow others full freedom to carry on their assignments from the same Source as come our own, knowing all are doing their best to create a network of harmony for the blessing and healing of the nations.

* * * * * * *

It is probable that every Light group receives correspondence from friends and members whose letters repeat the theme song of the time: "I am so sorry that I can do so little to help, but I live on a very small income and can only send you a small gift once in awhile." It must be the forces of darkness that have belittled people to the extent that they fail to recognize what can be done by many people together, each giving a little bit. There is no doubt of the power of little bits that have combined to build up the tobacco industry, the liquor industry, the coffee industry, the candy industry, the entertainment industries and the food industries. All these are material monuments of very impressive order which prove beyond the shadow of a doubt that many drawn together in support of either necessities or luxuries can achieve anything they really desire to attain.

Considering that this is true, it is also obvious that few among those who declare they find the works of the Light Groups indispensable to Life allow themselves to go without the material things that are thought essential, even though they are willing to accept the productions of the New Age forerunners gratis, while they set aside insurance funds for the purchase of soft and hard beverages, candy, tobacco and movies.

A time of decision has come upon us wherein the friends, members, followers and well-wishers of all the works of Light must come forth and prove their worthiness to be continued recipients of the distilled blood, sweat and tears of the comparative few whose whole lives are bound up in the struggle to set mankind free from fear, want and violence.

It cannot be denied that humans, and not robins or alligators or boll weevils have built up these immense industries catering to the pleasure and comfort of the physical body of man. Let it now be shown that the small change of the world can build up an enduring monument of devotion and thanksgiving to the Father of us all, for His goodness in setting before us so many way stations of spiritual food across the lands where all may be supplied if everyone will come to the rescue with pennies and other little coins, which TOGETHER can furnish sufficient support for all works and workers on the side of Light, wherever they are found.

You are not too proud to drop pennies in the collection plate at church. Why then hesitate to further the works of Aquarian inspiration in the same manner? All groups of Light need postage stamps. All such groups badly need one hundred and one things such as pencils and pens and stationery and typewriter ribbons and paper clips and filing cards. Pennies put together will buy or replace all these basic essentials. All Light groups need everything other groups need in as great a supply as they can get IF they are to carry out God's work on the scale He desires!

Please realize that I am constituting myself a voice for ALL works and workers for the Light Forces, wherever they happen to be and whatever aspect they are engaged in developing. This certainly includes many lone workers whom you must seek out and help as ardently and continuously as you must support all the other Light workers who happen to be merged into groups, IF YOU WISH TO KEEP SPIRITUAL LIGHT BURNING, and don't want it to disappear from lack of your recognition of responsibility so that we fall back into spiritual darkness!

Encourage, support and praise New Age scientists, physicians, ministers and priests, teachers, organic farmers, health food promoters, vegetarian restaurants, dentists, psychologists, government officials, laborers, entertainers and all others in every field who are attempting to make this world a safer, saner, healthier, happier and more beautiful place for all creatures who live upon the surface. Help them all! Strain! Don't stop at what is convenient for you to give. Give all that is possible which gives you a chance to measure up comparably with all those who sacrifice every hour of their daily lives so that the light may keep burning for you as long as they can hold body and soul together. In this way, if no other, the meek owners of pennies, pence and centavos can surely inherit the earth if they can help in the salvage of it!

God loves you and so do I,

Barbara Steele

CHILDREN OF THE NEW AGE

By Maurine Sellstrom

Foreword

We are offering our readers a most unique treat this month in the form of a communication from the Intelligence of an unborn child. Maurine tuned in to her daughter's coming baby a month before the birth. We have heard of rare instances previously where it was known such communication could be undertaken, but this is the first time we have been given the privilege of sharing a firsthand experience in this realm.

Please allow your mind to dwell upon the naturalness and reasonableness of these mental-spiritual adventures. They are intended to belong to all people everywhere, and they will after the few who dare to pioneer and publish the results of their experiments are accepted on good faith as heralds of things to come.

Keep your mind open, accepting and willing to be shown something that defies tradition as you know it.

Cosmon Research Foundation

Dear Cosmonites —

I am sharing my Christmas Present with you. This is a letter I received from my new Granddaughter — born January 23, 1964. Letter received December 24, 1963.

Dear Mother, Father, and Grandma,

Thank you for inviting me to come and live with you. I could not have come to Earth except I was sure of my welcome. I feel your warm love getting ready to nurture me and help me to learn about life on Earth.

Grandma I am like the little kitten that crawled on your lap today, I need the nurture and comfort of a warm and loving body. All three of you will be a great help and solace to me in this respect. My new father was chosen for his Norwegian serenity and strength. I need the gentleness to be found in all of you.

Some of us come to Earth with a job to do which necessitates keeping our sensitivity. You three will help me to keep mine, while you can help me to develop the strength and physical well-being to endure the Earth's currents and emotional forces without making those same sensitive nerves bear too big a load.

I love the water too, Grandma, and as for you it can be a reminder for me that "in Him we live and move and have our being."

Mother, help me to know and keep the great joy and vitality in life which you so buoyantly wear. This I know you can do, and for this reason I greatly value the privilege of growing up with your wise and loving guidance. I will need strength and vitality, for what I must do will take a great deal.

I will also need the integrity that I can learn from my Grandpa, the kind that will give me the firmness to do what I must, even when it is unpleasant and I would rather not. Mother, remember this need in my training, and help me to make habits which cultivate this kind of strength.

This is Christmas Eve, when the carols sing of Peace on Earth and Good Will to man. But to bring this peace to Earth many people must carry both good will and strength to do what is right and resist what is wrong. My work will be in that field. To accomplish this I need love, and strength, and serenity and integrity as well as the ability to endure discomfort and disapproval. I will need love and understanding. I will need a lot of ability to accurately estimate those with whom I deal in a way that is as "wise as a serpent and as harmless as a dove." I need the strength of a good body, and a serene mind which is freed to think all it is capable of thinking unimpaired by anxiety and needless nervousness.

Grandma I will want to know and develop an understanding heart. Pray for me and send me the currents of help as you have learned to do. The task of our generation is a great one, but if we are successful we can be the ones who help to establish the New Age and fulfill your long dream of the Kingdom on Earth as it is in Heaven.

This is probably the last communication of this adult level I will be able to send for a long time. As I become completely involved in learning to use a new body, my mind must go through the age level processes to claim the hereditary body which you have all given to me. Of course you know we are all adults really at the moment of birth. In this late time wise and developed adults are coming to the Earth in great numbers. But we must become as little children open to instruction, direction and discipline and training in learning the ways of Earth.

Help me and be patient as I show slowness to understand. Know that I can understand, and communicate to me as a whole person. Silently and subjectively communicate when you feel the objective training is going slowly. If you can do this, I may be able to show speed and alertness to all my needed training.

My love to all of you. I will see you soon. I am looking forward to our life together.
          Sincerely,
          Your emerging Christ Child

After receiving the letter there was added awareness about the needs for these children of the New Age. There were many kinds of wisdom that understanding adults could help them to acquire.

These children will need the ability to deal with brilliance and stardom. They will need to resist the temptation to project their abilities on others and make stars of them. They must learn to be responsible for their own talents, instead of projecting upon others a "fan" type of admiration.

It is easier for us to take back the projections of criticism. We can all do this as we develop the ability to know God's will and have the humility to be guided in prayer and meditation. But we are more afraid of our projections of ability and the accompanying response-ability that responding to ability entails.

Many of us feel overly responsible, when in truth we are really balking at the response life is asking of us. Man cannot begin to respond to all of the abilities God has endowed him with. We need to flow into action into life; this is the real secret. Respond to our joy, to our interests, to our obligations and to our loves. When we do this life can flow with us, from us, through us and around us to create the abundant life.

Our men in their building and caution are needed to give us the balancing stability that will preserve the vitality and keep the giving in proportion.

The world is growing into the New Age where old concepts of conservatism and liberality must be laid aside for new and more dynamic ones. The Conservatism should not be to conserve old forms, but conserve the original basic purpose and God-given endowment that each man brings with him to his birth. The Liberalism should not be government handouts, but individual handouts of vitality, and love and interest, until all men feel love support and oneness with their fellow men. We can all be liberal with the energies and abilities God gave us in the first place. It is only as we use those energies that there is any room for more in the limited cup of our personalities.

These children of the New Age can absorb all the wisdom we can give them, for they are capable of great sensitivities and too wise to need crucifixion as a learning experience. They will need all of our ability for objective observation to give them the skills to make objective force unnecessary, for they can know with whom they deal. They will be capable of knowing and dealing with all people as whole persons. Both the objective and the subjective sides will be taken into consideration.

Grandmas can be a great help with this training of the New Age children if they can lay aside their own self-pity and vanities and demands for consideration and respect. They can give the wisdom of their observations and the love and acceptance to help develop these sensitive potentialities in their grandchildren.

If we can give these children the appreciation to see and know the fields in which they play, they can be the ones to establish the Kingdom of Heaven on Earth and all souls can bask in the beauty of the new dimensions.

There was a sense also that with each generation the children will individually contain a better balance of masculine and feminine qualities. They will at the same time live wisely in the masculine or feminine role which their body designates. Both men and women will be able to use as needed the conceptual and building and active phases of living, which have been termed masculine, as well as the nurturing, sustaining, accepting and appreciating qualities which have been termed feminine. We will see them expressing in response to the polarity established in various groups.

Either men or women will be able to make balances. When in the presence of another who is conceiving and building, they can be appreciative and accepting. When it is their turn to conceive and build, they will find then associates able to help with the accepting, sustaining and appreciating.

As we can help to develop these skills and wisdoms, we will be truly following Jesus' instruction of "giving unto these my little ones, for of such is the kingdom of Heaven." It is time for us to enter into this project and enjoy the beauty of its bounty, for this is the true giving to the future. As we can do this and count not the cost, it will be our Father's good pleasure to give us the kingdom, pressed down and running over.

Thus those entering from other dimensions must become as little children to learn the ways of Earth, and as we mature we in turn must become as little children to enter the Kingdom of Heaven, or the New Age. No soul can enter into a new dimension without a childlike attitude of learning and taking instruction in ways and concepts we have not before understood.

ANOTHER COUNTY HEARD FROM

A friend of ours knows the woman whose message from a young girl on the Other Side of Life is presented to you here. Sam is the Spirit Guide of the Channel. What follows is self-explanatory. We hope to have further material from Mrs. Joan Dixon, whose interesting communication was forwarded to us by a mutual friend.

— Barbara Steele

Sam brought a teen-ager home to tell me her story. We thought you might be interested.

Hello, my name is Kathy. I was fifteen when I died. Although I've been over here several years I'm still a teen-ager at heart. You see, time goes faster over here. So we mature more slowly than you do, although we learn at about the same rate. Now don't ask me to explain that further. It's way over my head.

My life in your world was a very good one, from the material point of view. I had about everything a teen-ager could ask for. My folks had money, which didn't hurt me a bit when it came to popularity. In fact I always had boy friends hanging around. I was a cheerleader and attended all the games. Oh, I had lots of "school spirit". (That's a joke, in case you didn't catch it.)

One night we were going to hold an all-night pep rally. It started raining and most of the kids went home. But I insisted on being one of the last to leave, even though I got soaked to the skin. The next day I had such a bad cold that mama didn't want me to go to the game. I told her everyone was counting on me being there. And besides I didn't want to stay home. That night it rained again and I got wet and cold. I was plenty tired when I got home. But I didn't sleep good. I kept having nightmares. I must have hollered for mama because she came into my room and turned on the light. I'll never forget the look on her face when she saw me. She said to Daddy, "I don't care if it is 2 A.M., I'm calling the doctor, she looks terrible." That's about the last thing I remember clearly, except for a pain in my chest.

I'll never forget my awakening. It was weird. I was sitting on the grass and it was a sunny day. Real picnic weather. There were trees nearby and over to my left some buildings. The place looked ordinary enough, but there was something unusual about it. I couldn't put my finger on it. Naturally I wondered where I was and how I'd gotten there.

There was a girl sitting near me. I started to ask her a question, and then I saw her eyes. They were sort of glassy and she was staring into space like she wasn't really seeing anything. It really shook me. I noticed other people then, some sitting, some walking around like sleepwalkers.

I decided this was no place for me and got up and hurried toward the buildings. On my way I thought of the opening scene in "The Snake Pit" when the girl wakes up and wonders where she is and doesn't know she's in an insane asylum. That really scared me.

On the steps of the nearest building stood a kindly-looking woman, a small plump gray-haired lady with smiling eyes.

"Well, hello there," she greeted me happily. "I see you're wide awake."

"I seem to have lost my way," I told her politely. "Could you tell me where I am?"

"You're still a little disoriented," she replied still smiling. "But don't worry. It will come to you."

That wasn't the kind of reply I wanted to hear. I began to wonder if she was a patient too.

"Where's my mother?" I demanded. "I want to see mama."

She turned away so I couldn't see her face. "You're a long ways from home."

"That isn't the kind of evasive answer I want," I snapped. "Why don't you tell me the truth?"

There were people going in and out all the time. She called to one of them. "Here's Dr. Long. Maybe he can help you." Aha, I told myself, so this is a hospital and he's one of the psychiatrists.

Dr. Long was a tall dignified gentleman with a serene face and the wisest, calmest eyes you can imagine. "What's the trouble, young lady?" he asked.

"Where am I anyway? Is this some sort of hospital or what?"

He didn't answer right away, just looked at me. I got the feeling he wasn't looking at me, but right through me or inside of me. At last he said slowly, "No, this isn't a mental hospital, or anything like it. There's nothing at all wrong with that mind of yours except, I believe, you've had a good hard case of over-protection and find it difficult to face reality. Especially when things don't go the way you want."

I didn't know how to reply to this. For once I was speechless. Then he asked, "What's the last thing you remember before waking up over here?"

I thought a moment. "Well, I went to a ball game. Then when I got home I was tired and went to bed. Oh, I remember mama and how her face looked when she saw me. And there was an awful pain in my chest."

"Yes. I believe you had pneumonia. A fatal case."

Now I think I knew what he meant, but I just wasn't ready to listen. I looked at the people around us. Most of them were kids like myself, about high school age.

"What is this place, a boarding school?" I wondered.

"You can call it that if you like," he answered. I got the feeling he meant I could call it anything I wanted and it still wouldn't make any difference.

The kindly lady (later she told me her name was Ruth Anson or, as most of the kids called her, Aunt Ruth) spoke up. "I see you were a cheerleader. You must have been pretty popular over there. I'm sure you'll find the teen-agers over here just as easy to get along with."

I looked down at myself and saw I was still wearing my cheerleader's uniform. "That's a silly thing to wear to a boarding school," I commented.

"I think you know better than that," Dr. Long replied. "I believe you now realize where you really are and how you got here. But you're doing all you can to avoid the truth. This is entirely wrong. You're letting yourself in for a lot of unpleasantness. But until you find the strength within yourself to accept what's real, nothing we say or do can help you very much."

Then he spoke to Aunt Ruth. "Don't worry about her. Just treat her like anyone else. It's going to take time, but she's got a lot of common sense and a good sense of values, in spite of the fact they've been suppressed for many years. Right now she wants to be treated like a spoiled child. But she'll get over that. When she quits sulking she'll want someone around to talk to, to treat her like she's more than just another difficult case."

"Someone like her mother?"

"Definitely not. That's the root of her problem. No, someone her own age only more mature."

That was the gist of what he said. I don't really remember too clearly because at the time it was all over my head. But I've learned a lot about myself since then. And I think that's about the way Dr. Long had me sized up.

Then he left, and was I relieved! He had such a bad habit of saying things I didn't want to hear.

"This really is a school," Aunt Ruth was explaining. (I mean when I got around to listening to her again.) "We have classes in almost everything you can imagine. When you graduate here you go on to the University. Just like where you came from. Shall we go in and get you enrolled?"

"No thanks," I replied stubbornly. "Not until I talk to mama."

The smile faded and she looked away. "You're a long way from home you know."

"You already told me that," I yelled, getting madder by the minute. "But haven't you people ever heard of a modern invention called the telephone? You can call anywhere with it. Even Russia. That is, if I'm not already in Russia. From what I've seen of this place I'm not so sure."

I saw right away I was wasting my time. She didn't even bat an eyelash. "Dr. Long is right, you know," she replied calmly. "You can't run away from reality."

Well maybe not, but I sure gave it a try. In the weeks that followed I became one of the most anti-social creatures you'd ever want to meet. Although, come to think of it, I must have been pretty rational about it from the very beginning. I don't remember actually looking for a telephone. But I did lose my temper at a moment's notice. I yelled at people in public and did lots of other disagreeable things. Naturally people avoided me, but I didn't care. I missed my family and friends back home and spent many lonely hours brooding and worrying about myself and my future.

One day I overheard one of my classmates say to another, "Poor Kathy. She has so much potential. But at the rate she's going she'll be having a nervous breakdown before much longer."

Well, that pretty well floored me. I hadn't realized just how I'd looked to others. Me, the most popular girl in my class. But not over here. Here I was just another problem child. I did some serious thinking and decided that no matter what, I was going to be my old self again.

Of course things didn't change overnight. I'd still get so lonesome sometimes I could hardly stand it. But on the whole things improved. I even made a few casual friends. No one I really cared much about though.

One day I was sitting by a stream dreaming of home when a boy about my age came up and introduced himself. I don't remember his exact words, but he told me his name was Larry and he was studying to be a guide.

"A guide." I asked, "What's that?"

So he told me. And it sounded fascinating. And at the same time I realized how little thought I'd given to what I wanted to be. We talked all afternoon. And by that time we both felt like we'd known each other for years. From then on when I was lonesome I'd hunt up Larry. Sometimes I'd sit for hours just waiting for him. Sometimes he'd be waiting when I got out of class. School work was a breeze. My grades improved so, I could hardly believe it.

My first trip home was a shock. Larry warned me that it would be, but I had such dreams of homecoming I wouldn't listen. I guess I'd have been able to make the trip much sooner if I hadn't been so wrapped up in myself. At that I was lucky I guess. Larry says some people become "earthbound" and they're worse off than the ones that stay over here and get homesick.

Anyway, it was easy enough to make the trip once he showed me how. I walked right into my home like I still belonged there. I saw right away mama had rearranged the living room furniture again. Some pieces were missing, but I didn't know what. Larry told me to look in my room. I did and was I surprised! Everything was different. Nothing of mine remained. Not even a stick of furniture. I remarked about how different things were and Larry only nodded.

"I thought she'd be like that."

"Who?"

"Your mother."

I didn't know what he was talking about so I went into the kitchen. And there was mama cooking supper. I walked right up and kissed her on the cheek. Then I remembered what was missing from the living room.

"What did you do with my picture?" I asked. Not expecting an answer of course.

I went back into the living room and looked around. Nothing of mine was there.

"What did you expect?" Larry asked. "Did you think she would sit around and mourn for you the rest of her life?"

"Oh no. But did she have to get rid of everything?"

"Some people have a lot of forgetting to do."

"But even my picture."

"Don't worry. She keeps a picture of you in her heart."

Suddenly I got a vivid impression of what it had been like for mama these last few months, especially right after my death. I flopped into dad's old easy chair and began to cry.

"Are you doing this?" I asked, but Larry shook his head and looked worried.

"You must be getting something from your mother's mind. You have a lot of ESP and your presence here has stirred up old memories."

"Oh, quit talking like a doctor." I sobbed, and he took my hand and said, "Let's go." It was a long time before I had the courage to visit my mother again.

Well, that's about all. I'm still going to school and I've decided I want to learn to be a guide. Larry says I'll make a good one. I like to talk a lot. Or had you noticed?

I just want to add that I think people do their kids a great injustice when they give them all the material advantages but shelter them from the truth that life is hard and it takes a tough person to live and not be beaten down by it. If people really want their kids to have the very best they'll have to start early to teach children the character-strengthening virtues of faith, hope, love, fortitude, temperance, justice, and above all, self-discipline. Give them these and they'll get all the material things they need. Like I said, I've been here several years and I've learned a lot. I wish I had known these things when I first came here. It would have helped.

THE CREATIVE PROCESS

By Maurine W. Sellstrom

> These ideas are the result of a group meditation where we experienced a visit in fantasy with J.W. as he showed us the creative process on his planet.

We have been meeting regularly as a research group to work with fantasy, imagery, prayer, and channelling in order to see what new and creative ideas we could find to help us with our daily living and to help in our work of understanding human emotions. We have also been seeking for better understanding for our newly formed church, our Congregation of All Faiths.

Our Minister, Howard Carey, Eileen Charlton, and others besides myself have been meeting regularly. Our group varies from three to five people. We each open with an invocational type of prayer asking for guidance and instruction from those unseen who will better help us to understand the will of God for our work.

Our Minister some time ago has received the gift of tongues and often has a communication in a beautiful language which is unknown to us. Eileen frequently sees pictures or fantasy images as he speaks. It seems that my part is to have some understanding of the meanings or interpretations of what we are contacting. Others who are present from time to time make various clarifying contributions. I am sure each one present lends energies and helps us to focus our attention to receive more clearly the gift of the new ideas that are presented to us.

In one of our recent sessions Eileen had the distinct impression that J.W. of our Cosmon group was contacting us and had something to show us. She felt his great love for us, and his sorrow that so frequently our personalities keep us from clearly understanding what he would communicate. He also seemed to want us to understand that on no plane does anyone have all the answers, so that even though we do contact intelligences beyond our present development, they too have limitations. They are limited both in what they know and in knowledge of how to impart their knowledge to us.

Her first impression was of two space ships. One was a huge and shining metal one, such as we would imagine to be the most advanced type of vehicle our scientists on Earth could imagine and build. It left the Earth and at a certain place in space was exploded into bits by the pressures of the atmosphere and the currents moving rapidly around the Earth. The second ship was a nearly invisible shield of concentrated and rapidly moving energies with which we could learn to surround ourselves. This formed a shield or vehicle in which man could project himself, not physically but in thought form into other realms.

She said she saw J.W. try to explain this by using two graphs showing vibratory movements. The graph illustrating Earth vibration had wave lengths that were short, rapid and jerky and very close together, while those of space and of Jupiter were very wide waves or scallops, indicating a smoother and much less rapid vibration. It seemed that the force of the quick short wave lengths could be used like a jet to propel us through the current barriers which would explode the solidified form of any metal plane we could build. Then the fantasy moved on.

In the next scene she viewed, we were being shown a crystal clear large waterfall, perhaps on the planet Jupiter. It was frozen solid! The illusion of ice rather than a flowing waterfall seemed to be due to the difference in vibrational length and because our Earthly vision is used to the more rapid wave length in the movement of energies.

Next with a beam of light from the center of his forehead, J.W. cut out a square piece of the ice. As he took it out it looked like clear plastic. He carried it to a centrally located place and laid it on a block that seemed to be an altar situated where there was a focal point of the planet's energies. As this piece of solidified energy was laid on this altar and all the energies of the planet focused upon it, a new creation or form of life arose out of it! This seemed to be symbolic of a creative process. It could come out as a flower, or a woman, or any other form, all depending upon how those energies were directing its form.

I felt the purpose of the fantasy was to show us how creation happens. The movements of the two planets may be very different, so that our currents move at so rapid a rate that before we can see the form our wishes, desires and plans create, they have changed. The process is so rapid in our Earth vibrations that we lose sight of the process. Our creations flow away like our water, with our emotions and our ever-changing desires, and do not come to solidified form without work and building materially. By seeing this process in another vibration we could witness how creation is accomplished. Out of solidified idea or emotional longing, our vital energy is frozen or solidified into form. Our concentration of attention upon our concepts of how to bring it about is how we break this portion of energy from the flow all around us. As this piece of energy is brought to the altar which focuses the planet's energies, our attention shapes the substance from this native desire into the forms our experience and concepts have projected upon it.

We on Earth are living in a much more fluid and heated world, using the passions of love and hate and fear which have melted our waters. They are not in a state of solidity so we cannot see them as crystal, clear and pure. But we are still using these substances which are our energies in a similar manner, though working in a different and more fluid vibration. Whether we realize it or not, we are creating forms with our desires and with the energy of our sustained attention and with the beam of our vision, however limited the shapes of those forms which we experience in our living.

Eileen felt that J.W. verified this conclusion as the concept he was trying to impart. He added that it was so hard for us because our vision keeps changing with the fluidity of movement in Earth vibrations.

It seems that almost before we can catch the vision of one thing which our desire uses our energies to form, desire has already shifted and our longing is focused on something else.

Until we can become willing to give what we desire our intellectual and physical participation, it cannot bear interest as money or any form of abundance for us. People want to give form to a certain concept, or hold a particular job, or write some kind of book, because they believe there is money or wealth connected with such an enterprise. They say, "I have a right to that kind of activity because there is a return in it for me."

They want to make this claim before they have learned the right way to do what they desire. Once they have learned the right way to do any task, that is the way RIGHT with all the laws of the correct use of this creative energy. Then the return is inevitable. But return cannot come in any abundance until man can say with Kipling:

"And no man shall work for money
And no one shall work for fame
But each for the joy of the working
And each in his separate star
Shall paint the thing as he sees it
In the name of the gods as they are."

It seems that until one can work in this spirit he only receives the interest and the stimulation of the working. It does not bring the really abundant return that is longed for.

Yet many say, "Until I see there is something in it for me, I will not do anything." This state of mind indicates that they have not correctly used the science of creation and their work will not really prosper.

The truly creative process has to do with how we break off this piece of crystallized energy and hold it in the light of our attention and focus the energies of our beings. The imagery that persists in the beam of attention determines the form our creation takes.

Eileen felt that J.W. wanted to admonish us not to give up too easily. Because this is not an easy process for us, and our attention creates whether it is sustained on one desire or not. If it is too scattered what we seem to create is confusion!

Then our fantasy moved again and I saw each man as a block of such crystallized energy broken from the whole of life by the desire of God. Each of us seems like a living altar of such clear icelike energy. Then I saw that out of the center of the block that seemed to be me, energies in the form of emotions and longings began to heat up and create a kind of volcano. From this heated center in the midst of the block arose a mist as the ice melted in the flame of vital energy. The mist ascended and as it became more solid or heavy, fell down around the block into the shapes and forms of my world.

I saw that as we can bless this process, the forms so created turn toward the block from which they emerged, holding out their hands with gifts or fruits; thus bringing abundance into living. However, when we curse the process and bemoan the forms the mist takes, they turn their backs to the senders and hold out their arms loaded with gifts to a still more remote circle of forms, or projections. So as we curse that which forms from our energies, we see another circle of projected forms receiving what we have longed to have. Thus, by our self-pity, we give away the fruits of our creative process.

Eileen felt that this means we must work for our creations, or another will receive them.

What held my attention as important was that we must let our energies melt out the images of our desires, into a flowing living stream. If we remain static and frozen, nothing happens, our creations remain formless within us.

Each of us becomes a living altar, a piece of energy formed by God's desire. Whatever in our living receives our active emotional interest and participation stimulates the creative process, so that our imagery comes out as mist to take form in our life. As we have integration of desire and unity of purpose, the process is more rapid and less conflicting. When something matters very much we need to meditate and focus our energies to concentrate on the forms we are creating.

At this point we realized that in forming a Congregation of All Faiths we had pledged our energies to the form of accepting people as they really are. We could no longer stand as individuals in an ivory tower feeling that those different from ourselves are queer. We must really understand the forms of other people's ceremonies and beliefs if they are to be in our circle of accepted forms.

J.W. at this point made some humorous observances: "How about accepting ideas and beings whose forms you cannot see, or those who perhaps are formless. Can you accept an abundant life that does not take the form of monetary or earthly goods, but is just abundant life?"

He said, "Man wants to say, 'Presto chango, come a woman, come a building, come a flower,' but can he say yet, 'Come what is'? When he is willing to do that, he will more nearly move with the creative plan for the Universe. The rose has many petals, 'In my Father's house are many mansions,' the soul has many facets, the entity has many forms.

"Can a minister believe in an abundance that doesn't come in an offering basket; can a counselor believe in one that is not in a fee; can a head of a non-profit organization believe in abundance that does not come in donations?"

Then we saw that each of us, through our living, receives what has become the most precious. To one it may be love, to another faith, while still another seeks to find new truths.

J.W. observed that man has trouble letting his energies flow out into form when they would come in a form he does not want to recognize.

We see another man like a building with lights shining out of his windows. We long for the bright light we see another show. Yet as we let our own light shine, as we send forth our prayer backed by our emotions and our energies, God gives us back a return for our investment in what is most precious to our hearts. For one it may be a healing for a loved one, for another an inspiration, for someone else a new discovery which will improve or lighten his business. To each of us our blessing comes in the form most precious to our hearts.

If we will open the block of life that is ourselves and let the energies flow out with our prayers, we will each bring our blessing into the field where we stand. To the scientist it will be a scientific contribution, to the minister a sermon or greater faith, to the doctor the ability to heal in new ways, to the mother help for her children, to the counselor a better understanding of human relationships. As we each work and pray and understand this process more fully, we will become a magnet for the creative energies for the things we do know and understand. We may think what another attracts is brighter, but God has put each of us here with our special job to do, and the magnet to attract those energies we need to give form to our longings.

OUR IVORY TOWERS

By Violet Dale Cavell

This article is reprinted from The Beacon magazine of January, 1943
by courtesy of Foster Bailey and the Author, my friend of many years.
— Barbara Steele

How often these days do we hear persons say, "They have retired to their Ivory Tower" but have we asked ourselves if we have one? Before we answer that question might it not be well to analyze what an Ivory Tower is built of, what it looks like and where it is located?

The foundation of every Ivory Tower is pride, its long uneven stairs are constructed of the fears of past ages; the Tower has no windows, for when we climb these stairs, we do not want to look out upon the world of suffering, we are seeking for the separate self, peace; we do not want to be disturbed, shaken loose from our moorings, that Anchor that holds us to the Past, old habits, old traditions, old forms of government, money luxuries for the few, and starvation for the many. But why should we be concerned about the many, when we have our Tower where we can retreat into a life of Wishful Thinking, where the lights of glamour ever shine, and we can dream, and let the other fellow do the straightening of a world that got itself all bloody, why should we be annoyed by all that noise and mess, we had nothing to do with it — or did we?

Where is the Ivory Tower located? On an Island (of separateness) surrounded by water that is a bit too rough to hold a clear reflection (of the soul) and on these waters we see the black Swans (of selfishness). As we stand at the one entrance that our Tower has (the lower mind) we can see across those rough waters, if we hold the mind and eye very steady, the mainland (of reality) where the conflict (the pairs of opposites) rages, but we have an idea that cannot touch us, we do not belong to that seething mass of humanity, we are idealists, we do not like War, and we will not kill other human beings, we wrap the cloak of Pacifism tightly around us, and we can in fancy see a faint halo around our heads, for in our innermost hearts we have a real loathing for those who kill; in our blindness, in our windowless Tower we cannot see the utter selflessness of those who are willing to give their all, including life that others may live in safety. What would we call the warriors, if not — idealists? For they are striving to bring their ideal down and make the way clear for right human relations; theirs is the real Will to Good.

Perhaps we are artists or musicians, with highly sensitive emotional and physical bodies, and the dissonance of strife hits us like hammer blows; so, we take to the Ivory Tower. Oh yes, we admit it is an escape effort, we do not like reality, we prefer to dream and put our dreams down in colors on a canvas or black notes upon a sheet of paper; we have never achieved greatness, but we are sure if we remain in our Ivory Tower long enough we will; we have carefully avoided reading the life stories of all great geniuses, how they have sunk their teeth deep into life and suffered, and out of that suffering have come strength and — a vision that they have been able to hand on to others, and because of the genius born of privation and pain, others have had a glimpse of Heavenly Hosts; but we do not want to suffer, we are content with our mediocrity.

Then too, we may be advanced students of a universal philosophy, we have acquired great knowledge and some Wisdom, we enjoy our isolation so much that we have completely lost touch with reality, and have ascended to the very top of our Ivory Tower, and decided that we will not return to this world again. No reincarnation for us; but we have lost track of what Initiation would have to be taken before we have the choice of the Paths — which are Seven, and that choice is only made possible because of our Oneness with all that is, not a wish to escape from the destiny of the Whole.

We may belong to the favored few who have vast wealth, which we have used to surround ourselves with beauty, comfort and security; our walls are high so that the masses may not see the beauty that our money has gathered from all corners of the earth; why should the struggling, suffering people be permitted to see beauty, they could not desire or appreciate it, they are poor, only I have the power to have these things, they are mine, mine; no, I will not share, I'll stay in my Tower and the rest of the world can go hang. But can it? Don't you hear the walls cracking? Humanity is on the march — the sleeping giant is awakening.

There are those among us who have developed extraordinary minds. Ah, how that sets us above other people; what power it gives us over them. Kindness, Sympathy, that is the way of the weakling. I can sit in my Ivory Tower and make slaves of those who can be swayed by my voice, I can make them do my will. Come down from the Ivory Tower, humanity has grown up mentally, and will no longer be pushed around.

To us the Ivory Tower of our making is a thing of great strength and beauty, and very white; what does it look like to others? Perhaps a bit shoddy and its color a murky gray. People laugh a little when they speak of it, and remark that it is fortunate for the human race that there are so few. One of these days their laughter and tolerance will reach us on our Island, and we will awake and discover that we are terribly alone and lonely; without our stirring heart we long for the fellowship of sharing in experience, even if it is the fellowship of suffering; then we descend from our Tower, humility has taken the place of pride. As we stand at the shore of our Island, we hear the crumbling of the Tower that we have turned our backs upon, the Swans are now White, the water calm and blue, we long for that mainland of reality and our minds strive higher, ever higher to find a way across the intervening space. To our amazement a radiant Bridge appears, and we know that we can now become a part of the Whole, and our heart overflows in a new Comradeship of Joy.

WHY THEY CAME

By Eugene Hurtienne

Since 1947, when the first saucers were sighted, many aspects of this phenomenon have been developed by persons or organizations which are now devoted to a religious or a scientific view and are, in a sense, carrying out a necessary program in regard to the UFO phase.

UFOs have been seen in many places and in different forms. Their occupants have made personal contact on occasion. Many of us have come to accept the reality of their existence.

Many regard the appearance of the UFOs as an event correlated to our "start in space", the explosion of the atom bomb, and the end of the Piscean Age. Yet there are millions who are afraid to believe or even to admit the fact that life can exist outside the Earth's atmosphere; for to do so would be to necessitate total destruction of the illusory world they have created from their thinking, and annihilation of the world's present forms of economic security.

Innumerable questions have been asked concerning the coming of the UFOs, but truly, few answers can be given, for each answer comes from one's own insight and understanding. This article is my point of view on their coming, through my observation of current events and past events.

Most of you will agree that there is a general theme brought to the people of Earth through the appearance of these UFOs; that theme being... If we don't start to live the life we were taught by Christ (Love and Brotherhood) there will soon be no living beings left upon this planet. The Visitors have stated that there is more to Life than just the material plane. They have showed us the world contains seven planes of existence (the lowest of which is the dense, — our realm of vibration). By putting into action the love and brotherhood aspects, we, as persons or nations could raise our vibrational frequencies closer to their levels of existence.

Unfortunately for us, so many today regard love and brotherhood not as actions suited to heartfelt and mind-realized truths, but as mere subjects for lip service. We could say, then, that the coming of these individuals from other Systems and planets, was purposeful and that they came to reawaken us at the level of our material consciousness; to point the way to long life and peace as once taught by the Sages. Their coming also gave insight to the dawning New Age. Even as we have a personal plan to follow in our spiritual development, so, we are told, does each Solar System and each planet comprising these systems.

The time is at hand for emphasis upon the individual plan for Planet Earth. It is said that the Being Who ensouls our Earth, was given a choice between endeavoring to meet the requirements of the Universal Plan or to remain at the same point in order to give the human and other beings dwelling upon its surface a further opportunity for self-unfoldment.

We have been told that since we, as a race, have failed once again to bring love and brotherhood into manifestation — by which action we were to have earned the privilege of accompanying this Earth into its new vibratory relationship with the Universal Plan, many Souls will be removed from this planet to reembody themselves upon some other world or worlds; to enable them to "take over" those classes in understanding which they failed to pass upon this Earth.

Those among our humanity who can and are sincerely trying to live according to the Laws of Universal Love, will, we have been told, be allowed to assist in the ushering in of this New Age. (Those who live the Law of Love and Brotherhood will have earned the right to be pioneers; thus through their own merit they will be permitted to remain.)

There are certain requirements for fulfillment of this Law of Universal Love:

1. <u>Sincerity</u>: to be always sincere in everything you say, do or think.

2. <u>Appreciation</u>: to show honest appreciation for all things in the Universe.

3. <u>Kindness</u>: to be kind to all self-conscious and un-self-conscious living beings.

4. <u>Tolerance</u>: to be tolerant toward all ideas and beliefs held by others.

5. <u>Integrity</u>: to act honorably to all life everywhere.

Once these laws of behaviour are put into operation, the love aspect will become a living force in your life; thus becoming your "pass" to a new concept of life upon a renewed Earth.

In closing, let me say this: <u>Space</u> is the true home of man. Thus, we can say that Space is the womb of Creation and its consciousness the Divine fire of Life. All forms, visible and invisible, are of the One Consciousness which gave them birth.

CHAPEL IN COSMON

The above is Colonel Arthur J. Burks's title for a lecture he will give on the evening of May 2nd, 1964, 8:00 P.M., at

COSMIC STAR AUDITORIUM
6118 Santa Monica Blvd.
Los Angeles, California

Our friend Col. Burks has written and published a booklet under the same title which will be on sale at the Cosmic Star Auditorium. He will tell you what he discovered during an hour spent alone in our Chapel in Cosmon Research Foundation.

We hope our many friends in the Los Angeles area will be able to attend this lecture, especially as it holds great interest for all who are concerned with the future of COSMON, its spiritual purpose among the many Light groups, and the opportunities for those who are giving now of their time and strength to expand and extend the work started by Gloria Lee and J.W. of Jupiter.

Following is a list of other California Lectures to be given by Col. Burks during early Spring of 1964. We hope you will attend and enjoy them all.

C.R.F.

Monday, April 13th, 8:00 P.M.
  Place - R. R. Reynolds
          38941 Cherry Valley Blvd.
          Cherry Valley, California
  Title - Healing Class Meeting
Saturday, April 18th, 8:00 P.M.
  Place - Anderson Research Center
          301 So. St. Andrews Place
          Los Angeles, California
  Title - To Be Announced
Sunday, April 19th, 2:00 P.M.
  Place - Izaac Walton Hall
          Dexter Drive, Fairmount Park
          Riverside, California
  Title - You Know It All
Monday, April 20th, 8:00 P.M.
  Place - Home of Esther Stilgebouer
          3469 Spruce St.
          Riverside, California
  Title - Wisdom Pool Class
Saturday, April 25th, 8:00 P.M.
  Place - Understanding Unit #15
          Women's Club House
          840 Java St.
          Inglewood, California
  Title - To Be Announced
Sunday, April 26th, 1:30 P.M.
  Place - Understandorama
          Harmony Grove
          Escondido, California
  Title - Portals to the Infinite

THE BOOK CORNER

A Free Gift for our Readers

Ask for your copies of two booklets describing the work of Col. Arthur J. Burks. We requested this information from the Colonel's publisher, Ed O'Neal of CSA, Lakemont, Georgia, that we might give you a valuable gift and help spread the word of Col. Burks's teachings, Lesson Course and Lectures and Life Readings.

Ask us to send your free copy of <u>YOU KNOW IT ALL</u>, a beautifully printed booklet by Col. Burks. This is illustrated with rare prints of scenes and portraits from ancient civilizations.

Send for your copy of the <u>WISDOM POOL</u> brochure listing the many publications authored by Arthur J. Burks. Free for the asking. In this second booklet you are told how to discover your own Wisdom Pool, and in it the purpose for which you were set forth in this life pattern with all its perplexing questions.

We would appreciate having you furnish 6¢ postage if you are able. This will cover both books.

Write while we have a good supply of material.

We are also selling one of Col. Burks's newest releases, THE INVISIBLE PHYSICIAN, giving you the background story of how the Invisible Physician came to be and some of the remarkable healings he has performed. Price $1.00 each. Postage and handling, 10¢. Add 4¢ sales tax if you live in California.

Manual Labor

Our friend, Bret Gray, whose poetry you have read in our newsletter, has just completed one of the most fascinating books you have ever had the privilege of reading. He has written a <u>New Age</u> Manual for Professional Tutors. This is not only a book for professional tutors, but an inspirational source of ideas for teachers of all kinds, for parents, for social workers and creative craftsmen searching for new wells of stimulation. Bret offered COSMON an opportunity to buy some of these fabulous books at a discount for resale, as a donation, and sent one to us to review before placing it on sale. Bret was able to have a modest number printed and in so doing his first edition is put out at a cost to him of $8.00 per book — and worth $10.00 if I ever saw <u>anything</u> worth $10.00. He offered to let us resell it below cost. I refuse to do this on the grounds that I would always be ashamed of myself to have missed out on an opportunity to bless this wonderful friend's work and to publicize his efforts, so that many of you may become acquainted with him direct and buy out his first edition at no less than $10.00 per copy (plus $.25 each postage).

This is a must for all you New Age school teachers as well as tutors of professional calibre! You take it from here.

Excerpt from the "Orlando Evening Star"
February 25, 1964

"The author lost two careers when polio struck in 1948. But by using methods of learning revealed in A MANUAL FOR PROFESSIONAL TUTORS, Bret

Gray rebuilt his life and two new successful careers — though still in a wheelchair...

"Gray, a retired Army officer, has faced life with optimism and a smile from his wheelchair for the last sixteen years. A polio quadraplegic, he feels a driving urge... to prove that he is still a contributing member of society. He sets an example for all by working 80 to 90 hours a week, on behalf of others, and stresses that today's trifles must be ignored if we want tomorrow's triumphs.

"It is vitally important, he says, that all students invest their capital of time and strength in fields of general usefulness, tending toward realization of God's plan for mankind...

"Modern education must, according to Gray, provide the necessary spiritual values for youth to live by. This is a basic responsibility of all who consider themselves educators, and it must be done in spite of the anti-spiritual attitudes of certain Supreme Court Justices.

"How this can be done is explained in Gray's MANUAL FOR PROFESSIONAL TUTORS, a book that all teachers and parents, as well as high school and college students can use to good advantage.

"Copies of the Manual are available from William B. Gray, Jr.
Special Services Division, M.F.A. Co.
Box 1311, Winter Park, Florida 32790"

O.K. FAMILY! Let me see you support Brother Bret in high style and generous outpouring so that he can speedily get another edition off the press. Also if there is any news of the inspiring doings of other members of the family who can measure up to Bret for courage and service, let me hear about it. COSMON will happily give a boost to anyone who is sincerely trying to better conditions with his or her own earnest efforts.

Write to Bret direct at above address. We are not going to handle his books at COSMON at this time, because we want the FAMILY to buy out his first edition and save him mailing costs.

Your family member,

Barbara Steele

"The more we organize our schools and seek to perfect them, the more dead they become," was the despairing remark recently of an eminent educator. "What is the matter?" he asked. The answer is to be found in the question itself. To be alive a thing must be organic; that is it must follow the law of natural growth. Organized structures are of their very nature dead structures. The trouble with our schools is that we seek to dictate their form instead of letting that come as the free expression of a growing, expanding life.
ADDING A NEW DIMENSION TO EDUCATION
Cora L. Williams

YOUR HEALTH

NUTS

By Ronaldo Mineo

An item for you who are interested in eating natural food.

The best way to eat nuts and seeds is to grind them in an electric grinder. This process allows you to eat a large enough quantity as a meal, which would otherwise require hours to masticate properly.

There are two fine nut grinders on the market. The Moulinex, which sells for around eight and ten dollars, the latter being stainless steel; and the Carosello, which is stainless and costs only $7.95.

Here are the precise directions to follow which will make this endeavor worth while and easy to perform.

First obtain a wide-mouthed refrigerator jar, the size which will hold the ground amount that you use in 2 or 3 days. This type of jar expedites the emptying of the grinder after each run, by merely turning the grinder upside down directly into the jar and giving a fast turn on and off to shake the nut meal into the jar. The amount put into the grinder varies. For instance, Almonds grind into a finer meal if not placed past the blade; also, the motor has a tendency to overheat when making a few days' supply, but if caution is used in not overloading, your grinder will last longer. Sesame and Sunflower seeds grind much easier. You may fill the bowl with a greater quantity. Walnuts, Pecans and Filberts also taste delicious ground. You will be able to create some gourmet treats with these marvelous natural flavors.

Some people might be wondering how best to clean the grinder. This way works: unplug the unit, turn the warm water on full force and let the jet of water clean the bowl, angling it of course so the water does not splash everything, especially the motor. This is easy when done with a little dexterity. Then dry it well and there will be no particles to turn rancid. The big secret to this operation is to clean as soon as you are finished grinding.

If this routine is implemented in your food preparation, it will allow you to fulfill a very important area in the nutritional pattern, especially for those who wish no animal products in their diet.

When buying nuts, ask for this year's crop or new crop. If you want to purchase nuts for less, go to the wholesale nut distributors. (There are some in downtown Los Angeles.) They will sell them to you. There is a 50% markup on nuts in stores. If you have a group doing the same thing, buy 10 or 20 pounds at a time. You will appreciate the savings. (We are speaking of shelled nuts.) Remember also to keep your unground nuts and seeds in another set of jars in the refrigerator. They stay much fresher this way.

Here now is the best part. How to eat all these ground nuts and seeds. The Sunflower seed and Sesame meal are satisfying sprinkled over green salads or with avocado. The nuts go well eaten as a mixture with chopped dates, dried figs and raisins, or just spooned out of the jar for a meal in itself. Slightly less compatible, from an extreme point of view, is nut meal with ripe mashed bananas or blended with papaya and coconut milk.

Work and perfect this routine by spending 15 or 20 minutes every second or third day making sufficient quantities of grade A building food in a totally usable form.

CORRESPONDENCE FILE

AFTERMATH

Dear Barbara,

In reading the February newsletter, I was frozen with concern over the letter from the man wanting information on how to become a sorcerer. You gave him such correct advice.

The forces of evil will command his soul!!

Since a small child I've been scared to death of darkness (in the house, or outside).

About two years ago I had a life reading made. At the end of the psychic's reading you may ask questions. One of the questions I asked was, "Why am I so terribly afraid of the dark?" (To my knowledge I have never been scared on purpose, by my brothers or anyone else.)

The answer was quite surprising and amazing. It seems I am reaping what I had sown long ago!

The answer went way back to the Atlantean period, in the latter days, in that second portion that remained after the first breaking up in that land. Abiding in the city called "Alta".

It seems I was quite a sorcerer. I used patterns and symbols on the floor and stood in the middle of these, drawing forth spirits and reciting magic phrases. I used magic and psychic ability to call forth, send out and invoke these spirits to influence others, using my power of mind and will over other people to make them do as I chose. This in turn achieved the end of the entity. (Meaning me.) The reading went on to say my fear of darkness is one of the karmic debts I am paying for that one misguided life without God.

So now after all this time I am still paying for all those misdeeds! (Subconsciously I fear that these same spirits I used, are after me, the reading said.)

Barbara, do you know I can be reading the ads in "Fate" magazine or "Exploring the Unknown" and run across an ad on "How to put others in your power" or books on Black Magic to send for, etc., I can actually feel my flesh crawl from fear, realizing how away from God's plan this is. And wishing the people that put these ads in would realize the immensity of karma they are taking upon themselves, teaching these things, and realizing just what you told that man in the newsletter about all the karma he will be piling up against himself, for lives to come, just for one very foolish and selfish lifetime.

... "You can lead a horse to water, but you cannot make him drink!" I believe it is the same way with we humans most of the time. We learn and profit by our mistakes and experiences it seems. That and our prayers for God's guidance, so we can live and learn according to God's plan...

If this letter would help the gentleman to make up his mind on magic you are welcome to send it to him. Please omit my address from it.

Sincerely,

R.W.
California

Dear R.W.:

Thank you for your letter. Since it deals with a rather widespread human problem, I will print your experience and warning so many can have the advantage of your candid statements.

As a matter of fact there is also a heavy

karma for those who are accessories to the spiritual crime of spreading information which can influence individuals toward acceptance of suggestions of this kind. I am thinking of the magazines (collections of individuals) who accept ads of this nature by which to help pay the costs of their publications.

Your letter gives a clear reason why, since Atlantis, there has been a withdrawal of public knowledge concerning the greater mind powers which are potential in all humans. We have not far to look, to see how selfishness utilizes the power of money, alone, without the added dimension of developed mind powers. It was this greed for power and influence over others that led Atlantis to its frightful doom.

Before Atlantis, Lemuria met her engulfing by reason of the same misuse of godly powers.

We are now in a repeat cycle where all lands saturated and infested by negative force and abuse of spiritual power will be subjected to the cleansing forces of earthquakes, volcanoes, floods and fire. It is the people, themselves, who unleash these punishing forces and there is nothing mysterious about it.

Do you realize that wherever individual workers on the side of Light and/or groups dedicated to Light are located, these aid in releasing and transforming the negative accumulations of force, thus holding off the violent upheavals that would otherwise devastate the areas wherein they are working? Have you not wondered why there are so many Light groups operating along the great fault lines? It is due in part to their capacity for changing negative forces to positive energies and thus protecting the innocent whose time has not yet come.

Again I thank you for speaking up.

Barbara Steele

HELLO TO NEW READERS

In many cases, your friends have asked us to send you a sample copy of COSMON newsletter. From now on, we shall no longer place anyone automatically on our mailing list, unless you apply in person, and ask us to continue because you really like our publication and feel it fills a need. The sample copy you receive will be your last unless you notify us of your interest.

We do not charge a subscription rate or fees of any kind. Those who are able, support the work of Cosmon Research Foundation, and we continue to serve you with faith that our work will be expanded and our needs met so long as we try to progress, as individuals, and to raise our sights constantly toward a higher and more inclusive goal.

Your friends at C.R.F.

CO-WORKERS IN THE VINEYARD

White Star
P.O. BOX 307
JOSHUA TREE, CALIF.

January 10, 1964

GREETINGS...! A PERSONAL HELL'O TO ALL OF YOU:-

Because of shifting patterns here on the physical that have demanded much attention, we have not kept in as close touch via the mails as we would like to. To all who have written and have received no answer, PLEASE UNDERSTAND. We will be in a position to do better in the future, as your scribe is now back at the desert focus to carry forth the necessary functions. We begin this New Year with the SINCERE desire to fulfill without delays the schedule that has been given to us for the release of material. We are dedicated to putting this material in your hands on a MONTHLY basis, and if you are interested in this, PLEASE let us hear from you. This is for you, but we need your help in meeting the costs of publication and mailing. You can be sure that we have mailed material to you in the past as it was financially possible to do so, and have borrowed and hocked to the hilt many times to do so. Also, in the future we desire to keep you posted on the information which we feel is IMPORTANT, and calls for your meditative attention, and LIGHT ACTION in prayer. THANK YOU.

Danter point in the East Indies location. Sumatra, Java, Burma, Borneo, Formosa, Indonesia, etc. We have been informed of this as a coming "CIRCLE OF FIRE". Also, KRAKATOA, a present SLEEPING MONSTER OF THE SEA, (volcano) is to be watched. This warning was received January 8, 1964. This is something to give attention to during your periods of sending forth STABILIZING LIGHT.

Your scribe has been taken into great subterranean VAULTS in the WEST INDIES, Cuba area, and has seen ARSENALS concealed there. (A regular FEEDING LINE of trouble) This is an amazing sight, for this archipelago has many craters that have under-water fissures that can only be entered by submarine or frog-men, and once inside these extinct craters there are caverns large enough to house whole cities. Some of these have massive lakes inside with their beaches etc. THIS IS SOMETHING THAT PEACE LOVING PEOPLES SHOULD BE MADE AWARE OF. The huge stock piles of supplies and ARMS are beyond believing, and one wonders about this???? Remember the warning in BULLETIN #9...?

We appreciate you putting your address on the letters you send to us, as when we get around to answering them it saves time for us as we do not have to DIG in the files. Regarding the files: Our files are private and considered sacred, your names and addresses are given out to no other groups, nor are they available to outsiders. This has always been our policy. Please do not forget to send us your ZIP CODE NUMBER. Important! Thank you. We hope that you have all the BULLETINS and other material on file, as reference will be made from time to time. If your files are not complete, notify us and we will be happy to supply the missing links. To date we have published three ILLUMINATORS, and if some of you do not have these, please ask. Since your scribe takes care of all the office work etc, loose ends dangle once in a while...sorry.

Oh yes... that very unusual COMET that appeared on the scene in 1957 will make another pass this MAY. INTERESTING? Arend Roland, as science has it named, but it has a more familiar name to some of us. MORE ON THIS LATER.

> We give our lives in SERVICE, but we cannot serve you unless you join with us, and SUPPORT the work you believe in.
>
> OUR LIGHT IN CHRIST DEDICATED SERVICE
> WHITE STAR

ANNOUNCEMENT OF PUBLICATION

For the fourth time in nearly 110 years, the "HISTORY OF THE ORIGIN OF ALL THINGS" is again being published. During each period that it has been available, there have been a relative few who have accepted it and benefited from its eternal truths and priceless spiritual treasures. It comes from the press in 1961, in a period of uncertainty and crisis in our country and the world, and it is hoped that more will profit from its availability since pressures have caused many to search for the meaning of events, and the need is greater.

... So a new printing of this book has been made. Many there be who will profit by it — profit in joy and gratitude for a truer and a more satisfying interpretation.

* * *

TO. W-M PUBLISHING
BOX 247, KENTFIELD, CALIF.

Please send # _____ copy(s) of "HISTORY OF THE ORIGIN OF ALL THINGS" (430 pages - cloth bound) at $4.00 Ea. postpaid $ _____.

My check, money order or cash is enclosed. (California residents kindly add 4% sales tax)

_____
(Name - Please Print)

_____
No. Street   City   Zone State

If not satisfied, return within ten (10) days and money will be cheerfully refunded.

LECTURE TOUR

Our friend, Ernst Heinrich of Hamburg, Germany requests us to make a note of the following in the newsletter:

"In the next few weeks, Joseph Busby, editor of the New Age newspaper, 'Voice Universal', England, starts a lecturing tour in the U.S.A. Its purpose is to contact leaders of all spiritual fraternities and religious organizations for the promotion of unity. He also will introduce conceptions of S.U.N. Temples. This immense program, lasting some months, should be supported by all goodwill groups. More information about this is available from:

1. Mr. Wolfgang Schkoll
   6222 East 21st Street
   Indianapolis, Indiana

2. Rev. Eva Taylor
   5030 Workman Mill Road
   Whittier, California

3. Frank Corral
   New Age Information Service
   Box 693
   Oakland 4, California

4. Ronald Hunt
   Shrine of Radiance
   2024 North Hillhurst Avenue
   Hollywood 27, California"

(Request received by C.R.F. on March 3rd)

Food For Freedom

(A people-to-people program of world good will — Meals for Millions Foundation, 215 West 7th St., Los Angeles 14.)

"LET THERE BE PEACE..."

Meals for Millions sometimes gets involved in the most marvelous — if slightly offbeat — projects. Take song-writing, for instance. Who would ever dream that we who are usually up to our necks in soybeans, vitamins, refugees, soup kitchens, and 3¢ meals, should all of a sudden be concerned with a popular song, two songwriters, a young and beautiful vocalist, and an idea that seems to be catching on with teenagers like a chaparral fire?

But that's our story — and here it is in brief: Jill Jackson and Sy Miller, famous husband-and-wife team, wrote a song called "Let There Be Peace on Earth and Let It Begin With Me".

The blaze of its popularity began with a circle "sing" of 180 teenage leaders of all faiths and races in a human relations workshop, sponsored by the National Conference of Christians and Jews. Since then it has become the theme song of hundreds of groups across the country because it expressed so perfectly their feelings about brotherhood, offering to each a way of implementing such a dream. "Let there be peace on earth/The peace that was meant to be./...Let me walk with my brother/In perfect harmony./Let peace begin with me..." On the way it picked up a Brotherhood Award, and a George Washington Medal from the Freedoms Foundation at Valley Forge.

Choruses began to teach the song to audiences and conventions. National radio and TV programs featured it. The People to People program, initiated by President Eisenhower, sent it out on magnetic tapes through World Tape Pals, 4H clubs, International Farm Youth, and numerous missionaries of every faith. U. S. Information Agency used it in a film for Japan. It was translated into 26 languages, and letters poured in to the Millers from all over the world. "Suddenly," said Jill, "we didn't have just a song — we had a Movement!"

One of those who heard the song was a young, idealistic actress, Roberta Shore, who promptly recorded it for DOT Records. When she sings it, the song becomes almost a prayer — for simple goodness, peace between people and nations. Because Roberta felt that one of the most important steps toward peace is feeding the hungry, she donated all her royalties (and so did the Millers) to MEALS FOR MILLIONS.

So now you see how it is we got in the song-writing act, if only by the back door. And what a lovely door it is too. If any of you would like to purchase either the record or the sheet music, you will find it at all music stores — and you'll be feeding the hungry at the same time. (Also, don't forget the Share Banks and Life House at the front of the cafeterias as you go out.)

— 3¢ Buys a Meal —

DOT Record #45-16483
Via Music Stores Only

OVEREATERS ANONYMOUS

P. O. Box 3372
Beverly Hills, Calif.

"O.A. is a fellowship of men and women who meet to share their experience, strength and hope with one another in order that they may solve their common problem and help those who still suffer to recover from compulsive overeating."

Our readers may be interested in
THE TWELVE STEPS
they suggest as a program of recovery:

1. We admitted we were powerless over food — that our lives had become unmanageable.
2. Came to believe that a Power greater than ourselves could restore us to sanity.
3. Made a decision to turn our will and our lives over to the care of God <u>as we understood Him</u>.
4. Made a searching and fearless moral inventory of ourselves.
5. Admitted to God, to ourselves and to another human being the exact nature of our wrongs.
6. Were entirely ready to have God remove all these defects of character.
7. Humbly asked Him to remove our shortcomings.
8. Made a list of all persons we had harmed, and became willing to make amends to them all.
9. Made direct amends to such people wherever possible, except when to do so would injure them or others.
10. Continued to take personal inventory and when we were wrong, promptly admitted it.
11. Sought through prayer and meditation to improve our conscious contact with God <u>as we understood Him</u>, praying only for knowledge of <u>His</u> will for us and the power to carry that out.
12. Having had a spiritual awakening as the result of these steps, we tried to carry this message to compulsive overeaters and to practice these principles in all our affairs.

BEACON LIGHT HERALD

We present to our readers, William Kullgren, well known to many in the New Age groups of Light. Mr. Kullgren is a server with a background of astrological studies and a mine of rich personal experience. Like many others, this leader publishes a periodical to which you may wish to subscribe. At this time we have four publications to offer you through Cosmon, from our friend. If you wish to subscribe or have personal questions, write to William Kullgren direct at the following address:

Drawer 8
Atascadero, California

THE BEACON LIGHT HERALD
January - February 1964
Price — $1.00 per copy

THE BIBLE SPEAKS TO AMERICA
God is the divine Architect. He gave us a perfect blueprint for our everyday life, individually and nationally.
Price — $1.00

THE DAWN OF A NEW AGE
A compilation of contemporary revelations through the instrumentship of many well-known Channels.
Price — $2.50

MESSAGES FROM HIGHER PLANES
Further revelations. A second compilation for your interest and instruction.
Price — $2.50

Please add 10¢ postage to each book order. If you live in California, remember to add 4% sales tax to the total price of your order.

INVITATION TO READERS OF COSMON NEWSLETTER

From Rev. L. Garfield Wildren, a Jesus-appointed disciple (by letter, automatic writing, October 1955) to our Foundation Church of the New Birth, requesting that I evangelize and distribute His writings and His books. In doing this I offer you some or all of His now over fifty recent sermons, correcting much of the Bible's 1400 errors; telling what He did preach when He was on earth. These sermons are exclusive to our Foundation, so write me for them (a card will suffice). They are highly spiritual. Get that much-needed spiritual uplift now. No obligation. First sermon called "Way to Immortality".
Address me:

    P. O. Box 619
    Kirksville, Missouri

Publisher's Note:

In each aspiring, sincere and dedicated heart or group of human hearts, glows a facet of the glorious diamond of TRUTH. Each one of infinite approaches is a step on the Path of Returning to God. We share space with others who wish in their turn to share their joy of discovery with you.

    C.R.F.

FOR NEW AGERS ONLY

FOR SALE: 30 of the loveliest acres you ever saw, in a mountain forest in Oregon State. Virgin wilderness, with plenty of water, rich fertile soil, wild flowers, ferns, foot trails, wild creatures. Superb views. (No hunters allowed!) Near roads and towns.

Owner of this parcel writes: "I have had a lot of people who have wanted it, but they were either hunters or people who were NOT even remotely interested in the New Age type of things. We hope that we will get someone who wants to start a New Age center where people can come to learn, etc."

Price: $9,900.00. Terms or cash. The buyer could sell or lease lots for at least $500.00 each. Owner must have $2,000.00 cash down with $50.00 monthly payments.

If you want more information write to:

    OREGON PROPERTY
    c/o Cosmon Research Foundation
    P. O. Box 483
    Oro Grande, California 92368

Your letters will be forwarded unopened to Owner.